Common Theological Topics

Loci Communes Theologici

recently compiled and revisited

by Philip Melanchthon

Common Theological Topics

Loci Communes Theologici

recently compiled and revisited

by Philip Melanchthon

1535

translated from the original Latin by Paul A. Rydecki

2019

Repristination Press
Malone, Texas

Original title: *Loci Communes Theologici recens collecti et recogniti a Philippo Melanthone* (1535). Published by permission of the translator; all rights reserved by Repristination Press. No part of this publication may be reproduced, stored in a retrieval system, or transmitted in any form or by any means, electronic, mechanical, photocopying or otherwise without the prior written permission of Repristination Press.

REPRISTINATION PRESS
716 HCR 3424 E
MALONE, TEXAS 76660

www.repristinationpress.com

ISBN 1-891469-78-9 (10)
978-1-891469-78-7 (13)

Table of Contents

Introduction to the English Translation 7
Translator's Note 11
Dedication to King Henry VIII 15
Common Theological Topics 27
Catalogue of Topics 30
God 33
God is One 35
Three Persons of the Godhead 37
Creation 55
The Cause of Sin and Contingency 59
Human Powers/Free Will 63
Sin 70
Original Sin 71
Punishments 74
Actual Sins 78
The Divine Law 82
The Division of Laws 85
The Law of Nature 96
The Use of Divine Law 104
The Difference between Commandments and Counsels 107
Poverty 110
Chastity 113
The Gospel 116
Why the Promise of the Gospel is Needed 120
Grace and Justification 126
Good Works 138

The Promises of the Law	146
The Difference between Mortal and Venial Sins	164
Predestination	168
The Difference between the Old and the New Testament	172
The Spirit and the Letter	176
Christian Freedom	178
The Sacraments	190
The Number of Sacraments	194
Baptism	196
The Baptism of John and of the Apostles	197
The Baptism of Infants	198
The Lord's Supper	204
Eucharistic Sacrifice	210
Repentance	215
The Sin against the Holy Spirit	219
Confession	226
Satisfaction	229
Ecclesiastical Power: The Keys	236
The Church	243
Human Traditions	250
Mortification	255
Scandal	258
The Kingdom of Christ	262
The Resurrection of the Dead	268
Afflictions: Bearing the Cross	274
Prayer	284
Civil Magistrates and the Dignity of Civil Affairs	294
Ecclesiastical Polity	310

Introduction to the English Translation

The need for publication of a translation of this edition of Melanchthon's *Loci Communes* has been readily apparent for some time; it has been a goal of the publisher since the *Melanchthonjahr* in 1997, which was celebrated the 500th anniversary of the birth of the *Praeceptor Germaniae*. While several translations of the 1521 *Loci* have been published since the mid-twentieth century (most notably, the unsurpassed work of Charles Leander Hill), and Melanchthon's later revisions of the *Loci* were translated by J.A.O. Preus (initially published as a translation of the 1543 edition, but later republished as a translation of his 1559) and C. L. Manschreck (1555), nevertheless, the most important edition of the *Loci* has been neglected.

Comparing the 1535 edition with the 1521 demonstrates the development which had taken place in Melanchthon's understanding of the articles of the faith. In 1521, Melanchthon ordered the commonplaces of theology as follows: (1) Free Will; (2) Sin; (3) The Law; (4) Divine Law; (5) Counsels; (6) The Vows of Monks; (7) Judicial and Ceremonial Laws; (8) Human Laws; (9) The Gospel; (10) The Power of the Law; (11) The Power of the Gospel; (12) Grace; (13) Justification and Faith; (14) The Efficacy of Faith; (15) Love and Hope; (16) The Difference between the Old and New Testaments; (17) The Old Man and the New; (18) Mortal and Daily Sin; (19) Signs; (20) Baptism; (21) Repentance; (22) Private Confessions; (23) Participation in the Lord's Table; (24) Love; (25) Magistrates; and (26) Offense.

Even a cursory comparison of this enumeration of theological topics with that which is provided on pages 30 and 31 of the present work demonstrates how significantly Melanchthon's understanding of theology had grown in the intervening years, especially in the course of the controversies with the Zwinglians in 1529 and the confrontation with the Papists at the Diet of Augsburg in 1530. The 1535 *Loci* provides an outline of Christian dogmatics which is familiar to modern Lutheran theologians, and for a good reason: Melanchthon's work establishes the model for Lutheran dogmatics. Nevertheless, Melanchthon's *Loci Communes Theologici* is intentionally less exhaustive than the later works of the Age of Lutheran Orthodoxy. The result is that Melanchthon's *Loci*—like the Augsburg Confession and its Apology—remains accessible to a broad audience and offers a good starting point for theological study, when used in conjunction with the Book of Concord.

When one considers the fact that Melanchthon's contributions to the Book of Concord were written between 1530 and 1537, the contents of his 1535 edition of the *Loci* can be seen in their confessional context. Furthermore, while the 1521 *Loci* was quickly rushed to print when students prematurely published notes from Melanchthon's lectures on Romans, the 1535 *Loci* was a thorough revision of the earlier work and played a significant role in discussions between Lutheran theologians and the court theologians of the king of England, Henry VIII. As John Schofield observes in his *Philip Melanchthon and the English Reformation*, the dedication of this work to the English king was a "breakthrough" in relations between England and the Lutheran Schmalkald League. Three representatives of the king—Edward Foxe, Nicholas Heath, and Robert Barnes—were sent to Germany as emissaries, and attended a meeting of the Schmalkald League; Melanchthon and the three representatives "worked tirelessly" toward agreement, and, in April, 1536, "a document that came to be known as the Wittenberg Articles, based on the Augsburg Confession and the *Loci*" was produced. Schofield notes that "Luther approved the Wittenberg Articles as being 'in agreement with our teaching' in a letter to Elector John Frederick."[1] The mercurial temperament of Henry VIII ultimately scuttled such efforts to bring England into the fold of the Augsburg Confession, but the publication of the new *Loci* marked a significant point of development in the ongoing Lutheran Reformation.

---

1   (Burlington, Vermon: Ashgate, 2006) p. 61, 66, 67.

The careful student of the Unaltered Augsburg Confession and its Apology will recognize much that is familiar within this edition of the *Loci*. Melanchthon often uses the same phrases which appear in the confessions, and then offers further commentary, providing further context to the works which he contributed to the Lutheran *corpus doctrinae*. Luther's assessment of the *Loci* in the winter of 1542–3 should stand as enduring testimony to this work's significance:

> If anybody wished to become a theologian, he has a great advantage, first of all, in having the Bible. This is now so clear that he can read it without any trouble. Afterward he should read Philip's *Loci Communes*. This he should read diligently and well, until he has its contents fixed in his head. If he has these two he is a theologian, and neither the devil nor a heretic can shake him. The whole of theology is open to him, and afterward he can read whatever he wishes for edification. ...
>
> There's no book under the sun in which the whole of theology is so compactly presented as in the *Loci Communes*. If you read all the fathers and sententiaries you have nothing. No better book has been written after the Holy Scriptures than Philip's. He expresses himself more concisely than I do when he argues and instructs. I'm garrulous and more rhetorical.[2]

Rt. Rev. James D. Heiser
Bishop, *The Evangelical Lutheran Diocese of North America*
Festival of St. Timothy, A.D. 2020

---

2   Martin Luther, *Table Talk*, ed. and trans. by Theodore G. Tappert, 55 vols., (Philadelphia: Fortress Press, 1967) vol. 54, p. 439–440.

Translator's Note

The 1535 edition of Philip Melanchthon's *Common Theological Topics* reads more like an extended letter than a theological textbook. The dedication to King Henry VIII is not at all perfunctory; Master Philip has clearly arranged this entire work to convince the King of England that the teachings of the Lutheran Church are both Scriptural and reasonable and not at all at odds with the teachings of the Church catholic. Frequent citations in Greek and references to both Greek and Roman poets and philosophers help to establish Melanchthon's credentials as a teacher worthy to be given audience by a king.

The translation of this work is straightforward, but a few notes may be in order.

The Biblical citations in this work all come from the Latin Vulgate, although sometimes with Melanchthon's own paraphrasing. Therefore, the English rendering may differ at times from modern English translations and even from the Vulgate itself. All the chapter numbers given by Melanchthon have been updated to match the numbering of the King James Version, meaning that, in most of the Psalms, the number given here is one higher than the number given in the Vulgate. Where Melanchthon quoted Scripture but did not provide a reference, it has been added in brackets.

Melanchthon makes frequent use of the term *pius* in its various forms (*pius, pietas, impius, impietas*). There is a tragic lack of understanding of this concept in the modern world. It implies devotion to one's duty, especially one's duty to God. Many English Bible translations use the word "godly" as a translation of the Greek word εὐσεβής, but English readers are often surprised to learn that the word lacks any etymological connection to the word "God." In a small attempt to bring the term "pious" back into more frequent use, I have intentionally alternated between the terms "godly" and "pious," "godliness" and "piety," "ungodly" and "wicked," "ungodliness" and "wickedness."

One of the most important theological words used throughout this work is the adjective *gratuitus* (used 34 times), with its related adverb *gratis* (used 62 times). Both words are derived from the noun *gratia*, which is usually rendered as "grace," a derivation which is easily recognizable in Latin. Whereas the meaning of the noun was hotly debated in the sixteenth century, especially between the Lutherans and the Roman Catholics, both the adjective and the adverb clearly emphasize that something is or is being given "free of charge." Melanchthon uses the terms freely in connection with God's promise of reconciliation and justification. Indeed, the adjective may be translated as "free" and the adverb as "freely," but, in my opinion, those words do not always clearly convey the notion of "free of charge," as the previous sentence illustrates. What is more, they have no transparent relation whatsoever to the important theological term "grace." Therefore, I have chosen in every case to render the adjective *gratuitus* with the less commonly used word "gratuitous," and the adverb *gratis* with the even less common English word "gratis," borrowed directly from its Latin root. For as odd as these words may appear to the modern reader, I believe they will prove invaluable for communicating Melanchthon's obvious intention to explain his—and the Lutheran—understanding of the concept of grace.

In no other sacrifices does God delight as much as in the pursuit of the pure doctrine and Word. Therefore, O Lord Christ, receive these hymns with a kindly heart and refresh our minds by Your Holy Spirit.

14

To the fairest Prince, Lord Henry VIII, King of England and France, Lord of Ireland, Prince of Wales and Cornwall: Greetings.

Whenever one endeavors to teach, there is great advantage in having topics arranged in a rational order and drawn together into a method suitable for teaching. Therefore, I, too, have gathered together the chief topics of the Christian doctrine and those topics which I thought to be most useful for promoting godliness in the daily life and exercises of the godly—topics which should be especially prominent in the churches and impressed in sermons. In doing so, I have curtailed and avoided curious and useless questions. Indeed, even in the remaining topics which I deemed necessary to be explained, I have expounded the matters themselves, as much as I was able, with great honesty and simplicity, without any sophistry. For I, too, despise it when people who gather many inextricable, perplexing, paradoxical, absurd, and monstrous arguments, mostly from their own deceitful debates, succeed only at disturbing consciences, even as they fail to teach.

However, although my only plan was to gather together the doctrine of the catholic Church of Christ concerning necessary matters, namely, the doctrine passed down in the apostolic writings and in the received ecclesiastical writers, nevertheless I considered it necessary at this point to say ahead of time that I gladly leave the judgment concerning all my efforts to the catholic Church, that is, to all godly, educated, and learned men. For even as Paul commands that each one should know the manner of faith given to him by God, so my own weakness is surely not unknown to me, and therefore I have not made prejudicial pronouncements about any dogma without citing authorities, nor shall I ever scorn the judgment of the Church.

At the same time, it is not a novel practice to develop methods for teaching the Christian doctrine. For also among the Greeks, Damascene[1], and among our own theologians, Lombard[2], left behind writings of this kind, for which this one thing has produced favor and notoriety: that methods of teaching are in great demand. Therefore, we observe that they have been counted among the first-class writers. Books of this kind existed even before these men—the detailed expositions of Cyprian and of others in the Creed. And several men elegantly gathered the sentences of Augustine on every article in a book entitled *De fide ad Petrum*. There also exists an ancient writing of Origen entitled *Peri archon*, which he so named because there he arranged and attempted to explain the chief topics of Christian doctrine in an orderly way. What is more, Paul develops a certain method of teaching in Romans, offering a precise argument concerning the cause of sin, the use of the Law and the benefit of Christ, what the proper benefit of Christ is, how we obtain the forgiveness of sins and reconciliation. The creeds were initially also formed for this purpose, that there might be a brief summary of Christian doctrine in which men could observe and embrace the topics necessary for godliness set forth all in one place in a single document. For this is the only way to teach effectively. Therefore, I am not the originator of a novel practice in the Church; the notion of a novel practice greatly vexes my spirit.

The greater the need there is of a method of teaching, the more avidly all students of all ages have sought out and received such instruction, the more purposefully and religiously they had to be written. For what is more difficult than to explain clearly the weightiest controversies

---

[1] John of Damascus (676-749) was one of the most significant theologians of the Byzantine church. His works are cited extensively by later Lutheran theologians such as Johann Gerhard. (ed.)

[2] Peter Lombard (1096-1160), author of *Libri Quatuor Sententiarum* or *Four Books of Sentences*, which formed the basis of much of the theological study undertaken in medieval universities. (ed.)

of the religion? What is more dangerous than to select the most correct things when surrounded by so much variety of opinion? What is more natural, what is more characteristic of man than to fall, to wander, to be deceived by what all too often only appears to be right? It often occurs that, even when teachers understand something correctly, nevertheless, in explaining it, it is as if they forget themselves and are unable to express adequately what they mean. They often yield to the burden and are unable to explain what they are thinking. Thus when ignorant men later imbibe these less-than-helpful opinions, a great many scandals arise in the Church. Those who read the ancient writers with discernment know that my complaints are not without merit. There hardly exists any ancient writing in which either perspicuity or care is not sometimes lacking. How many passages there are about which we would like to speak with the authors themselves, if it were possible, and ask them openly and in person what they were thinking, which authorities they had consulted! But especially in this kind of writing, in methods of teaching, how many are rather openly censured! How many times is Origen brutally taken to task for his book *Peri archon*! And not even his own students have shown mercy to Lombard. Indeed, some things he has written are condemned by law!

Therefore, since there is so much difficulty and so much danger in composing a method of teaching, it has often occurred to me that it should not be the work of one man, but of a council in which the most learned and noble men deliberate a matter together, concerning all those articles in which controversies have often arisen and in which there is some disagreement among the ancients themselves, and then carefully pronounce judgment, setting forth the whole doctrine of the religion. As Plato said, "The princes of the republics should especially see to it that their citizens are both happy and friendly to one another." For achieving this noble state of the Church, there is nothing more important than having such a godly and simple form of doctrine set down in writing with weighty authority. For such a form of doctrine could both heal hesitant minds and restore the concord and tranquility of the Church, fortifying the same for the future. It is fitting that the authors of this most sublime benefit among men should be not only bishops, but also the greatest princes, that they may both extol the glory of God and look after the salvation of all the nations, especially since a great work such as this cannot be accomplished without their resources.

Nor do I doubt that, as every prince is most wise and noble, every prince is dreadfully affected by the dire circumstances that plague the Church, for they are neither obscure nor so trivial that they can be considered without sharp and severe pain. Certain ancient illnesses fester in the Church and must not be ignored. For the fact is that certain notable articles of the Christian doctrine have lain in ruins for a long time, buried under a dense fog. Now that the works of some learned and good men have begun to roll out of this fog, there has arisen in some places an unusual ferocity which is unworthy of the mildness that should characterize the Church. Not only are learned and good men being slaughtered and the abuses of them endorsed, but the study of Christian doctrine is being altogether extinguished. From this, dissension has arisen, which not only gives birth to countless other problems, but also this chief problem, that it provides an opportunity for men who are otherwise considered unlearned, seditious, and fanatical both to initiate wicked theological battles in the Church and to sow false opinions in civil affairs, which are harmful to religion and to the civil society of men, as they openly transform religion into a horrible barbarity. Surely it is fitting for good and wise princes to seek appropriate remedies to these great atrocities. Should they not also provide a Church to those who come after them? Unless reason steps in, so that a godly and reliable form of doctrine is passed on to posterity, the Church will be torn to pieces in countless ways.

There is extant in the writings of Xenophon[3] a speech, full of grav-

---

3   Xenophon, *Hellenica*, Book VII.

ity and spirit, concerning the Laconian Archidamus, who, by his virtue, restored the ruined and nearly hopeless city of Sparta. Before that battle in which he greatly benefited his country again, after the battle line had been drawn up and he had already ordered the signals to be sounded, he exhorted the army with these words: "Men, citizens, now that we have become good, let us look up with our gaze firmly fixed! Let us repay those who are assaulting the fatherland!" O noble word, worthy of the Spartan king and of his son Agesilaus, with which he testifies that great and brave men should take up the greatest battles, that they may leave behind to their posterity a safe republic as a dependable home! How much more fitting is it for Christians and princes and teachers to be so moved that they desire to leave behind for their posterity a Church that is rightly ordered and peaceful! Indeed, there should be no greater or more venerable concern for great men, especially those who sit at the helm. If only such men, in the midst of such great calamities of the Church, would ever take up for themselves this most honorable word, "Let us look up with our gaze firmly fixed! Let us repay those who are assaulting the Church!" But this cannot be accomplished unless the doctrine is rightly explained. For violent debates neither provide healing for hesitant minds, nor are they profitable for establishing a lasting peace. And although insolence must be held in check and those who sow or who love ungodly dogmas or who incite rebellions should be punished with severe examples, nevertheless we must see to it that ferocity is not equally and indiscriminately exercised against the good together with the evil.

But to return to the point from which I digressed, I, for my part, sincerely hope that a council will someday consider a comprehensive method of teaching. But I have seen around me such a wide variety of opinions and debates that I have concluded that whole areas of Christian doctrine must be revealed to unlearned men, and that they must be safeguarded against pernicious and ungodly opinions. Therefore, I have, with proper study, put together these topics in a compendium, and, as much as I was able, I was careful to provide an order and a path suitable for teaching. I have carefully enclosed myself within the confines of this method. Although it is also weakness of ability which forces me to do this, nevertheless I have a certain reason for my plan. For although there are some men who are gifted with extraordinary abilities, who add the splendor and light of prayer to their method of teaching, for illuminating the size of things, just as Phidias assigns to his statues not only a proper harmony of members, but also dignity and breadth, nevertheless this good fortune belongs to very few. I measure myself by my own foot, and I know myself well enough, that I am not able to fashion that divine form and model of Phidias. Indeed, I readily suffer myself to be numbered among the hobbyists and craftsmen of tiny works, wherefore I seek those traces of art with greater care and zeal.

I know many others find more delight in free declamations and flee from the narrow straits of a method of teaching. But a great many, while they indulge themselves, often stray from the goal, and while they utter many things off-topic with a loud voice and gesture with the whole hand, they teach the reader nothing certain. I truly despise that license of disputing according to the academic custom, which some take up for themselves, who also blasphemously distort and alter the things that have been rightly taught by others, and without right, without discrimination, without ancient authority, they say whatever they please. As Euripides said of Tantalus, "He had an unbridled tongue, a most shameful disease."[4] Surely in a theologian an unbridled tongue is a most shameful disease. We should remember in which theater we wander: We have Christ for a Judge, angels as spectators, and the weak as the audience, whose spirits are easily wounded.

Therefore, I have zealously pursued religion and the faithfulness which we should apply to sacred matters. And lest I, too, should further complicate matters that are in some respects already complex, I have

---

4   Euripides, *Orestes*.

employed the proper signification in explaining them, as much as I was able. Indeed, for this reason I have used words that are customary in the Church, and at times I have borrowed certain words from the schools which must be condoned because of the times. Besides this, I have taken great care to use clear speech; I have not mixed in foreign arguments. For although I believe that those who have not been instructed with a liberal education are not sufficiently suited to expound religious doctrine; and although there are, in several topics, certain things from other fields of study which must be addressed; and although certain religious declarations must at times be compared with philosophy; nevertheless, as in other matters, so also here, there is a procedure that is most pleasant. Let us receive assistance from the other arts in illuminating these very matters, in establishing divisions, or, if I may, in laying out the very design of the building. For the unlearned cannot divide complex matters properly, but often combine things that do not belong together, or tear apart things that do. Nor do they always see what the essence of the controversy is, or where they should disagree. In these situations, many topics become clearer by means of a comparison with philosophy. And yet, the different arts should not be confused with one another; Christian doctrine must not be overwhelmed with foreign arguments. I, too, have selected only sparingly, as needed, certain things from other fields of study, lest I should wax on needlessly. Paul wants those who pass on religious doctrine to be "able to teach" [1 Timothy 3:2], which surely no one can accomplish using the instructor's baton of foreign fields.

Therefore, although there are other, more excellent virtues—godliness, life skills, experience in spiritual battles, wisdom—nevertheless they are also impudent who, in professing to be interpreters of Christian doctrine, are not careful to add a liberal education, which is not only an ornament for the Christian Church, but also sheds some light on the doctrine itself. Indeed, I openly judge the Anabaptists to be worthy of hatred, along with any who may be like them, who attempt to import into the Church a certain unskilled and barbaric theology, and who contend that there is no need of learning other fields of study. That is why everything they say is confusing and lacking in art. They show no knowledge of antiquity; they make no comparison from other disciplines. Indeed, they have their own theater! For the common people, since they hate the arts by nature, rejoice when the dignity of the arts is maligned. But this persuasion not only impedes the studies of higher education and civic life, which the rest of the arts have in view, but it also harms religion. For education is not only beneficial because it sharpens one's judgment, because it shows a pattern of teaching, but it is also advantageous for the sake of morality. For to the degree that a person is educated, to that degree he measures the size of things with his mind, increasing his care and concern for teaching rightly. On the other hand, ignorance fosters carelessness in good men, and in the bad it strengthens their audacity. There is no greater plague on the Church than that. For evil men raise their voices and make pronouncements much more confidently where they are able to claim authority for themselves without doctrine. Therefore, I judge that in every contention, all who wish to be of useful service to the Church should be urged to a proper method of learning and to the true pursuit both of religion and of other noble arts.

But extraordinary works are encouraged by examples, according to the saying of Hesiod, "Neighbor vies with his neighbor." Therefore, although my writings are not polished, nevertheless, even if I accomplish nothing else, certainly a method of teaching is able to remind readers that the other fields of study and the arts are also needed in order to expound such great things.

Moreover, that this commentary may go out into the public more auspiciously, I have decided that it should be dedicated to your name, O famous King, especially for this reason: A number of men in other nations—some of them unlearned, some of them wicked—are inciting the minds of the highest kings indiscriminately against all those who do not approve all the fantasies of the monks, and they are doing so with wondrous skill. So I have decided to apply my own skills so that I may furnish you, the most learned of all kings, with this writing, in order that Your Majesty may form a judgment about me and this whole manner of doctrine in which I conduct myself on the basis of this writing rather than on the basis of the accusations of others. We understand that you have been well instructed both in Biblical literature and in the remaining philosophies, and especially in that beautiful art of considering the celestial movements and operations. We read that the greatest and wisest kings in every age have taken great delight in this field, studying it with keenest zeal and highest prudence, both because of the dignity of the subject and because of the practical usefulness of it. To this great doctrine of the most excellent arts are added also the remaining virtues worthy of a great prince: justice in ruling, concern for keeping the peace, greatness of spirit, godliness, zeal for aiding and advancing the Christian religion, clemency and exceptional kindness, which is not only discerned in other business, but also shines forth in this matter, that in your kingdom, no brutality is said to be exercised against good and temperate men who are zealous for a purer ecclesiastical doctrine, whereas in other lands the wrath of princes has flared up beyond measure. I will not complain about their actions in this place. I will only say this: It seems to me that unjust cruelty does not befit the Church, nor will it help to restore tranquility. Therefore, your moderation, worthy of a good and wise prince, is certainly pleasing to God. For even as God commands that fanatics and wicked men should be restrained by force, so also no parricide is crueler than to slaughter godly men and members of Christ together with the wicked, to harass the true Church, and to wipe out good and useful things from the Church.

Nor can it be denied that many things that are useful for godliness have been rediscovered by good and learned men. When the prophet Isaiah prophesies that there will be godly kings—*nutricii*, foster fathers of the Church, he calls them [Isaiah 49:23]—he demands that the kings protect the godly against unjust brutality, that they take pains to spread the right doctrine. What titles, what trophies should be more highly prized by great and wise kings than that this sweet name should be ascribed to them by the heavenly voice, that they should be foretold as foster fathers of the Church of Christ? It is high praise and full of dignity to be given the title Africanus, Macedonicus, and other such names. But it is more glorious by far to be called *Pater Patriae*, the father of the fatherland. Our true and lasting fatherland, however, is the Church of Christ. To be the father of this true fatherland and, as the prophet uses the word, the foster father of it—that is high praise indeed, and kings especially should aspire to it. These are the duties which kings render to God. These duties are the sacrifices which are pleasing to God. But those who unjustly put to death the true members of the Church, that is, godly and learned men, and who wipe out the doctrine in which the true forms of worshiping God are revealed, are not the foster fathers of the Church, no matter how much they disguise their cruelty under the name of the Church. Therefore, not only should your moderation and clemency themselves be praised, but also your discernment and wisdom, in that Your Majesty fosters the tranquility of the Church, and in such a way that Your Majesty favors pious pursuits and understands that certain abuses are in need of correction.

Therefore, since I knew that Your Majesty excelled in doctrine, and since I understood that, in these dissensions, you have employed singular moderation and clemency, which are well-suited to a man of learning, I decided that this writing should be sent to Your Majesty in particular. While I leave it entirely to the judgment of Your Majesty, I do hope, nevertheless, that it will demonstrate that the wrath of kings is being unjustly kindled against us. I have no doubt that Your Majesty desires a resolution that will at once bring glory to Christ and peace to the Church, and that you have thought long and hard about remedies for this discord. Therefore, it will surely be helpful for you to consider more than just the writings of those who discredit our cause with unjust accusations. This is done, not only by certain impudent people and by men of the lowest station, but also by many others who walk onto this stage under an assumed persona of singular gravitas and wisdom, who were supposed to use their authority, not for the destruction of good men or to inflame the cruelty of the ignorant, but rather to extol the glory of Christ, to properly cure the diseases of the Church, and to turn the minds of the princes toward Christian mildness. For it is most shameful for great men to deceitfully employ the ruse of gravitas, which they do who cleverly conceal the accepted abuses and artfully distort the pious and useful warnings which our men have issued. From my heart I revere the catholic Church of Christ, and I zealously cherish its opinion, nor have I ever wanted to dissent from the judgments of good and learned men in the Church. Therefore, I offer this commentary of mine to Your Majesty, not as my defender, if indeed I err, but as a censor in the weightiest controversies, whose judgment I thought would be right on account of your doctrine, free and equitable on account of the reputation of Your Royal Majesty. I pray, therefore, that, with this in mind, Your Majesty would not hesitate to accept my writing, in which I hope you will see that I have included things that are useful for godliness, and that I am most desirous of peace and concord in the Church.

May Christ keep Your Majesty safe and prosperous, and may He guide Your Majesty, that the glory of Christ may be extolled and that the Church may dwell in safety.

In the year 1535.

COMMON THEOLOGICAL TOPICS

Just as in the other arts it is beneficial to have the chief topics arranged according to a method of teaching and a logical series—and once these have been learned, the beginnings, the progressions and the outcomes of the arts can be foreseen—so also it is advantageous to develop a method of teaching in Christian doctrine. For the fact is that this is the one proper path for excellent teaching, celebrated in the writings of all learned and wise men. But some people, when they assemble theological topics, import only topics from moral philosophy. They make a list of virtues, such as justice, temperance, kindness, and similar things. But Christians should know that, even though these philosophical topics are properly related to a certain part of God's Law, there is a vast difference between Christian doctrine and the teachings of philosophy. Much greater things must be sought here which are unknown to philosophy, as will soon be apparent in the catalogue of topics.

Indeed, if a person considers the very order of the books of the Bible more closely, he will notice that they are aptly arranged. The first starts out speaking of the beginnings of things. It teaches that the world was made by God. It describes man's nature and dignity. It reveals the beginning, the cause, and the punishments for sin. It also describes the beginning of the Gospel, how from the very beginning was promised the Seed which was to free us from the tyranny of the devil, that is, from sin and death. These are already the first beginnings of the Church. Afterwards, there follow in the histories many proclamations of Law and Gospel, namely, of the judgment of God, of the punishments of the wicked, of the rewards of the godly, of eternal life.

Such is that first proclamation to Cain: "If you do well, you will be acceptable; but if you do wrong, it will yet be revealed, even if it is silent.

But let sin be under you, and may you master it" [Genesis 4:7].[5] This proclamation combines commands, rewards, and penalties. It testifies that God will be the Judge. It also indicates that judgment will be postponed, that the wicked will flourish for a time, that the righteous will be sorely afflicted, but that some judgment will be inflicted. Therefore it prophesies dimly about the last judgment, about eternal life. It teaches likewise that sin clings to a person's nature, but that God, nevertheless, approves of this beginning of obedience in which we believe that God forgives us and in which we resist sin. You see here the whole purpose of the Gospel, for the promise of the Seed must be added from the previous chapter, on account of which God testifies that He again receives men into grace and forgives sin. This promise is revealed little by little and thus is set forth more and more clearly.

The Law, too, is renewed in the book of Exodus. The histories then contain examples of Law and Gospel, wrath and mercy, that God truly punishes sins and forgives those who repent, that He does good to the righteous. In the same way, all the sermons of the prophets are spent on two topics: on the Law, and on illuminating the promise of the Christ. They rebuke sins and then set forth the consolation, teaching about the benefits of Christ. These same things are later more clearly revealed in the Gospel and spread to all nations. When one notices this sequence, it is not at all difficult to perceive that the matters which are necessary for godliness are handed down in the Scriptures with a certain order in mind. In the end, Paul is clearly a master craftsman as he employs a method of teaching in his arguments. He demonstrates the distinction between Law and Gospel, etc. We will imitate these examples and list, in order, the chief topics of Christian doctrine, closely following the order that is presented in the Symbols of the faith.

Moreover, it must be understood that, concerning these things

---

5   The reader will note that, in several of his citations of Scripture, Melanchthon renders the passages somewhat freely. (Trans.)

which the Holy Scriptures bid us to understand and concerning the articles of faith, it is not enough to have ambiguous opinions; we must have a certain and firm understanding. For doubt gives birth to impiety, and despair along with it. "Everything that is not of faith is sin" [Romans 14:23]. Also in Romans 14, "Let each one be certain about his faith." Indeed, faith is not doubt, but ἔλεγχος, that is, a certain conviction (*assensio*) concerning things with are not seen. Therefore, the custom of the Academics and the Sceptics must be roundly rejected, for they refuse to affirm anything and command men to doubt everything, or certainly ἐπέχειν, that is, to suspend the giving of approval. It destroys religion entirely when someone bids us to doubt concerning the will of God, insofar as it has been revealed in Scripture, that is, to doubt concerning the threats and the promises. One must conclude the same thing concerning the rest of the articles which the Scriptures set forth.

Catalogue of Topics

God

God is one

Three Persons of the Godhead

Creation

The cause of sin and contingency

Human powers / Free will

Sin

Original sin

Punishments

Actual sins

The divine Law

The division of laws

The law of nature

The difference between commandments and counsels

Poverty

Chastity

The Gospel

Why the promise of the Gospel is needed

Grace and justification

Good works

The promises of the Law

The difference between mortal and venial sin

Predestination

The difference between the Old and New Testaments

The Spirit and the letter

Christian freedom

The Sacraments

The number of Sacraments

Baptism

The Baptism of John and of the Apostles

The Baptism of infants

The Lord's Supper

Eucharistic sacrifice

Repentance

The sin against the Holy Spirit

Confession

Satisfaction

Ecclesiastical power: the Keys

The Church

Human traditions

Mortification

Scandal

The kingdom of Christ is spiritual

The resurrection of the dead

Afflictions: Bearing the cross

Prayer

Civil magistrates and the dignity of civil affairs

Ecclesiastical polity

GOD

The most concise introduction to this topic is provided in Christ's admonition in which He responds to Philip's question about the greatest and weightiest matter of all, that is, about the nature of God: "Lord, show us the Father!" [John 14:8]. Christ calls him back from investigating God's hidden nature and teaches him how God is to be sought and known. For He says, "He who sees Me sees the Father also. Or do you not believe that I am in the Father, and that the Father is in Me?" Speculations about God stir up great tumults in the minds of men when they argue about God's nature and will apart from God's Word and the signs which God has set forth. For although there are certain traces of the Godhead impressed on the nature of created things, nevertheless the infirmity of human minds is so great that they are not sufficiently influenced by those traces. And when they see that things go badly for the good and well for the wicked, they doubt whether God is concerned with human affairs, or whether all things actually happen by chance. Besides this, that will of God which a person must know in order to be saved cannot in any way be discerned by reason, namely, that God wants to forgive sins. For this determination—this will of God—has only been revealed by the voice of God in the promises and in the Gospel.

Therefore, in order that human minds might be able to grasp God in some way and discern His will, God has always set forth some word and sign to which the minds of men might turn and grasp God through the word and the sign. Thus, in the First Commandment: "I am the God who led you out of the land of Egypt." He sets forth a recent and memorable deed so that they may know which God they should call upon and worship, namely, this God who led the Israelites out of Egypt and gave them this word. Yes, all of His deeds and all of His signs were testimonies and types of the coming Christ. Therefore, this very Christ has now been born to us; He suffered, was crucified, died, rose again, and is now set forth. We should keep this Christ and His word in view by faith whenever our minds begin to doubt and debate what the nature or will of God is. For if the minds of men allow themselves to be deterred from this aim, attempting to measure and comprehend the divine nature without God's word, with human thoughts, they will fall into dreadful darkness.

Then, concerning the will of God, the matter itself suggests that men cannot, without the Gospel, by the judgment of reason alone, find out about the mercy of God. That is, they cannot know that God wants to forgive. Therefore, the Gospel sets forth for us this access to the knowledge of God, of which Paul speaks when he says, "Since the world, in wisdom, did not know God through wisdom, it pleased God to save those who believe through foolish preaching" [1 Corinthians 1:21]. For he bids us not to seek out the answer in nature, but to acknowledge God's will set forth in Christ. Once this is done, then the presence of God is truly discerned, along with His goodness and power in us. This knowledge should not consist in idle speculation, but when terrified minds are aware of sins, they are raised up again by the voice of the Gospel, and they flee to Christ and grasp mercy. There, when they receive comfort, the presence and goodness of God are discerned.

This method of teaching does not progress from the starting point, that is, from the hidden nature of God to the knowledge of His will, but from the knowledge of Christ and the mercy revealed in the Gospel to the knowledge of the presence of God. It is much better and a much better procedure to exercise and confirm this knowledge in one's whole life, in all dangers, in all one's affairs, and to arouse the mind to fear, faith, and invocation, than to stir up idle speculations and to quarrel about scholastic devices which still do not explain the hidden nature of God. And since many of these devices are impossible to sort out, they undoubtedly end up destroying consciences, not building them up. Therefore, it is most beneficial to have a limit to these discussions.

And yet, in order that the true forms of the worship of God may be retained, it is necessary to have divinely revealed decrees about the unity of the divine essence, about omnipotence, about the natures of Christ, and about the Holy Spirit. But I will not prepare long disputations concerning these things. Instead, I will repeat the decree of the Christian Church. And that the consciences of the godly may have testimonies ready at hand, I will gather together the relevant topics from the prophetic and apostolic Scriptures, that they may at once both confirm faith and instruct us about that practical knowledge. For the godly reader will always remember that one must not tarry in idle speculations, nor it is beneficial to dwell on them. But the mind must immediately be carried back to Christ and to a recognition of mercy, so that we may exercise faith and invocation. There God is more clearly seen, even as Christ commands that we look at Him when we seek the Father. For He says, "He who sees Me sees the Father" [John 14:9]. And again, "No one comes to the Father except through Me" [John 14:6]. And in Matthew 11, "No one knows the Son except the Father. Nor does anyone know the Father except the Son, and the one to whom the Son chooses to reveal Him."

GOD IS ONE

If we gather together the descriptions of God that are found throughout the Scriptures, they will provide a definition. For the Scriptures testify that God is a spiritual substance. As Christ says, "God is Spirit" [John 4:24]. They ascribe to Him eternity, infinite power, infinite wisdom, infinite goodness, infinite justice, infinite mercy. Furthermore, "substance" should not be understood here as something that suffers accidents, for in God there is nothing accidental (*caducum*). "Substance" in this instance most properly signifies an essence (οὐσίαν) that subsists by itself. Wisdom, goodness, mercy, and righteousness are not accidents in God, but just as we do not divide power from the substance, so we do not separate either wisdom or goodness from the substance. For in effect, power is wisdom, goodness, and similar virtues, as I will demonstrate.

Now we shall seek testimonies about the unity of God.

Deuteronomy 6, "Hear, O Israel: The Lord your God, the Lord is one."

Isaiah 44, "Thus says the Lord, the King of Israel and his Redeemer, the Lord of hosts. I am the First and the Last, and besides Me there is no God."

Isaiah 45, "I am God, and there is no other besides. Besides Me there is no God. I am God and there is no other, forming light and creating darkness." Likewise, "There is no other God besides Me, a righteous God and a Savior. There is no other besides Me. Be converted to Me and be saved, all you ends of the earth. For I am God, and there is no other."

1 Corinthians 8, "We know that an idol is nothing in the world, and that there is no other God but one. For although there are those who are called gods, whether in heaven or on earth, just as there are many gods and many lords, nevertheless there is one God the Father, from whom all things are, and we in Him. And there is one Lord Jesus Christ, through whom all things are, and we through Him."

Ephesians 4, "One God and Father of all, who is over all and through all things."

Manichaeus attacked this article, among others, because it did not seem appropriate to him that the same One should be the Author and Creator of good and evil. Therefore, he imagined two principles, both coeternal, that is, two gods, the one good and the author of good, the other evil, the author of evil. Against this impiety one must hold to the decrees about the unity of God. We will explain under the article on creation how one should respond concerning the origin of evil. The Valentinians, too, imagined a prodigious multitude of gods. Such things can easily be refuted.

THREE PERSONS OF THE GODHEAD

Scripture teaches that God is one, and yet it attributes the divine essence to three persons. It must be stated, therefore, that there is only one divine essence, and that these persons have the same essence, that they are *homoousioi*, to use the [Nicene] Council's word. Moreover, in this discussion, the Church Fathers do not use the word "person" as it is sometimes used in Latin or in the theaters to signify the distinction of a certain character or role, as when we say that Roscius sometimes plays the person of Ajax, other times the person of Ulysses, or the person of a king, or of a servant. But the word "person" in these ecclesiastical discussions is used for an indivisible, intelligent substance.

Nazianzus writes that the Latins used the word "person" for *hypostasis*, since they had no better word, although the Greeks even afterwards preferred to say *prosopa* rather than *hypostasis*. There are, then, three persons of the Godhead, immense, coeternal, *homoousioi*, Father, Son, and Holy Spirit. The Son is called "the Word", the *Logos*, by John. In the Epistle to the Hebrews, the Son is called the "express image" of the substance of the Father. And one can easily understand that it is talking about the divine nature of the Son when it says that all things were made through the Son. In Colossians, He is called εἰκὼν τοῦ θεοῦ, the image of God the Father. From this we can understand why the Son is called "the Word." The Father, understanding Himself, begets a certain thought which is His image, just as our thoughts are also images of things. But we do not pour out our essence into those images. God the Father, however, pours out His essence into that image. This thought is the image and effulgence (ἀπαύγασμα) of the Father and is called "the Word." For this reason, John calls the Son the *Logos*.

The third person is called the "Holy Spirit." In John, He is said to proceed from the Father and the Son, not to be born of them. Indeed, these names which indicate the differences between the persons must be carefully observed and retained. The name "Spirit" indicates something about how this person is different from the others. For the word "spirit" elsewhere signifies an activity or a moving force.

However, since Christ is often mentioned later on in the testimonies, I have decided that a discussion of the distinction of persons should be added here. At the chosen time, the Son assumed the human nature from the virgin Mary. Christ is that Son, one person, consisting of two natures, the divine and the human. The Father did not assume the human nature, nor did the Holy Spirit assume the human nature. The Spirit is the Mover by whom the Godhead warms and vivifies, as He is described in the very beginning by Moses. It is helpful to add this passage, because the godly and learned have always adapted it in order to describe the persons in some way and to indicate the differences between them.

"God said" [Genesis 1:3]. Here is mentioned the Word which God spoke before the created things. That is, He decreed something by thinking it. And in that thinking, the image of the Father, which is the Son, shines forth. Then the Holy Spirit is mentioned: "The Spirit of God was hovering over the waters" [Genesis 1:2]. The Jews misrepresent this as a physical wind. But even though this passage is somewhat obscure, it indicates, however dimly, that it is talking about some divine force that was warming and preserving the waters, especially when it explicitly adds, "the Spirit of God." For this reason, godly men understand this passage to be about the Holy Spirit. And from this they have taken up these descriptions: The Father creates things through the Word, and the Godhead warms, moves, and vivifies by the Holy Spirit.

Testimonies

Matthew 28, "Baptizing them in the name of the Father, and of the Son, and of the Holy Spirit." He lists the three persons by name and attributes to them equal power and honor. For it is certain that Baptism is a testimony about God in which God indicates that He forgives us and receives us into grace. We, in turn, confess that He is God whom Baptism proclaims to be God, that He is to be called upon, and that salvation is to be expected from Him. Therefore, when "in the name of the Father" is said, we confess that Father to be God who has now forgiven us, who has received us into grace, who is to be called upon, who is omnipotent, who can and will give us eternal life. We who have been baptized ought to trust that the Father provides these things, and we should call upon Him with confidence.

This is the understanding of the words of Baptism. Therefore, since those words profess that the Father is God, is omnipotent, is to be called upon, and since Christ adds the Son and the Holy Spirit to the fellowship of this honor, He testifies that their power is equal. And since the power is equal, He indicates that they are *homoousioi*. It is clear, then, that the Father and Christ the Son are distinct persons. So, too, a distinct person is indicated with the name Holy Spirit. For if the Spirit signified only the Father Himself as the one propelling or moving things, then the Father would have been twice named, and this would have been a useless tautology. Indeed, Basil[6] wisely and convincingly proceeds in a rational way from this saying of Christ to the understanding that the Father, the Son, and the Holy Spirit are *homoousioi*. "For it is necessary that you be baptized, as we have received; that you believe, as we are

---

6   Basil of Caesarea (330–379 A.D.), one of the Cappadocian Fathers, was an important theological opponent of the Arians.

baptized; that you praise, as we have believed, the Father, and the Son, and the Holy Spirit."

But since there are proofs scattered throughout the Scriptures, some of which speak only about the Son while others speak about the Holy Spirit, the testimonies about the Son will have to be gathered first. The chief proof is in the first chapter of John, who, they say, was compelled to write his Gospel by the fact that Ebion,[7] and then Cerinthus,[8] had spread around a Jewish opinion and had removed from Christ the divine nature, pretending that He has only a human nature. But before I turn to John, I will propose two reasonable arguments, drawn from the Scriptures, which are useful, in my opinion, both for teaching and for comforting the godly.

The first is this: It is necessary to confess that Christ is the natural Son of God, because the Scriptures distinguish adopted sons from Christ the Son. For John calls Christ the only-begotten Son, John 1, "… glory as of the only-begotten." Now, since He is certainly a natural Son, it is necessary for something of the divine nature to be in Him substantially. But whatever is outside the person of the Father, which, nevertheless, is something of the divine nature, must necessarily be a person.

The second argument: The whole Scripture, with great consensus, commands us to worship Christ, to call upon Him. It enjoins us to trust in Him. Therefore, it attributes to Him infinite and divine power, that He is present everywhere, that He looks into hearts, that He hears, that He justifies, that He saves. So there must necessarily be a divine nature in Christ. Moreover, there are clear testimonies about the invocation of Christ and trust in Christ. Matthew 11, "Come to Me, all you who labor and are burdened, and I will refresh you." John 3, "He who believes in the

---

7   Ebion was a Judaizing heretic who denied Jesus' divine nature.
8   Cerinthus was a first century Gnostic who claimed that the Christ descended upon Jesus at His baptism, and departed from Him at His crucifixion.

Son has eternal life." Isaiah 11, "In that day, the Root of Jesse will stand as a sign for the peoples. The nations will pray to Him." Psalm 45, "And the King will desire your beauty, for He Himself is your God, and they will worship Him." Psalm 72, "And they will fear Him, as long as the sun and the moon." Again, "They will pray before Him always."

In these and similar testimonies it is clearly stated about the everlasting kingdom of Christ that He is to be called upon forever, worshiped forever. Therefore, this worship cannot be understood about an external demonstration of honor, as is shown to a person, as to a king who holds a physical or civil kingdom. But these decrees must be ascribed to the kingdom of Christ, who reigns in the power of God, as Psalm 110 says: "Sit at My right hand." And since it testifies that Christ is to be called upon, it obviously attributes to Him divine power. Therefore, let us sustain ourselves with these arguments of reason, for at the same time they both teach us what kind of honor belongs to Christ, and they comfort us, showing the benefits of Christ. Invocation ascribes omnipotence to Christ. Therefore, this argument must be kept in view and continually set against the accusations which remove the divine nature from Christ.

Now let us proceed to the statement of John. John testifies first that the *Logos* is eternal when he says, "In the beginning was the Word." For if the *Logos* was in the beginning, before the formation of all created things, then the *Logos* is not a created thing, but is coeternal with the Father. He also adds that the *Logos* was with God. Here he distinguishes the persons, God the Father and the *Logos*, since he says that the *Logos* was with God. (We shall demonstrate this distinction more clearly later.) Then he adds also that "the Word was God." Here he plainly testifies that the *Logos* is God. Indeed, the Greek article teaches how this particle should be construed. For the *Logos* should be the subject of the sentence, while "God" is in the predicate, so that the word "God" serves as a definition, describing the *Logos*. Thus it is rendered, "The *Logos* was God." For the article belongs with the subject.

This testimony is perfectly clear. For this entire narrative of John was arranged particularly for the purpose of describing the nature of God. Therefore, although in other narratives which do not speak about God's nature, but about divinely ordained human duties—or occasionally there is a metaphor in the name "God," as when it says, "I said, 'You are gods,'"—nevertheless, in this narrative of John, the word "God" must necessarily be understood in its most proper sense. Therefore, we should remember this testimony which expressly proclaims what the nature of the Word is, namely, that the *Logos* is God by nature. Indeed, this one statement clearly refutes the Arians, who, although they conceded that the *Logos* is a person, nevertheless denied that He is God by nature. But after you concede that the *Logos* is a person, this sentence, "and the *Logos* was God," then forces you to confess that the *Logos* is God by nature. Therefore, we must, above all, highlight the fact that the *Logos* is a person. For this is the principal controversy in this matter.

Many heresies have arisen against the Trinity. But some are so monstrous, like the Valentinian heresy and the delirium of the Manichaeans, that they allege nothing that is in any way even superficially demonstrable. Therefore, they can easily be judged and refuted.

Paul of Samosata,[9] on the other hand, cleverly and craftily contends that the *Logos* is not a person. But just as, in a man, the thought or speech of the man is not a person, but a certain passing quality or emotion of the man, so he contends that, in God, the *Logos* is not a person, but only a thought of the Father, which is the Father Himself, even as we say that the mind or the goodness of the Father is the Father Himself. Or if a vocal utterance is understood, he absurdly argues that the substance and person is understood for a voice and a movement of the air or a thought revealed to others. Afterwards, he adapts John to this interpretation. "In the beginning was the word." The "word," he says, is a thought or purpose of the Creator God. It indicates that He wanted to reveal Himself

---

9 Paul of Samosata was a third century anti-Trinitarian heretic who was deposed from his position as bishop of Antioch by the Synod of Antioch in A.D. 269.

through the formation of the created things. Likewise, that He wanted to reveal Himself in Christ in order to become known in Him and save men through Him. This thought, he says, was God Himself. And by this thought, by this purpose, he claims that all things were made. As it is written in Genesis, "God said, 'Let there be light, etc.'" In the same way God proceeded to carry out all things with His voice, speaking to the fathers—Adam, Noah, Abraham—then sending out the promises to the prophets, until at last God revealed Himself in Christ. There the word became flesh, that is, that purpose of revealing Himself in that Christ, or that promise about Christ, is now accomplished; it becomes the flesh in which God wants to reveal Himself. Indeed, he says that John begins in this way in order to show that the Gospel is not a human invention; it was the eternal purpose of God to offer this Son to the world, that He might be made known in Him and save men through Him. The promises and all the revelations were made for this reason, that they should be testimonies about this coming Christ.

This is Samosata's interpretation, which, because he makes a clever allusion to a human example, deludes the ungodly because of its charm. Firm testimonies must be gathered against this, and minds must be fortified with pious study against this sophistry. Therefore, let us list the testimonies which show that the *Logos* is a person, and that it truly signifies such a Word in which the image of God is a person or a *hypostasis*—a person who speaks with the fathers and the prophets.

It is easier to refute the Arians. For if a person grants that the *Logos* is a person, as the Arians admitted, John clearly goes on to testify that the *Logos* is God. But both the Arians and the Samosatenes can thus be refuted by gathering testimonies about Christ. For since it has been proved that the divine nature is in Christ, that nature and person must necessarily be God, and that, by nature.

Scripture testifies that the *Logos* is a person, for it says in several places that all things were made through the Son. Thus there must be a divine nature in Christ through which all things were made. For it is clear that the world was not made through the human nature of Christ. John 1, "He was in the world, and the world was made through Him." Colossians 1, "All things were made through Him and in Him, and He is before all things; all things hold together in Him." Hebrews 1, "Through the Son, whom He made Heir of all things, through whom He also made the worlds, who is the brilliance of His brightness, and the exact likeness of His substance, sustaining all things by the word of His power." These sentences clearly testify that a divine nature both is and remains in Christ by which all things were made. Therefore, the *Logos* does not signify a purpose or thought outside the substance of Christ, nor does it signify a passing voice (*vox transiens*). It signifies a nature that remains in Christ, a nature that makes and preserves things. Therefore, the *Logos* is a person.

There is nothing ambiguous about these testimonies, although I am not unaware how certain clever men elude them. But when they invent their interpretations, they slander and corrupt the simple and plain sentences of the apostolic Scripture. Moreover, this matter should be judged, not on the basis of human opinions, but from the divine testimonies. I will add here the saying of John in his Epistle. "That which was from the beginning, which we have heard, which we have seen, which our hands have touched, the Word of life—that we have announced." Here he also testifies that that Word which was in the beginning is and remains in Christ Himself.

Servetus[10] tries to pull the wool over the reader's eyes, as if the most ancient, accepted writers understood the *Logos* not to be a person before He put on the human nature. Indeed, he cites Irenaeus and Tertullian. But he does an injustice to both. For Tertullian, in *Adversus Praxeam*, openly poses the question whether the *Logos* is a subsisting nature, or as

10   Servetus (Miguel Serveto) was an anti-Trinitarian heretic who lived from 1511 to 1553; he began publishing his heretical works in 1531. John Calvin had him burned at the stake in Geneva, Switzerland in 1553.

we now say, a person. He answers in the affirmative, that He is a person or a *hypostasis*. He discusses this matter with many words. This is what he says: "Therefore, whatever the substance of the Word was, that I call a person, and I claim for it the name 'Son.' And in acknowledging Him as Son, I maintain that He is second from the Father, etc."

Irenaeus also openly affirms that the *Logos* was a person before He assumed the human nature. This is what he says, cap. 20. lib. 3.: "I clearly show that the Word who existed in the beginning with God, through whom all things were made, who always aided the human race—Him God sent in these last days according to the predetermined time, united by the Father to His own form, made into a man who is able to suffer."

Origen, too, *Peri archon*, expressly affirms that the *Logos* is a person. He says, "No one should think that we call anything impersonal when we call the Wisdom of God by name." And afterwards, "Therefore, if it was once rightly accepted that the only-begotten Son of God is His Wisdom, He must subsist substantially." He affirms the same thing afterwards when he discusses the incarnation.

But I return to John where he says, "The Word became flesh." First, he testifies that the Father and the Word are not the same person. For the Father did not put on the human nature, as the Scriptures testify in many places. For the Father says of the Son, "This is My beloved Son." Secondly, since the Word became flesh, He is speaking of a person, not of a thought or a passing voice. For surely it is not a thought which is the Father Himself, or a passing voice that becomes flesh. There are, then, two natures in Christ, the *Logos* and the human nature, united in such a way that Christ is one person. The more recent authors use the word "united." The ancients also, at times, say that the natures were mingled, which, if understood correctly, is said with a proper meaning and does not conform badly to the essence of this statement, "The Word became flesh." Although Origen denies that a proper analogy of this connection can be cited, nevertheless, he compares it to red-hot iron. As fire penetrates the iron and thoroughly mixes with it, so the Word, in assuming the human nature, is resplendent in all of it. And the human nature, like a lamp that has been lit, is united to the Word. Therefore, Christ is the Son of God by nature. But if we hold that Christ is the Son of God by nature, we will also easily be able to defend the claim that there is a divine nature in Christ and that the *Logos* is a person.

John 20. Thomas openly calls Christ "God," saying, "My Lord and my God."

Romans 9, "Who is over all things, the blessed God." And lest anyone argue that "God" is understood metaphorically, let those testimonies be added which attribute to Christ the things which are proper to the divine nature, namely, to give life, to sanctify, to hear, to save, and similar things.

John 5, "Just as the Father raises the dead and gives life, so also the Son gives life to whom He wishes."

Also, "Whatever He does, the Son does these things likewise." Here He openly testifies that He acts, creates, etc., equally with the Father.

John 10, "I give eternal life."

John 14, "Whatever you ask in My name, I will do it." Here He openly testifies that He both hears and does what we ask, both of which are undoubtedly proper to a divine and immense nature.

Also, "We will come to him and make Our dwelling with him."

John 16, "The Holy Spirit will take from what is Mine." But the Holy Spirit gives life. Therefore, if He takes from Christ's power, then Christ must necessarily have divine power.

John 15, "Without Me you can do nothing." This sentence testifies that Christ is present, that He moves and governs. These are proper works of God.

Matthew 18, "Wherever two or three are gathered together in My name, there I am in the midst of them."

Also John 20. He gives the Holy Spirit. But that is also a proper work of God.

John 10, "I lay down My life and take it up again."

John 6, "I will raise him up on the last day."

And then, "If you see the Son of Man ascending to where He was before."

John 8, "Before Abraham was born, I am." Here He testifies that He existed before He put on the human nature.

John 17, "Father, glorify Me with You with the glory I had with You before the world."

Colossians 2, "In Him all the fullness of the Godhead dwells bodily." Although God dwells in others spiritually, that is, He produces new impulses in them, He dwells bodily in Christ, that is, essentially or substantially or, as we say, naturally, so that Christ's very nature or substance is divine.

From the Old Testament

Jeremiah 33, "And this is the name which they will call Him: The Lord Our Justifier (*iustificator*)." Here he ascribes to Christ both the proper name of God and the name Justifier. Therefore, he ascribes to Him the glory of God, which belongs to no one but God.

Micah 5, "His going out is from the beginning, before the days of the world." Although this testimony is obscure, it, nevertheless, signifies that the Son of God existed before the world was formed. Therefore, He is eternal. Indeed, He is God.

Isaiah 7, "His name will be called Emmanuel, that is, God with us." But that which follows is even stronger.

Isaiah 9, "His name will be called Wonderful, Counselor, Mighty God, Father of the Coming Age." The Jews contend that the word *El* is not only ascribed to God. Therefore, let us press that which follows: "Father of everlasting life." If He is the author of everlasting life after this life—as He Himself says, "I give eternal life"—then He must necessarily be God.

Isaiah 53, "The knowledge of Him will justify many." If knowing Christ justifies, He must necessarily be God. For this knowledge signifies not only to see or to hear Christ when He is present, but it signifies trust and invocation. As Isaiah says elsewhere, "In Him the nations will hope." Thus the Scriptures rather often teach us in a practical way about the divinity of Christ. And they commend to us His offices, so that they may stir up faith in us and teach us about genuine worship. For in such practice we recognize Christ better than in idle speculations.

Psalm 45, "And the King will desire your beauty, for He is your God." Here he calls Christ the King "God."

Psalm 72, "And they will fear Him as long as the sun and the moon."

Also, "And all the kings of the earth will worship Him." Here divinity is attributed to Christ, for it speaks, not of the services rendered to present kings, but of the everlasting kingdom and invocation of one person, for Christ is worshiped forever, even though He does not dwell among us visibly. Indeed, many similar passages are found in the Scriptures which the godly reader will readily acknowledge.

Psalm 110, "The Lord said to my Lord, 'Sit at My right hand.'" From this passage Christ proves that He is not only the Son of David, but the Lord. Indeed, the whole Psalm must be included here. Afterwards it describes the kingdom of Christ, "Sit at My right hand." But if He will reign with the Father with equal power, it follows that Christ is God, since His power is infinite.

Psalm 2, "Today I have begotten You." This is said of Christ alone. He is, therefore, the Son of God by nature, and for this reason, there is truly a divine nature in Christ.

One may raise the objection that the divine nature does not suffer or die; but Christ died. The solution is both common and necessary. Since there are two natures in Christ, certain things are proper to one nature; but these do not prevent the other nature from being present. These things are proper to the human nature: to suffer, to die, and similar things. For this reason, Peter also said, "Christ suffered in the flesh." From this has come the principle of the communication of attributes, used in the schools, which is very useful. It is, moreover, a figure of speech by which a property that applies to the other nature is attributed to the whole person. For example, God is man, Christ is dead. Irenaeus says this: "Christ suffered while the Word rested, so that He might be able to be crucified and die." This seems to me to be a very appropriate manner of speech. It meaningfully describes the humiliation of the Son of God, of which Paul speaks to the Philippians when he says, "He emptied Himself," that is, He did not use His power, His gifts, His glory. He did not exert His might in His suffering. Therefore, it seems to me that this response is also useful at times, that some sayings speak properly about the humbled Christ, as when He begins to be troubled and distressed. Likewise, "My God, why have You forsaken Me?" For these sentences must be maintained: that the Son of God is the Redeemer, and that He is humbled.

That other response is also highly necessary: that certain sayings have the offices in view. For example, "The Father is greater than I." Here Christ is speaking, not of His nature, but of His office. The Jews were accusing Christ of teaching against the authority of God. Here it was necessary for Christ to cite the authority of the Father. For this reason,

He testifies that He was sent by the Father, that He had received authority from the Father, as one who is sent receives authority from the one who sends. In this sense He says, "The Father is greater than I," that is, I was sent by the Father. I received authority from the Father. So, then, He speaks, not of His nature, but of His office.

Let this be sufficient admonition concerning the interpretation of dissimilar sentences. I will omit here many scholastic debates, for one must think and speak reverently about that hidden and wondrous humiliation of the Son of God, which can certainly be neither understood nor defined by means of profane discussions. But we will thus acknowledge both the afflictions and the power of Christ, since we will be participants in His hardships and will also be raised up again and comforted by trusting in Him.

Now, I admonished above that these two arguments must be kept in view: that the Scripture distinguishes Christ from adopted sons, teaching that Christ is, by nature, the Son of God; also, that since the Scripture commands that Christ be called upon and that one should trust in Him, it attributes omnipotence to Him. These two arguments clearly testify that there is a divine nature in Christ. They are also profitable for invocation and for the true exercises of faith, which include the true honor of Christ and the true forms of worship.

The Holy Spirit

The name "Spirit" generally signifies a movement or a moving nature or force. But the word is used in various ways in Scripture. Sometimes it signifies wind; other times, life; [and] often the created impulses or moving forces of men, both good and evil. Here it signifies a spiritual nature. "God is Spirit" [John 4:24]. Indeed, in this passage the name is common to the Father and the other persons. For this reason, discernment must be shown in gathering testimonies, and one must judge prudently where the Scripture properly speaks about the Holy Spirit, whom the Gospel proclaims is given through Christ that He may vivify and sanctify, and whom the Church acknowledges to be a divine, vivifying, sanctifying person.

Indeed, it must be stipulated that the Holy Spirit is a person. For there have been many cunning men in the Church who have contended that the Holy Spirit is not a person, but signifies only a created movement in men, or that, perhaps, it signifies properly the Father Himself, who is powerful, that is, who alone moves, without another person. But Christ distinguishes between the persons when He says, "Baptizing in the name of the Father, and of the Son, and of the Holy Spirit" [Matthew 28:19]. For if the Holy Spirit were the Father Himself, He would be repeating the name "Father" in vain. Likewise, to be baptized in the name of the Father and of the Son and of the Holy Spirit is to confess that the Father and the Son and the Holy Spirit save, hear prayers, etc. Therefore, since equal honor is ascribed to the Father, the Son, and the Holy Spirit, it follows also that the Holy Spirit here is understood to be God; not a created movement, but a saving person, just as the Father and the Son also save.

The persons are distinguished quite clearly in the third chapter of Luke. The Father says, "This is My beloved Son." Thus the Father is one person, the Son is another. The Holy Spirit, moreover, descends in the likeness of a dove. If the Holy Spirit were a created activity in the mind, He would not appear with a peculiar bodily likeness. Or if He were the Father Himself, then the Spirit would not be distinguished from Him. But it says, "The One upon whom you see the Holy Spirit, etc." [John 1:33]. Christ is obviously called the Son of the Father, not of the Holy Spirit. And Christ says, "He will take from what is Mine" [John 16:14]. In the same way, He is distinguished from the Father: "I will ask the Father, and He will give you another Paraclete" [John 14:16]. He appears at Pentecost in the peculiar form of tongues. In my judgment, there is great force in this argument. For surely the pious must confess that the Holy Spirit was truly there in the form of that dove or those tongues, and that this person was neither the Father nor the Son. The Holy Spirit, then, is a third person, proceeding from the Father and the Son.

John 14, "I will ask the Father, and He will give you another Paraclete." And a little later, "The Paraclete, the Holy Spirit whom the Father will send in My name—He will teach you all things." If the Holy Spirit signified a created movement, then He would be the teaching itself. But here Christ calls Him a Teacher. "He will teach," says Christ. He calls Him the Paraclete. He also says, "He will speak the things He hears." These things properly apply to a person. And when He says, "another Paraclete," He distinguishes the Holy Spirit from the Father. Therefore, the Holy Spirit does not signify the Father Himself as He stirs and moves, as Samosatene contends, but another person.

1 Corinthians 12, "One and the same Spirit effects all these things." Here he distinguishes the Holy Spirit as the originator from the effects, namely, from the created gifts and spiritual impulses.

I like this testimony as well. Acts 2, "I will pour out from My Spirit on all flesh." For when He says, "I will pour out," He testifies that the Spirit who sanctifies and stirs up the godly is not the very person of the Father. And yet when He says, "of My Spirit," it signifies that the Spirit who is efficacious in the godly is a divine nature.

1 John 5, "There are three who testify in heaven: the Father, the Word, and the Holy Spirit, and these three are one."

This passage from John 15 teaches that the Holy Spirit proceeds from the Father and from the Son: "When the Paraclete comes, whom I will send you from the Father, the Spirit of truth, who proceeds from the Father." Christ confirms that the Spirit is sent from Himself, and that He proceeds from the Father. He is distinguished, then, from the Father and the Son.

Peter clearly testifies that the Holy Spirit existed before the Son of God put on flesh. He says concerning the prophets that the Spirit of Christ foretold in them that the Christ would suffer. Here He is expressly called the Spirit of Christ, who was in the prophets. By the same Holy Spirit, then, both the fathers and the apostles and the godly in succession have been sanctified.

Moreover, just as the Scripture teaches us about the divinity of the Son, not only speculatively, but practically, that is, it commands us to call upon Christ and to trust in Christ—for thus divine honor is ascribed to Him—so the Scripture also wants us to recognize the divinity of the Holy Spirit in His work of comforting and bringing to life. It commands us to ask that He be given to us, that we may be sanctified, edified and vivified through Him. Christ said: "He will give the Holy Spirit to those who ask Him" [Luke 11:13]. In this way, then, we will afford true honor to the Holy Spirit, when we ask that He be given to us as Paraclete, Teacher, Guide, and Sanctifier. This is how we will truly recognize Him, when we pray in this way and when we edify and comfort ourselves with the Word, by which the Holy Spirit is efficacious. This is what the sentence in the Creed teaches us: "I believe in the Holy Spirit," that is, I believe the Holy Spirit, who testifies in the Church by the Gospel. I believe that He is efficacious through the Word, teaching and vivifying believers. I pray that we be taught and guided by this Spirit. This is also what Paul says: "The Spirit testifies with our spirit, in whom we cry, 'Abba, Father.'" [Romans 8:15-16]. That is, the Holy Spirit edifies and comforts us and causes us to recognize the mercy and presence of God. It is beneficial to consider these works of the Holy Spirit, which both bring us comfort and demonstrate His divinity in the very work He does.

I have now gathered testimonies about the Son and the Holy Spirit. And although there are more and clearer testimonies about the Son, the ones I have provided are sufficiently clear. It belongs, moreover, to the pious mind to consider the weight and force of the testimonies, not only the number. We do well to remember that the sayings of Scripture are divine oracles. Therefore let us assent to them and not twist them with sophistry.

The inexperienced should also be warned not to number more than three persons of the Godhead. For the Valentinians, after they saw that the Father, the Son, and the Holy Spirit were distinguished, went on to imagine a vast multitude of gods, having collected innumerable words which are attributed to God, as Hesiod did with Chaos, Night, Erebus, and the like. In this way, Valentinus divided up these things—eternity, mind, truth, good, power, wisdom, righteousness, and many other things. Therefore, either Valentinus thought that the Father, Son, and Holy Spirit only differ in names, not in persons, so that he retained one person, according to the Jewish custom; or he also imagined for himself innumerable persons. All men should reject these delusions. Indeed, the godly should know that the words "power" and "virtues," as also "righteousness" and "mercy," are equally common to all the persons and are not things that are distinct from the very substance of the Godhead. The power of God is the very substance of God. We must think the same thing about righteousness, mercy, and similar virtues. Therefore, the Church only declares there to be three persons of the Godhead: the Father, the Son, and the Holy Spirit. And it teaches us to discern these persons by their offices. It wants us to keep the offices in view rather than argue about their nature. When we consider our Baptism, when we list in the Creed Father, Son, and Holy Spirit, we will remember that the Son is set before us as the Redeemer and Mediator through whom we approach the Father. We will remember also that the Holy Spirit is set forth so that the godly may be sanctified and guided by Him. Let us also set forth for ourselves the Scriptures which command us to call upon the Son and which teach that He is a Son by nature; likewise, the Scriptures which command us to ask for and to worship the Holy Spirit as Teacher and Guide. In this invocation, in these exercises of faith, we will acknowledge the Trinity better than in idle speculations in which people argue over what the persons do among themselves, instead of focusing on what they do with us.

CREATION

God made all the angels and all bodily natures out of nothing. This is called "creation." Indeed, creation is described often, not only in Genesis, but in other places as well. Psalm 33, "By the Word of the Lord were the heavens established, and all their might by the breath of His mouth." And then, "He spoke, and they were made. He commanded, and they were created." Here it means that things were made out of nothing by the Word of God. For things came into existence or arose as God commanded. Therefore, they did not arise from some pre-existing material. John also says, "All things were made through Him" [John 1:3]. Therefore, all these things must have been made out of nothing.

But the following must be emphasized in this article: The creation should not be understood as if God rested from His work as a builder rests from a house he has made or a ship he has built. No, God continually sustains and preserves the natures of things. This understanding of creation is necessary and proper for the godly. Therefore, in the article of creation, the continual preserving and sustaining of things must always be understood. "I believe in God the Father Almighty, the Creator of heaven and earth." Here understand, not only the making, but the continual governing and preserving. Every year He makes the earth fertile. He brings forth crops from the earth. He continually supplies the living creatures with life and movement. Indeed, this preservation of things is called a general activity of God.

It is very helpful to have testimonies concerning this article for training faith in the exercise of invocation. Acts 17, "In Him we live and move and are." Hebrews 1, "Upholding all things by the Word of His power." Colossians 1, "All things are held together in Him." In 1 Timothy [6:13], it says that God "gives life to all things." Likewise, "We hope in the living God, who is the Savior of all men, especially of those who believe." Again, "In the living God, who provides us with all things abundantly for our enjoyment." Matthew 10, "They sell two sparrows for a penny, and not one of them falls to the earth without your Father. And the hairs of your head are all numbered." Psalm 104, "All things look to You to give them their food in due season. When You give them, they gather. When You open Your hand, all things are filled with goodness. When You hide Your face, they are thrown into confusion. When You remove their spirit, they pass away and return to their dust. Send out Your Spirit, and they will be created, and You will renew the face of the earth." Psalm 100, "Know that the Lord, He is God. He Himself has made us, and not we ourselves. We are His people and the sheep of His pasture." That is, we are not born, we do not live by chance or by our powers alone, but because God vivifies and preserves us. Psalm 33, "The Lord has looked from heaven; He has seen all the sons of men. He fashions their hearts, one by one; He understands all their works." Psalm 147, "Who covers the heaven with clouds and prepares rain for the earth; who produces grass on the mountains, tender grass for the servitude of men. He gives to the beasts their food and to the chicks of the ravens that call upon Him." Psalm 36, "You will preserve men and beasts, O Lord."

Finally, the Lord's Prayer teaches this very thing, where we are commanded to seek daily bread from God. We confess, therefore, that God supplies life's nourishment, that nothing is sustained, that nature is not fertile, unless God grants His aid. Indeed, this is confessed in all the statements that teach that we are nourished and protected by God. For example, "Cast your care upon the Lord, and He will sustain you" [Psalm 55:22]. This presence of God in created things, that is, His preservation of created things, is not discerned by reason, but must be discerned by faith. Thus the Scripture teaches us not only about the creation of things, but about their continual preservation. Nor is creation rightly understood unless we also believe that the created things are continually sustained and preserved, that movement and life are supplied to the created things by God. Indeed, this faith is the true understanding of creation, which is also beneficial for invocation. For how can a human spirit seek from God nourishment, life, powers, protection, etc., unless he believes that God is present, that He governs, maintains, and preserves nature?

After the mind has been confirmed by the Word of God itself with the true and correct understanding of God and of creation, then it is both useful and gratifying also to seek the traces of God in nature and to gather the proofs which testify that there is a God. For surely the entire nature of things was created so as to point to God. Many clear proofs can be gathered as witnesses that the world did not come into existence by chance, that it is not governed by chance, but that all things are ruled by some immense and eternal mind. This is also what Paul says to the Romans. "The Godhead is observed in nature" [Romans 1:19–20]. And in Acts, he says much more significantly that God is so close that He can almost be touched with the hands. Paul surely intended to use such a momentous statement in order to incite us to this philosophy. For he adds that the proofs of the Godhead have been set forth in such a way that we learn to consider the presence of God in nature. Therefore, the whole universe of created things should be thought of as a kind of sacrament, namely, in that it is a testimony that there is a God, that He is wise, good, and righteous. The laws governing the motion of the celestial bodies are so manifold and so precise—the harmony of the higher bodies with the lower bodies, the change of seasons, the nature of each created thing being destined for definite purposes and uses, the preservation of determined species—do these things not sufficiently cry out that the nature of created things does not exist by chance, but was created and is preserved by a fixed plan?

But the clearest trace of God is the mind of man, and the knowledge impressed on the mind that God is honorable and just, and the terrors of conscience. For there must necessarily be another mind from which the minds of men and such knowledge arose. And since the human mind has the ability to discern between righteousness and unrighteousness, there must also be wisdom and righteousness in that eternal mind. Human minds, then, are images of the Godhead, or, so to speak, mirrors in which we ought to contemplate the Godhead.

The civil society of mankind also points to the presence of God. It is obvious that governments cannot be established or retained except by divine influence. We see murderers and tyrants divinely carried off to punishment. The knowledge of the law about God still shines in their minds—that there is a God, that He is just.

This knowledge would be much brighter if the nature of man were not afflicted with the disease of origin. Not that this disease has entirely extinguished that divine light in our minds, for a certain knowledge of natural law remains. But the disease of origin has spread a dark cloud over our minds. The godly must now see to it, first, that they rekindle that knowledge with the Word of God. Then let them also render that knowledge brighter by consulting the signs that have been written into nature. It is terribly uncivilized for a person not to desire to contemplate so much light in nature. In addition, since God Himself invites us to this philosophy, we must not entirely neglect it, especially since it is highly conducive to discipline and advantageous to morality. For it stirs up and confirms religion and reverent opinions in the mind about the presence and righteousness of God.

Now, these thoughts are made brighter and are contemplated more accurately when the true teaching of physics is applied. More traces of the Godhead become evident to those who studiously examine and consider nature and ponder it wisely. The Epicureans became atheists because they corrupted physics. But nature itself led others who pondered it rightly to this light: that they both acknowledged that there is a God and concluded that nature itself is divinely ruled and preserved.

The most distinguished discussions in favor of this opinion are found in Xenophon, who, after gathering many arguments, at length stated that from these things it is indisputable that nothing came into existence by chance, but that the world is the handiwork of "a wise Craftsman who loves life."[11] It is truly a very sweet description, to call God a Creator "who loves life." For he observed that all things were created for the benefit of men, and therefore that God cares for men. He reasoned, why would God work so meticulously at helping, protecting, and equipping mankind if we had only been created for the short span of this bodily life? To Xenophon, God's philanthropy toward us is apparent in the very nature of the created things. Therefore, we Christians should also contemplate nature and there perceive the presence and the kindness of God toward us. This study is very beneficial to discipline and confirms good and pious opinions in the mind. And yet this philosophy must be governed by the Word of God. Then it is a work of great piety to use the created things in such a way that we glorify God through them and proclaim His presence and His kindness in them, giving Him thanks.

I have said these things, by the way, in order to show how much I delight in this philosophy of examining the traces of the Godhead in nature, and I urge students to take it up.

THE CAUSE OF SIN AND CONTINGENCY

Both of these arguments—concerning the cause of sin and concerning contingency—have challenged the Church at various times and have caused great tragedies. Indeed, brilliant men put together many

---

11 Xenophon, *Memorabilia*, Book I, chapter 4.

inextricable and absurd arguments concerning both topics. And since these arguments are somewhat dangerous, the young should be admonished to set aside those infinite debates and seek rather the simple and pious understanding, which is useful for religion and morality. Let them hold firmly to this understanding, and may they not allow themselves to be led astray from it by the deceitfulness of such arguments.

Now, this is the godly and true understanding of both questions, and it must be genuinely maintained in every heart: that God is not the cause of sin, and that God does not want sin. The causes of sin are the will of the devil and the will of man. For it says in the first chapter of Genesis, "God saw all that He had made, and it was very good." And in the Psalm, "You are not a God who wants wickedness" [Psalm 5:4]. And Christ says, "The devil is the father of lies and speaks lies from his own" [John 8:44]. Therefore, He transfers the cause to the devil when He calls him "the father of lies." And when He says that the devil "speaks from his own," He distinguishes the vice from the nature which God created and preserves. For these things do not contradict one another: to say, on the one hand, that nature arose from God and is preserved by Him, and, on the other hand, that the will of the devil and of man is the cause of sin. For the will was able to abuse its own freedom and turn away from God. Other testimonies can also be added, such as Romans 5, "Through a man sin entered the world." And in the Epistle of John, "The lust of the flesh, etc., is not of the Father, but of the world" [1 John 2:16].

Nor are those figures of speech in the Scriptures troubling: "I will harden Pharaoh's heart" [Exodus 14:4] and similar passages. For it is certain, according to the Hebrew usage, that such words signify God's permission, not His efficacious will, just as we say in the Lord's Prayer, "Lead us not into temptation," that is, "Do not permit us to be led into it."

We must also agree with those who teach that sin expressly signifies, not the nature created by God, but a corruption or a defect, even as original sin is a lack of gifts and of righteous obedience in the nature of man. Now, however, God preserves man's nature such as it is, even though corruption has arisen from elsewhere. Disordered emotions are actual sins, namely, when the deficient will turns away from a righteous object. The sinful emotion itself or the action is called the material cause of sin while the defect or disorder is called the formal cause. But this is the reason for the vice. Sin properly signifies the guilt of that corruption and defect.

Since it has been firmly established that God is not the cause of sin, it clearly follows that contingency must be granted. For since sin properly arose from the will of the devil and of man, and since this was not done with God's approval or by God's coercion of our wills, it cannot have happened necessarily, by an absolute necessity. Indeed, our will, before the fall into sin, was truly free. The freedom of the will, then, is the cause of the contingency of our actions. For it is the contingency of our actions that is in question. This argument, taken from the cause of sin, is sufficiently clear and should be set against those arguments which entirely remove contingency and often stir up great turmoil in curious and clever minds.

The following must also, then, be granted, that the Scripture also now attributes to man, after the fall into sin, a certain freedom to choose the things that are subject to reason, for performing civil righteousness, as we will say later. Therefore, just as God created the whole of nature, so He also created this gift of nature, this manner of acting, namely, freedom. But freedom is, as we have said, the source of contingency in human actions. Therefore, God foresees contingent things and limits them in such a way that He does not remove the manner of acting that has been placed into nature, but limits the actions as they are done. He permits the will of Saul, for example, to act in a certain way and does not compel him to act differently, even as He determines where He will restrain Saul.

But just as the creation itself cannot be understood or judged by any creature, so neither can these things be perceived—how freedom remains, when God both endows nature with life and powers and limits the things that are contingent. All these things pertain to the understanding of creation and cannot be sufficiently explained. Indeed, those who argue more subtly over these things gather many prodigious arguments which only serve to disturb feeble minds. Therefore, let us keep in view that reasoning which I have mentioned, the reasoning which is plain and clear, namely, that contingency must be defended, lest we make God the author or cause of sin. To be sure, freedom is a gift of God, an orderly arrangement that God has placed in the will. Therefore, although God foresees and limits contingent things, nevertheless He so limits them that the will's manner of acting—its orderly arrangement—is not removed.

Furthermore, the following distinction is necessary. There is one kind of necessity that is of the consequent, that is, absolute necessity, such as, "It is necessary that God exists, that God is good, righteous, etc." There is another kind of necessity that is of the consequence, such as, "Jerusalem must be destroyed." The latter things are not necessary by their nature, but become immutable after they are decreed. For example, "The dead shall live again." Or they become immutable because they follow as the result of preceding causes. For example, "There must be heretics." Since the devil hates God and incites wicked men against the Gospel who yield to his influence, therefore there must be heretics. These things are contingent by nature, for this consequence does not remove the freedom of the will.

Nor should the Stoic fantasies about fate or about necessity (περὶ τῆς ἀνάγκης) be imported into the Church. For there is nothing true and certain in them, but they are mere juggling acts and heaps of sophistry. Accordingly, it is not hard to see how much harm this opinion does to piety and morality, if men reason in this way, as, for example, when the young servant of Zeno said that he should not be punished, because he was forced by Stoic fate to sin. Pious ears and minds should rightly recoil from these opinions.

HUMAN POWERS / FREE WILL

Valla[12] and several others improperly remove freedom from the will of man because all things are done by God's decree. Thus they remove contingency entirely. But the dispute about contingency is foreign to this topic of human powers. For here the question is asked in the Church what man's nature is like, whether he is capable of furnishing perfect obedience to the Law of God. The question is not asked concerning the hidden counsel of God as He guides all things, or about predestination. We are not here dealing with all things contingent. Therefore, the prudent reader should here disregard the disputes about contingency, and likewise about predestination, and keep them far away from this topic. Let us be mindful of ourselves and remember that we are now speaking about our infirmity. There is no use in trying to walk the air, delving into heavenly things concerning the manner of divine governance or predestination. Indeed, we must make provision, lest good and useful things be buried by foolish arguments that do not pertain at all to the matter at hand, as often happens when foreign topics are mingled together. Therefore, I will explain briefly here how the Scripture teaches us about the infirmity of human nature, for this must be recognized so that we may learn why we need the benefit of Christ.

Concerning the powers of man, the various divisions, which are not unknown, are taken from philosophy. In man there is reason, that is, the mind that forms a judgment; and the will, which either complies with or rejects that judgment and governs the lower powers. The lower powers

---

12   Lorenzo Valla (1407–1457), an Italian humanist. A humanist and Catholic priest, Valla was called to Rome to serve as the founder of the Vatican library. Among other accomplishments as a humanist, Valla demonstrated that the purported "Donation of Constantine" (which the Papacy used as part of the basis for its claim of superiority to all secular authority) was a forgery.

are the senses and the desires of the senses, that is, the emotions. They call "free will" the will combined with reason. When Scripture mentions the heart, the mind, and similar things, it includes the judgment and the actual desires themselves, not the contrived or external work.

But for the sake of avoiding quarrels over nomenclature, we must speak about the matter at hand. The question is, in what way is the will free? That is, how can it obey the Law of God? But this question cannot be answered unless the magnitude of the sin that is innate in us, that is, our natural infirmity, is considered; and unless we know that not only external, civil deeds are required by the Law of God, but the continual and perfect obedience of the entire nature. For if the nature of man were not corrupted by sin, it would have a surer and clearer knowledge of God. It would not have doubts concerning the will of God. It would have true fear, true trust. And, finally, it would furnish a perfect obedience to the Law. That is, all the impulses in man's nature would agree with the Law of God, as in the godly angels. Now, however, the nature of man is oppressed by the disease of origin. It is full of doubt, fog, and errors. It does not truly fear God, nor does it truly trust in God. And finally, it is full of evil impulses. The question that is being asked here concerning this infirmity is, how much can the human will furnish?

First, then, I respond: Since the capacity for judgment remains in man's nature, along with a certain ability to choose the things that are subject to reason or sense, there also remains the ability to choose external, civil works. Therefore, the human will is able, in a certain way, by its own powers, apart from renewal, to do the external works of the Law. This is the freedom of the will which the philosophers rightly attribute to man. For the sacred writings also grant this to men in a certain way. The Scriptures teach that there is a certain righteousness of the flesh, certain works of the Law, in those who are not reborn. Therefore, it grants that these works can be performed by human powers, apart from renewal. Indeed, it strictly requires this external discipline when it says,

"The Law is made for the unrighteous" [1 Timothy 1:9], and, "The Law is a schoolmaster" [Galatians 3:24]. We will explain a little later how many uses this schoolmaster has. For now, I will only add that this very freedom to perform civil righteousness is often overcome by our natural weakness, often impeded by the devil. For since his nature is full of evil emotions, men often follow their depraved lusts, not right judgment, as Medea says, "I see the better, and I approve; but I follow the worse."[13] Besides, the devil also drives the captive nature to various external crimes, even as we see that the greatest men, who tried to live honorably, are guilty of the most disgraceful lapses. Nevertheless, among these difficulties, however great they may be, there still remains a certain freedom to perform civil righteousness.

Secondly, the Gospel teaches that there is a horrible corruption in nature that fights against the Law of God, that is, it makes it so that we cannot furnish perfect obedience. Human will cannot remove this corruption from its nature by itself, just as it cannot, by itself, remove death—which is the most characteristic effect of that corruption—from its nature. Moreover, there is so much blindness in human nature that we cannot sufficiently perceive this corruption. Therefore, we do not notice how much infirmity there is in human powers. If we truly discerned it, then we would finally understand that men cannot satisfy God's Law.

With regard to free will, then, it must be acknowledged that men cannot satisfy God's Law. For the divine Law requires not only external deeds, but inner cleanness, fear, trust, the highest love for God, and, finally, perfect obedience, and it forbids all evil desires. But it is an established fact that men do not furnish this perfect obedience in this corrupt nature. We are speaking especially about this corruption, not about external deeds, when we minimize the freedom of the will. For it is very important that this corruption be neither minimized nor concealed, so

---

13   Ovid, *Metamorphoses*, Book VII.

that we may understand that men do not satisfy the Law, so that we may know that we are in need of mercy, etc.

Then this, too, must be added: Without the Holy Spirit, the human will cannot produce the spiritual emotions that God requires, namely, true fear of God, true trust in the mercy of God, obedience and patience under afflictions, the love of God, and similar attitudes. There are many testimonies that bear witness that our nature is corrupt and cannot satisfy God's Law, and that it cannot produce the spiritual attitudes that God requires without the Holy Spirit.

Romans 8, "Those who are led by the Spirit of God, they are sons of God." Likewise, "If anyone does not have the Spirit of Christ, he is not Christ's." These two sentences are sufficiently clear and plainly testify that the Holy Spirit is needed so that we are able to obey. Now, it is clear that the term "Holy Spirit" refers, not to human reason, but to the Spirit of God who is efficacious in our minds.

1 Corinthians 2, "Natural man does not perceive the things which are of the Spirit of God." For "natural man" signifies a person who lives with a natural life, that is, with natural sense and reason, without the Holy Spirit. For in this way Paul distinguishes in this passage the natural man from the spiritual man. For although the knowledge of God is imprinted on man by nature, it is so obscured that the mind does not sufficiently assent to it, but doubts whether God cares for us, whether He punishes, whether He wants to forgive, to hear. The result of this doubt is that minds do not truly fear God, etc.

John 3, "Unless a person is born again of water and the Spirit, he cannot enter the kingdom of God." John 6, "No one can come to Me, unless the Father draws him," and, "They will all be taught by God." Likewise, "Apart from Me you can do nothing" [John 15:5]. These testimonies teach plainly enough that human will does not obey God apart from the Holy Spirit, that is, that human will does not have spiritual attitudes, true knowledge of God, true fear, true trust. For we are speaking here especially about the attitudes of the mind, not about external deeds. But there is no need for a lengthy argument. Let each one consult his own mind. Let him search within himself and ask if, somehow, doubts about God do not affect his soul, if he does not struggle with extraordinary unbelief, if he truly fears and loves God, if he does not hate the fact that this feeble nature is afflicted with so many troubles, like aging and death, and that, in addition, the terrors of eternal punishments are presented to him. What does he think in the midst of those very afflictions? How are minds affected when they seem to be abandoned by God? At those times, do they really not doubt whether God cares about human affairs, whether He hears the prayers of men? These important attitudes of the mind must be considered when free will is discussed.

We do not say these things in order to set traps for men's consciences, or to frighten them away from the pursuit of obedience or from believing, or to prevent them from trying. Indeed, since we should begin with the Word, we certainly should not resist the Word of God, but work at obeying it, keeping the promise of the Gospel in view, which is universal. These things can be judged more clearly in true struggles than in idle disputations. For in the real contest, when we are distressed concerning the forgiveness of sins, we should build ourselves up and keep the promise in view. But, although the will struggles with weakness, nevertheless, since it does not cast the Word away, but sustains itself with the Word, it obtains comfort. There the Holy Spirit is efficacious through the Word. As Paul says, "The Spirit helps our weakness" [Romans 8:26]. In this battle, the mind must be exhorted to make every effort to retain the Word. It should not be dissuaded from making such an effort but must be taught that the promise is universal and should be believed. In this example, we see these causes joined together: the Word, the Holy Spirit, and the will—not the will as completely idle, but as it fights against its weakness.

The writers of the Church are accustomed to joining these causes together in this way. Basil says, "Only be willing, and God will go forth to meet you."[14] God goes ahead of us. He calls, moves, and helps. But we must see to it that we do not fight against Him. For it is certain that sin arises from us, not from the will of God. Chrysostom says, "He who draws, draws the willing."[15] This applies to the one who follows the guidance of the Word, not to the one who opposes or fights against it. We must surely draw this conclusion. For we should not indulge unbelief or the laziness of our nature.

Furthermore, if we were to speak of the whole life of the godly, even though there is great weakness, nevertheless there is a certain freedom of the will, since it now surely receives help from the Holy Spirit, and it can do something to avoid external lapses. Therefore, the Holy Spirit's aid should be magnified, and at the same time, our diligence should be sharpened, as Paul commands us to beware, "lest we received grace in vain" [2 Corinthians 6:1]. And Christ, when He says, "He will give the Holy Spirit to those who ask" [Luke 11:13], makes this promise, not to the idle, not to those who despise, not to those who oppose. God increases His gifts in those who use them rightly, as the parable of the talents teaches.

Finally, concerning discipline I said above that the will is able to perform civil duties by its own powers after a fashion. Indeed, God requires this discipline also in those who are not yet sanctified, and there is surely some benefit in it. For external offenses are punished with bodily and with eternal punishments. In addition, Paul says that the Law is a schoolmaster toward Christ. For this pedagogy is useful in order that men may hear and be taught the Word of God. Yes, since God is efficacious through the Word, many are called to true piety through these exercises.

---

14 Basil, *Homily on Repentance*.
15 Chrysostom, *De ferendis reprehensionibus*, Homily 3.

This understanding of free will makes perfect sense and is the genuine understanding, not only of other ecclesiastical writers and of the councils, but also of Augustine. It does not drive good minds to despair, nor does it deter them from trying. Indeed, it both magnifies the aid of the Holy Spirit and sharpens the care and diligence of our will. I do not approve of the delusions of the Manichaeans, who attribute no action at all to the will, not even with the assistance of the Holy Spirit, as if there were no difference whatsoever between the will and a statue. Indeed, from here statements about freedom can easily be assembled. Ecclesiasticus says, "God left man in the hand of his counsel, etc." [Sirach 15:14]. I declare that the will is not idle in pious actions and efforts, and yet it must be assisted by the Holy Spirit. In this way, it becomes more truly free.

To make these things clearer, I will add two sayings of Jerome. "If anyone says that God commands the impossible, let him be cursed." Certain unskilled men abuse this saying greatly. It is necessary, therefore, to add a suitable interpretation to Jerome's saying. We will take this up on the basis of the second saying of the same author: "Whoever says that we can fulfill God's commands apart from God's grace, let him be cursed." Here grace is to be understood, not only in that we are aided by the Holy Spirit, but also as the gratuitous imputation itself of righteousness, that is, the reception of it, namely, that we are accounted righteous for the sake of Christ. Then the incipient obedience is found pleasing, even though it does not satisfy the Law. In this way, the Law should be understood to be doable through grace. This interpretation is necessary so that we understand that the obedience of the godly is far from the perfection of the Law, and yet it is pleasing because the individuals who perform it are pleasing for Christ's sake. But let these things be more fully explained under their own topic.

SIN

Christ summarized the whole doctrine of the Gospel and practically shaped the method of teaching it when He commanded that repentance and forgiveness of sins should be preached. These are the chief topics of the whole doctrine of Christ, to which the remaining parts should be directed back as to the head.

Now, the preaching of repentance censures and condemns sin, as it is written in John [16:8], "The Holy Spirit will convict the world concerning sin, etc." Therefore, it must be diligently explained in ecclesiastical doctrine what the Scripture calls "sin." Indeed, it is for this reason that Paul spends almost the entire Epistle to the Romans comparing these three topics: sin, the Law, and grace. Therefore, we, too, have undertaken to explain this topic, especially since the Scripture judges differently than human reason or philosophy or civil laws about sin. There is need of extraordinary wisdom in this article. For there are also many theologians who have stumbled here, who understood sin only with regard to civil deeds. This error then gave birth to other errors. For the magnitude of the benefit of Christ cannot be understood unless we first understand our malady.

First, therefore, the unlearned must be instructed concerning the vocable. "Sin" in the Holy Scriptures does not only signify a certain deed, as it sounds in Latin according to the grammar. No, it signifies also a chronic illness (*perpetuum vicium*), that is, the corruption of nature which is at odds with the Law as well as the deeds which are at odds with the Law of God. Therefore, I must teach about the vocable, because some people, persuaded by a grammatical superstition, have removed the disease of origin, because sin, according to the Latin usage, signifies, not a chronic disease, but a certain deed. Nor do they see that the Hebrew word properly signifies something damnable, or something liable to punishment, so to speak, which, in Latin, is basically called a "crime" (*scelus*). Therefore, let sin be generally understood to be a chronic illness, or a deed that is at odds with the Law of God. Sin is divided, moreover, into the categories of original sin and actual sin. These terms are to be used for the sake of instruction.

ORIGINAL SIN

Many disagreements have arisen concerning original sin, because human reason does not see man's natural uncleanness. That is, it does not see that the things that inhere in the nature of man are damnable; namely, ignorance of God, to be devoid of the fear of God, to distrust God, etc. Since reason does not discern these enormous plagues, it imagines that only civil righteousness is required by the Law of God and that nothing else is a sin except for civil offenses.

Because of this, the unlearned distort certain sayings to this end. For example, "Nature is good," or, "Sin is not sin unless it is voluntary." These sayings are true, if they are spoken in their place, for God created nature good and whole. But afterwards, corruption entered through the sin of Adam, which prevents the natural powers from obeying the Law of God.

In the same way, "Sin is not sin unless it is voluntary." This properly refers to civil offenses. It should not be twisted to refer to original sin, even though Augustine also applies it to original sin with a rather subtle interpretation. He says that it is voluntary, not because it is in our power to accept it or to reject it, but because we are not as we are unwillingly. But there is no need for this subtle interpretation. It is sufficient to hold that it refers to civil sins. Such also is that statement: "We are neither praised nor blamed on account of the things which are present by nature."[16] I have mentioned these sayings because they are inappropriately cited by theologians in this discussion.

The scholastic teachers say many disputable things about original sin, but this is, in effect, what they think: that original sin is guilt, that is, the imputation by which Adam's posterity are guilty and condemned on account of his offense. Then they add that it is a certain weakness in nature. They call it "tinder" (*fomes*), and they deny that it is sin, that is, something that is, by its nature, worthy of condemnation. Instead, they make it a penalty of sin and a neutral matter. In addition, they teach that man is able to be without sin and to satisfy the Law. This is the sum of the thinking of the scholastics, which gives birth to many other errors, for it buries both the Law and the Gospel. For when they imagine that doubt, unbelief, and similar wicked impulses with which we are born are not sins, they obscure the Law. Then, since they imagine that only civil works are required by God's Law, and likewise that men are righteous by their own works, they destroy the Gospel concerning mercy. They likewise destroy the doctrine about faith, for they insist and teach that doubt is not a sin. Therefore, since the false persuasion concerning original sin has brought so much ruin, we must necessarily hold it accountable, so that the Law may be rightly understood and the doctrine about mercy made clear.

We, on the other hand, believe this: Original sin is not only imputation or guilt, but also the corruption of man's nature which makes it impossible for us to truly obey the Law of God and to be without sin. For although reason, which is still valid in these things that are subject to the senses, can do external and civil works, nevertheless there inhere in man's nature ignorance of God, doubt, distrust, hatred toward God, and other diseases which are at odds with the Law of God. Now, I call corruption, not a certain act, but a chronic disease. It is the same thing

---

16   A saying among the scholastics, later taken up and defended by Francisco Suárez (1548–1617), a Jesuit priest and philosopher.

which others sometimes refer to as defects, or covetousness (*concupiscentia*), or the unbridled appetite which now remains in man's nature. For the ignorance of God, the absence of fear, love, and trust in God are defects. But neither should we imagine that these defects are harmless to the nature that remains. For these very defects are horrible plagues and vices, and the most disgraceful impulses also follow, namely, distrust and hatred toward God, uncontrolled desires which fear and love carnal things.

But all these things will be clarified by way of contrast. Anselm rightly defines original sin when he says that it is the lack of original righteousness. Here righteousness should be understood, not only as imputation or approval, but also, in man's very nature, the integrity of powers in body and soul, the sure knowledge of God, perfect obedience, fear, love, and trust in God. Since this integrity has been lost, the powers of body and soul have been so corrupted that they are not truly able to obey God's Law. After man's nature lost the sure knowledge of God, ignorance, doubt, contempt, and hatred of God's judgment necessarily followed. And since it is now without God, it fears and loves carnal things and has multiple impulses that are at odds with the Law of God. This is how Anselm himself interprets his definition. He shows that he includes both the defects and the covetousness. And Bonaventure wisely says that there is no difference between these figures of speech, to say that original sin is covetousness, or to say that it is a defect. He adds that the one is signified by, and included in, the other. Therefore, the more recent authors quarrel for no reason, arguing that original sin is a defect, not covetousness, for it includes both. Indeed, they should know that the material of sin is both the covetousness and the defects, while the form of sin is truly and properly the guilt or imputation.

When Adam fell, he lost his natural integrity, since he felt the wrath and judgment of God and was subjected to the kingdom of sin and death. What is more, he was stripped of his earlier ornaments. He then begot such as were already of his own nature. Thus they contract the original illness by propagation, that is, they are guilty and have a diseased nature.

PUNISHMENTS

The Scholastics make covetousness a punishment for sin, not a sin in and of itself. We say that covetousness is both a punishment for Adam's fall and a sin in those who are born. Death, too, is a punishment. But the chief punishment is the tyranny of the devil, to whom man's nature is subject on account of sin. Genesis speaks of this punishment when it says, "You will lie in wait for His heel."[17] Therefore, the devil vents his rage on man's nature, assaulting it with terrors and with all kinds of troubles, and even killing him. In addition, he drives it to all sorts of shameful acts, to blasphemies, to ungodly opinions, to hypocrisy, to murder, hatred, etc. This is evident even in the most outstanding men who have tried to live with virtue, but who were eventually overcome by the weakness of nature and the power of the devil, falling into all manner of disgrace.

Testimonies That Original Sin Exists and What It Is

Psalm 51, "Behold, in iniquity I was conceived, and in sin did my mother conceive me." He is not lamenting the sin of his mother, but his own sin. I was conceived in such a way that, when I was formed, sin immediately existed in my mass, that is, in myself. Thus the prophet testifies that sin exists in men, that they bring it with them when they are born.

---

17   *Insidiaberis calcaneo eius*, a direct quotation from the Vulgate, in which Jerome was clearly influenced more by the Septuagint than by the Hebrew in this passage.

Ephesians 2, "We were by nature children of wrath, like the rest." It is a Hebrew phrase, "children of wrath," used for "the guilty" or "the damned." Paul says that Jews and Greeks alike are children of wrath by nature. Therefore, condemnation is not only the result of actual sins, but also of the disease of nature. Furthermore, in the same passage the greatness of that evil is described when he says that "the devil is efficacious in unbelievers." From this it can be understood what the chief punishment of original sin is, which the scholastics never touch on in their disputations. Indeed, men had to be especially admonished of this punishment—namely, that men are subject to the reign and tyranny of the devil—in order that, in recognizing the magnitude of the evil, we might understand that we need the benefit of Christ.

Romans 5, "By the offense of one man, all died." Therefore, all are guilty for Adam's fall. And, he adds, "Death spread to all, for all sinned." It is a Hebrew phrase, "they sinned," for "they are guilty," or, "they have sin." If only actual offenses were sins, then each one would only be guilty of his own deed. Now when it clearly says that we are guilty because of Adam's offense, it testifies that some other sin exists in our nature besides actual offenses. And lest that sin be understood only as guilt, the weight of these words must be observed: "Sin reigned, death reigned," and similar things. It means that men were oppressed by the wrath of God, that they have no sure knowledge of God, that they hate and flee from the judgment of God, that they die in terror of God's judgment. As Paul says, "The sting of death is sin" [1 Corinthians 15:56].

John 3, "Unless a person is born again of water and the Spirit, he cannot enter the kingdom of God." If regeneration is necessary, then the old nature is guilty and unclean.

Genesis 8, "The intention of the human heart is evil from childhood." This means that offenses are not only committed by habit, but that the sin that immediately erupts in the nature is there from the beginning.

Jeremiah's statement also belongs here: "The heart of man is crooked and unfathomable" [Jeremiah 17:9]. But Paul's statements are especially poignant in this matter in Romans 7 and 8, for they testify that sin exists. In those chapters, it is clear that he does not only accuse people of actual offenses, but of the sin that inheres in the members, of which he says, "I find another law in my members which wars against the law of my mind." Likewise, "In my flesh, I serve the law of sin." And again, "The mind of the flesh is death and enmity toward God. It cannot obey the Law of God."

These passages teach both things. They teach that men are born with sin, since covetousness is surely innate in us; and they testify that original sin is not only guilt, but also a disease that inheres in our very nature, no matter whether you call this disease a defect or covetousness. For in reality, there is no difference between the two, if you understand "defect" properly. There is nothing more serious than such defects in nature—ignorance of God, to be devoid of fear, love and trust in God. No disease can be named that is more serious than this.

These things concerning original sin are true and clear and are consistent with the Scriptures and with the Church fathers. But just as, long ago, the Pelagian philosophers inopportunely removed original sin, and just as the Scholastics, though they retain it superficially, actually remove it when they deny that covetousness is sin and pretend that man can satisfy the Law of God, so there are many poorly instructed teachers in our time who tenderly mock the things which we have said about original sin. For since reason does not discern that this weakness is a damnable thing, and since philosophy does not judge anything to be wicked that is not within our power, therefore they gather absurdities which appear to inhere in our statement and broadly attack them, judging this entire understanding of the Church to be mere fantasy. In opposition to these capricious spirits, minds should be carefully instructed from the Scriptural testimonies which we have cited. We must see to it that these testimonies not be cast off by the slanderous interpretations of those who transform the statements which were made about spiritual and hidden matters into philosophy and civil opinions.

It remains for us to interpret the common saying that they usually cite to minimize original sin. For original sin is said to be forgiven in Baptism. Because of this saying, they imagine that nothing wicked or worthy of condemnation remains after Baptism. For this reason, they also fail to teach about faith, pretending that a man is righteous by his own cleanness. But we must understand that saying in this way: In Baptism, the guilt is forgiven, and yet the disease itself remains. That is, the disease remains, but it is not imputed to the one who believes. In addition, when the Holy Spirit is given, we form new and godly impulses by which the disease begins partially to be remedied, and thus one must fight against this disease throughout one's whole life in a twofold way. First, he must be assured by faith that it is not imputed. Then, also by faith, the knowledge of God must be formed, both trust in mercy and comfort. When this is done, the disease is partially remedied and eternal life begins.

Now, I am referring to defects and covetousness as a disease, as I said above. For it is clear that both remain after Baptism, even in mature saints. For even the saints scarcely obey under the cross. They doubt. They distrust God. They seethe with anger over the fact that the wicked are allowed to prosper and are granted success in persecution, etc. These things testify that both defects and covetousness still inhere in our nature. We must know that these things are sins, that is, things that are truly worthy of the condemnation which corresponds to the nature of the disease itself. And yet we must also know that they are not imputed, if, by faith, we lay hold of mercy. For unless we acknowledge this sin, the benefit of Christ cannot be understood, nor can faith be exercised. The passages from Romans chapters 7 and 8, cited above, clearly testify that this sin also remains in the saints. Augustine teaches in the same way about the forgiveness of original sin in Baptism: "Sin is remitted, not in such a way that it doesn't exist, but in such a way that it is not imputed."[18]

ACTUAL SINS

Actual sin refers to the fruits of the diseased nature, that is, the impulses, thoughts, words, and deeds against God's Law. We should include at the same time both the person and the work. Therefore, although some wicked men do honorable works, nevertheless, since the persons are wicked, their works do not please God. In those persons there are inner vices—doubt, a lack of fear and trust in God. This is the case even in the greatest of men, like Pomponius Atticus or Cicero, who, although they have a certain knowledge of the Law, namely, that God is good and righteous, nevertheless, they are ignorant of the Gospel, that God forgives sins gratis, and so in great afflictions they conclude that they are rejected by God. Therefore, since they have inner diseases, their external actions are also contaminated. As Paul says, "Everything that is not from faith is sin" [Romans 14:23], that is, everything that is done by those who doubt that God cares for them, who do not believe that they have a propitious God. For faith means trust in mercy. Although it is not within the pale of our judgment to determine what God did with those excellent men—Solon, Themistocles, Fabius, Scipio, Pomponius Atticus, and similar men—whether, by a peculiar benefit, He provided them with some understanding of His gratuitous mercy, of the forgiveness of sins, and of true worship, nevertheless we should judge only according to the Word now proclaimed, that is, according to the Gospel, that no one is saved without a knowledge of Christ and without the mercy promised on account of Christ.

---

18   Augustine, *De nuptiis et concupiscentia*, Book I, ch. 25.

But here one may object: If honorable works are sins, what use is there in doing them? Likewise, why does God command them, since He does not approve of sin, according to that saying, "God is not the one who wills evil. You are."?

Answer: It is easy for us to answer these objections. Add faith to this discipline, and then it will please God, even though the obedience is actually imperfect. As I said above, since the person is pleasing, so also is the obedience in those who truly believe in the spiritual and bodily rewards in this life and after this life.

But if one asks about the wicked, this is my answer: We are not Stoics, who used to argue that all sins are equal. No, Nero sins more than Pomponius Atticus. And although it is up to God to judge the degree of inner vice, which certainly should not be minimized, nevertheless, God requires honorable external works, which are called works of the Law. He requires it, moreover, both for the tranquility of men amongst themselves and for discipline, that is, that men may be instructed and taught about the Gospel. As Paul says, "The Law is a schoolmaster" [Galatians 3:24]. And God blesses this pedagogy through outstanding bodily rewards, while, on the other hand, He punishes the external violation of the Law with serious penalties, both bodily and eternal. Therefore, it is useful to magnify this pedagogy and diligently to teach men to consider that God has set forth both rewards for good deeds and penalties for offenses.

The Scriptures teach about these rewards in the Decalogue itself: "Honor your father and your mother, if you wish to live long on the earth." On penalty of perjury, it says in the Second Commandment: "God will not hold him guiltless who uses God's name in vain." In the same way, it teaches about penalties whenever it speaks about the magistrate, for God has established it to retain discipline among men, and through the magistrates God punishes shameful deeds. He also punishes apart from the magistrate, with other troubles, as the curses in the

Law testify. Both the law of nature and experience bear witness to the same. For this very opinion is a law of nature, namely, to perceive that God rewards good deeds and punishes evil deeds. This judgment has remained among all the nations, and from this arose those most serious statements recorded in Hesiod and others about the penalties for offenses.

Furthermore, this, too, is clear: That those tremendously heroic virtues in the greatest men are truly peculiar gifts and works of God, such as the searching for God displayed by Xenophon; the greatness of spirit and of counsel in defending the fatherland displayed by Themistocles, Fabius, and Scipio; the self-control and faithfulness displayed by Lelius and Atticus. And since these are most certainly works of God, as are our eyes themselves, they certainly are not evil things. Therefore, the righteousness of the flesh is also worthy of its own praise, and men should be taught that God requires it and accompanies it with rewards.

Some, however, object that this righteousness is sin; but God does not require sins. I answer: God requires the work itself. Then it happens by accident, namely, on account of the diseased person, that this work is sin, so that the greatness of spirit in Achilles is a distinguished virtue in and of itself and is truly a work of God. But it becomes wicked, because the person is wicked who doubts whether God cares for men; such a person is without fear of God and without trust in God. Therefore, the work itself is not obedience toward God. But that is the righteous purpose of works that are truly good, to be obedience toward God. Therefore, God, indeed, requires that which is good, but the diseased nature contaminates the very thing which God requires.

There remains the distinction between mortal and venial sin. But we will say more about this distinction later, for it cannot be understood what is venial unless we first speak about faith. For without faith, the conscience cannot stand in the judgment of God. Therefore, all sins are mortal which accuse the conscience. As Paul says, "The law works wrath"

[Romans 4:15]. Likewise, "The sting of death is sin, and the power of sin is the Law" [1 Corinthians 15:56]. Nor can works be set against the judgment of God, no matter how honorable they are, because we cannot approach God without the Mediator Christ. Therefore Paul says, "The mind of the flesh is death" [Romans 8:6]. That is, even though man has some knowledge of God apart from faith, even though he has outstanding virtues, nevertheless in the judgment of God they do not vivify. Therefore, even though God requires this pedagogy or righteousness of the flesh, even though He blesses it with bodily rewards, nevertheless the assertions of our adversaries are false, for they say that such works merit the forgiveness of sins, whether done fittingly (*de congruo*) or truly deservingly (*de condigno*). They even teach that works of this kind merit the forgiveness of sins apart from trust in Christ. Thus, they imagine that the wrath of God is appeased apart from Christ. But Paul protests loudly against this. He teaches that sins are forgiven gratis, by faith, for Christ's sake, as he clearly testifies in Ephesians 2, "Gratis you have been saved, etc."[19]

Let these things serve as sufficient instruction for the present. Later we will have to speak more fully about the forgiveness of sins and justification.

In this topic concerning sin, the reader must be admonished concerning affections. The affections in man's nature are twofold. Some are simply at odds with the Law of God, such as desiring the things or the spouse of another, envying the benefits God has given to others, desiring undue glory, elevating oneself above others, distrusting God, seething with rage at the judgment of God, hating God. Such affections are properly the fruits of original sin and are simply evil and wicked and must be cast out of man's nature, nor would they have existed in man's whole and uncorrupted nature. There are other affections which are not

---

19   Melanchthon changes the ablative form of the noun *gratia*, used by the Vulgate, to the adverbial form *gratis*, emphasizing the free-of-charge nature of grace. See Translator's Note.

at odds with the Law of God, such as loving one's children, spouse, the deserving, or being angry at vices. For the uncorrupted nature of man would not have existed without any desires. To take away desires from man's nature is to take away movement and life. Therefore, even though these affections are also contaminated by the vice of origin, nevertheless it must be known that they, of themselves, are not evil and wicked, but that they are to be retained in nature. They must be purified. They are called by the Greeks "natural affections" (στοργαὶ φυσικαί). This distinction must be observed, lest we be deceived by hypocrites who condemn all affections without distinction as wicked and evil in and of themselves.

THE DIVINE LAW

The Law of God is the doctrine that tells us what kind of people we should be, what we must do and not do. It requires perfect obedience toward God, and it condemns those who do not furnish such obedience. As the Law says, "Cursed is everyone who does not continue in all these things which are written in the book of the Law" [Galatians 3:10].

Here we must first remember what the difference is between human laws and the Law of God. Human laws only require or forbid external deeds. Philosophy requires a bit more, namely, diligence, not only in controlling the external members, but also in bending the affections toward a settled evenness and calmness or gentleness. This is properly called ethics (ἠθικός). But it still does not find fault with natural uncleanness, nor does it pass judgment on those worst-of-all vices that are at odds with the first table of the Law—doubting God, unbelief, and similar diseases that inhere in man's nature.

But the Law of God does not only require or forbid external deeds.

It does not only require that diligence with which the philosophers demand that affections be restrained. No, it requires that man's nature be just as conformed to the Law of God as covetousness now fights against God's Law. It especially requires a sure knowledge of God, true fear of God, firm trust in God, perfect love. It censures wicked affections and the very uncleanness of man's nature; that is, the covetousness which gives rise to wicked affections. This is what Paul means when he says, "The Law is spiritual" [Romans 7:14]. That is, it requires spiritual things—true knowledge of God, true fear, true trust, perfect love. As the Law says, "You shall love the Lord your God with all your heart" [Deuteronomy 6:5]. Since the scholastic teachers did not consider this difference between the Law of God and human laws or philosophy, they gave rise to many errors.

First, they imagined that man's natural weakness, that is, covetousness, is not condemned by God's Law.

Second, they imagined that God's Law is satisfied by our external works, and, likewise, by the inner striving of the will, even though covetousness fights against it.

Third, they actually imagine that it is possible to satisfy the Law without the Holy Spirit.

Fourth, they pretend that doubt, distrust of God's will, and similar attitudes are not sins.

Fifth, since they think that man can satisfy the Law, they imagine that he is pronounced righteous on account of his own works, even without faith, that is, without trust in mercy. In short, they discern no difference between that righteousness which the Law of God requires and that which the civil laws or philosophy teach.

Sixth, from this sprang forth also the delusions concerning perfection, concerning counsels, concerning works of supererogation. For since they dreamed that they had already satisfied the Law, they went on to add how one can do even more than the Law demands. But I will speak of counsels and perfection later.

Paul goes to war with those Pharisaical opinions about the Law and shows that God's Law not only requires civil works, but perfect obedience toward God, and that it levels its accusation not only against actual sins, but also against the diseased nature. He contends that all men are guilty, that no one satisfies the Law. Unless these things are acknowledged, the benefit of Christ cannot be understood, as we shall say later. Consequently, he applies the type of the veiled face of Moses to this in Corinthians,[20] saying that the Jews do not look upon the end of the Law, that is, they do not view the Law perfectly, but that their minds are obstructed by a veil, understanding the veil to be this false persuasion itself, that is, the carnal or civil judgment that the Law only requires civil works and does not censure the diseased nature; that the Law is satisfied by this human diligence; that they are righteous by works, even if their hearts are meanwhile full of doubt and other sinful affections. He teaches that this veil is taken away through Christ, namely, when we acknowledge that we are subject to God's wrath and cannot satisfy the Law of God, and when we seek mercy and conclude that we are pronounced righteous for Christ's sake. Thus, freed from doubt, we truly acknowledge God and call upon Him, etc.

Therefore, since the scholastic teachers also teach those same Jewish and carnal opinions about the Law, they, too, look upon the veiled face of Moses, not judging rightly about the Law of God. Indeed, their doctrine is actually the very veil by which the Law is obscured, for it has been taken from a human and carnal judgment about laws.

The Gospel, however, uncovers the face of Moses, since, in the preaching of repentance, it shows what the Law truly requires, that it accuses all men.

---

20   2 Corinthians 3:7–18.

I have chosen to offer at the outset this brief instruction concerning the difference between the Law of God and human laws so that we may know what the Law of God requires and so that we may be able to judge rightly concerning the use of the divine Law.

THE DIVISION OF LAWS

First, these are the kinds of laws which are normally listed: the law of nature, divine Law, and human law. Divine Laws are the laws which are found everywhere in Scripture, both in Moses and in the books of the Gospel. Although, as I shall say later, Christians are free from the Law of Moses, nevertheless, for the sake of teaching, the Laws of Moses must be differentiated so that afterwards it may be more easily shown what the law of nature is and to which laws we owe obedience.

The Laws of Moses are arranged in three categories. Some are moral; others are judicial, that is, forensic; others are ceremonial. We call "moral laws" the ones which contain the commandments concerning the virtues pertaining to all men. And since the Decalogue contains the summary of such commandments, we usually understand with the name "Decalogue" the moral commandments, wherever they are found in the Scriptures, which command something concerning virtuous duties. The commands in Romans 12 and in other places belong to this category, for all statements of this kind are essentially an explanation of the Decalogue. Now, since, in any art whatsoever, it is advantageous to create methods of teaching so that we may gather widely dispersed matters under definite headings, we include all the moral commands in the Decalogue, so that we may have a method of teaching, and surely no better method of teaching can be devised. Indeed, is it sufficiently clear that this summary was composed, not by human, but by divine wisdom.

I have said these things so that the term "Decalogue" may not cause any controversy, but that the readers may know that we use this term in this way for the commandments about virtues and morals, wherever they are found, both in the Old and in the New Testament. This also helps students by providing them with a summary and a method of teaching the commandments, so that they may be able to see and comprehend, in order, all the laws and the fountains of all virtue, which is essential for drawing a proper conclusion.

It is easy to determine which laws are judicial and which are ceremonial. The judicial laws are the ones which make pronouncements concerning marriage rites, inheritances, punishments for crimes, and similar forensic matters. The ceremonial laws have to do with the temple and the rites which separate the people of Israel from the other nations. They consist in the kind of works whose immediate purpose should be to serve as signs and testimonies of one's profession or of one's faith toward God. Although we will explain later how one should understand the saying that Christians are said to be free from these laws, it should still be understood here in this summary that the judicial and ceremonial laws of Moses no do not pertain to us at all, except for the natural laws which may be found in them, as, for example, concerning spouses, when marriages of relatives and defined relations are forbidden. Since these pronouncements involve knowledge that has been written into nature, they cannot be repealed; they endure as part of man's very nature. For this reason, many people classify such commandments as moral, because a respect for blood pertains to virtues and ought to be observed by all nations and at all times. Moses himself testifies that these laws about degrees of consanguinity do not only pertain to the Israelites, but to all nations, for he says that the Canaanites will be wiped out on account of their unclean passions in that they married their relatives.[21] If the Canaanites are considered blameworthy for this, then such prohibitions must necessarily pertain to all people in common, and there must

---

21   cf. Leviticus 20:23.

be certain natural laws which forbid this kind of marriage, even before the Law of Moses, just as other natural knowledge also existed prior to the Law of Moses.

It is most helpful to remember these things concerning marriage and similar issues so that the laws of nature may not be violated under the pretext of Christian freedom.

The moral commandments apply to all people, not on account of Moses, but on account of natural law. Likewise, since the Gospel also preaches spiritual righteousness and obedience toward God, it, therefore, repeats the moral commandments which teach about cleanness of the heart and spiritual attitudes and duties. We will explain below how this should be understood. For now, we must show what natural law is, and we must compare the Decalogue with natural law. In order that the laws of nature may be more easily understood, we will first review the Decalogue, for, as I said, the Decalogue is a most excellent method of teaching in which all the moral laws can be included. Then we will accommodate the laws of nature to the Decalogue. Indeed, for this very reason the Decalogue was published, that it might interpret and shed light on the law of nature.

There are two tables, the first of which involves the works in which we properly deal with God, namely, the true worship of God, both internal and external. The second involves the works toward our neighbor, both internal and external. At times they are also distinguished in this way: The first table involves the spiritual life; the second, the civil life.

The First Commandment teaches about the highest and principal work, namely, true knowledge of God, true and perfect obedience toward God, perfect fear, trust and love. It embraces the two greatest matters: how we are to know God, and true worship.

The "how" is that God is apprehended through His Word and testimony. For since human reason seeks God and institutes forms of worship apart from His Word and testimony, it cannot be rendered certain, but doubts whether it has apprehended God, whether God is concerned with human affairs, whether these forms of worship please God, etc. Therefore, a definite Word and testimony has been set forth here: "I am the Lord your God, who brought you out of the land of Egypt." He testifies that this God, who delivered this Word and wanted to be acknowledged in this work, is the true God. So also Christ has been set forth for us, that we may know that the true God is the One who sent Christ, and on account of Christ His Son, He wishes to be kindly disposed toward us. Thus a sure Word and a sure testimony must be grasped so that He may be known by it.

Moreover, the forms of worship which are prescribed in the First Commandment are true fear, true trust, true love. He requires love when He says, "I am your God," that is, the One who looks after you, cares for you, saves you, etc. Likewise, "Showing mercy to those who love Me." Again, "You should love the Lord your God with all your heart." For statements of this kind are explanations of the First Commandment.

Furthermore, since He requires perfect obedience, it can easily be understood that this Law always accuses and condemns all men in this corrupt nature, which neither furnishes nor can furnish perfect obedience, perfect fear, perfect trust, perfect love.

But suppose someone says, "Yes, but it is necessary for those who are pleasing to God to keep this Law. How, then, is it done?" I answer briefly: This Law is never satisfied, not even by the saints. But Christ is the fulfillment of the Law. That is, after we have been terrified by a knowledge of our sins, we are raised up again by faith in Christ, for then we acknowledge God's mercy promised in Christ. We begin to know God, to fear Him, and to trust in Him. Here we begin to do the works of the First Commandment. And although we are far from perfection, nevertheless, on account of Christ, we are declared righteous, as remains to be explained below.

So it is that the First Commandment is kept imputatively, which is why the First Commandment cannot be kept—no, it cannot even begin to be kept—without the Gospel concerning Christ. For there can be no trust without Christ, since the Law itself always accuses and condemns. But it is helpful, for the sake of teaching, to summarize all the works of the First Commandment with these two words: fear and trust. For although trust actually produces love, the word "love" is more obscure than the words "fear" or "trust." For we must always experience love in repentance, and trust must be experienced in consolations.

From all these things, it is clear that, in the First Commandment, we are instructed about the highest and chief work, namely, about the inner worship of God.

The Second Commandment teaches about external worship, that is, about the proper effects of faith, about the use of God's name. Here I must include the following categories: invocation, thanksgiving, preaching the Word of God, and confession. These four categories make up the chief use of God's name, representing the chief outward form of worship. For these things are the sacrifices of praise about which the Scriptures everywhere preach. Psalm 116[:10–17], "I believed, wherefore I spoke… I will take the saving cup and call upon the name of the Lord… To You I will sacrifice an offering of praise, and I will call upon the name of the Lord."

Now, even though the commandments are spoken negatively, one must recognize the nature of speech. For a negative statement on the one hand requires an affirmative statement on the other. "You shall have no other Gods before Me." This requires that God be worshiped as God, that is, that the honor which is owed to God (namely, fear and trust) be ascribed to Him. This is why it says affirmatively at the beginning, "I am the Lord your God." So when He says, "You shall not use God's name in vain," it requires that righteous use of God's name. But the righteous use is in those four categories which I have noted.

The Third Commandment properly deals with the ceremonies which are part of external worship, for they are signs instituted both as a matter of confession and for the sake of the ministry of the Word; these ought to be the purposes of ceremonies. You see, then, how neatly arranged the order is. The First Commandment preaches about inner worship—fear and trust; the Second, about the principal external worship—invocation and the preaching of the Word, etc.; the Third Commandment, about the ceremonies which, as I said, were handed down both that we might confess the faith by them, and that they should help to preserve the ministry of the Word.

Now, the text speaks about the Sabbath Day, for since the Sabbath was instituted for the sake of the ministry of the Word, it is the chief ceremony, embracing the rest. For it expressly says that the Law was not only about resting on the seventh day, but about sanctification. "Remember to sanctify the Sabbath Day," that is, to come together for holy purposes, namely, for considering the Word of God and for other divinely ordained forms of worship. Therefore, some have astutely pointed out that the Third Commandment is partly moral, partly ceremonial. It is ceremonial insofar as it teaches about the Jewish observation of a defined seventh day. This ceremony, as we all agree, has been abrogated, just as circumcision and the rest of the Jewish ceremonies were, as Paul teaches expressly about the Sabbath Day in his Epistle to the Colossians.[22] But there is a moral component in this Law, which signifies that the divinely instituted ceremonies are to be preserved on account of the ministry of the Word, and that certain times are to be set aside for using those ceremonies and for hearing God's Word. This moral and natural commandment surely pertains to all men. The genus is of divine Law—that we should at a certain time use the divinely delivered ceremonies and come together for the ministry of the Word. But the species—on what day or at what time it is done—no longer has a divine command. I am not seeking an allegorical meaning in the commandment; I am pointing

---

22   Colossians 2:16–17.

out the main idea of it. For this commandment especially requires that we preserve the divinely instituted ceremonies and the public ministry of the Word of God. Therefore, it instructs us about the most important matters. For nothing is more necessary than the ministry of God's Word. It is, therefore, no trivial sin when the common people throw this entire commandment back to the Jews in such a way that, meanwhile, they neglect the evangelical ceremonies and the ministry of the Gospel.

Let these things suffice concerning the first table.

Now we must discuss the disobedience of the human heart in relation to each commandment. The security in the minds of men who are devoid of the fear of God, doubt, distrust in mercy—these things are in conflict with the First Commandment, as are trust in one's own righteousness and ability, as well as various false opinions about God and the idolatries which attribute to created things the honor, trust, and invocation that are due to God.

In conflict with the Second Commandment is the doubt of those who call upon God without faith, or who do not call upon Him at all, since they cannot rouse themselves to believe. Also against this commandment are wicked forms of worship, wicked doctrine, blasphemy, etc.

In conflict with the Third Commandment are the profanation of ceremonies and contempt for the ministry of the Word.

Now, clearly the world is full of all these vices. But the ones who especially sin against the first table of the Law are the ungodly teachers and priests who condone and support these great vices.

Contrary to the First Commandment, they teach that the natural uncleanness which causes us not to obey God perfectly is not sin. They teach nothing about trust in gratuitous mercy. Indeed, they teach that doubting and distrusting mercy are not sins.

Contrary to the Second Commandment, they defend the ungodly doctrines which abolish true invocation. They defend wicked forms of worship, such as the idolatry of the Masses and monasticism. Under the ungodly pretext of the divine name, they exercise the most wretched cruelty.

Contrary to the Third Commandment, they distort the use of ceremonies; they pretend that the ceremonies themselves merit the forgiveness of sins simply by doing the work, without faith. For this reason, they amass countless ceremonies, and meanwhile they overthrow the ministry of the Word, on account of which the ceremonies were primarily divinely instituted. I shall omit for now how many ceremonies they have dreamed up solely by greed or ambition. Such is the kingdom of the ungodly teachers and priests, which is plainly contrary to the first table of God's Law.

I mentioned above that these errors derive from a false persuasion, for men dream that only civil or external works are required by God's Law. This pharisaical opinion gives rise to the remaining errors.

The Second Table

The second table tells us what kind of people we should be toward our neighbor. Although this table, too, teaches about natural cleanness, nevertheless, it establishes here at the same time a social structure. The first level in this society of the human race is ruling power, so that some give orders while others follow them. Therefore, the first virtue is obedience, even among the philosophers, who call it "universal righteousness"—a most worthy name. Therefore, right here at the beginning, the second table gives us instructions about obedience. Indeed, it requires the highest work of obedience, namely, honor. For "honor" means to attribute to the other person wisdom and righteousness, from the heart; that is, to submit to his judgment and authority. It arises, moreover, from the first level of ruling power, namely, from parental authority. Then the other levels should be added to this. So it is that this commandment covers the things that are said about magistrates in Romans 13 and elsewhere. The highest virtues belong to this law, namely, to serve in one's vocation with restraint, that is, not to disturb the commonwealth or one's vocation through meddling or ambition. To this belongs devotion to one's parents, toward the commonwealth, and similar virtues.

The following commandments include the remaining virtues and duties that are necessary for the society of the human race. A particular righteousness is necessary, which properly includes not hurting anyone, and assigning to each one what it his. Therefore, the Law's next command is: "You shall not kill." This law forbids every private act of vengeance, for the magistrate afterwards has his own commandments concerning vengeance.

Furthermore, since the Law is not only speaking about the external work, but condemns every private act of vengeance, it forbids not only manifest injuries, but the desire for vengeance, hatred, jealousy, and similar feelings. This is how Christ interprets this Law in Matthew 5. Therefore, it embraces many virtues: justice, gentleness, loyalty, patience, clemency.

The Sixth Commandment, "You shall not commit adultery," sanctions marriage. There is no higher praise for marriage than what is contained in this law. For since it commands a person to stay away from another's spouse, it is evident that marriage is being protected. Therefore, the commandment commends marriage and grants the conjugal use of one's own wife. Nor could it have extolled marriage more highly than with this very honor; namely, that marriage is defended and protected by this law. For this reason, both things must be learned here, that this law both commends marriage and commands a man to stay away from another man's wife. Christ also proclaims this law in Matthew 5. Thus it covers many virtues: chastity, temperance, continence, sobriety, and similar things which forbid illicit pleasures, both sexual appetites and those of the stomach, for these vices are joined together by nature.

The Seventh, "You shall not steal," protects the ownership of property. Here, too, both things must be learned: First, that we know that a distinction in ownership is an ordinance of God. It is helpful to observe this in the face of the fanatics and mad spirits who contend with great and pernicious error that the ownership of property is removed by the Gospel. Second, the prohibition must also be observed, that we should not set our hearts on the things that belong to another. This law, too, covers many virtues which are at odds with wastefulness, avarice, and laziness, namely, frugality, sedulity, diligence, generosity. For all thieves are both wasteful and lazy, which is why they need to steal from someone else in order to provide for their expenses and leisure.

The Eighth, "You shall not give false testimony," protects judgments, which comprise the defense of all the things about which instruction was given above—body, marriage, and possessions. This law, then, encompasses the most beautiful virtue of all: truth.

The Ninth and Tenth Commandments add a declaration so that we know that the Law of God not only instructs about external works, but that it also censures man's diseased nature. For it requires there to be perfect obedience toward God in man's nature. But since man's nature is full of covetousness and evil emotions, it can easily be understood that no one satisfies God's Law and that all are subject to God's wrath, that it pertains to the weak nature.

Threats and promises have been added to the Decalogue, as can be discerned in the First and Second Commandments, and likewise in the Fourth. Both punishments and rewards must be set forth in the laws. Indeed, the sum of the promises is set forth elsewhere in these words: "He who does these things shall live by them" [Romans 10:5], or, "Do this and you will live" [Luke 10:28]. The sum of the threats is set forth in these words: "Cursed is the one who does not persevere in all things which are written in the Law" [Galatians 3:10].

But it must be understood that all the promises of the Law are conditional. And since the Law always accuses us, the promises would be made invalid unless we had the comfort of the Gospel, which teaches how and for what reason these promises of the Law are made valid: Since we are declared righteous gratis for the sake of Christ, we are reckoned as fulfilling the Law, namely, by imputation. Then the promises are valid, and we obtain spiritual and bodily rewards, both in this life and after this life. I will explain under its own topic what the difference is between the Gospel and the Law and the promises of the Law. You will also remember that, in civil righteousness, the bodily promises are valid, and the external offenses are accompanied by manifest punishment. God blesses external righteousness with bodily rewards, as attested by examples from all nations and by the statements of the wisest men. For God preserves civil order in the world. Therefore He Himself carries out punishments, even when men fail to do so, etc. For this reason He expressly adds a bodily reward in the Fourth Commandment, which establishes civil order: "If you want to live long on the earth, etc."

Thus far I have briefly reviewed the Decalogue. I have explained that it pertains to all people, for it is the law of nature. I have likewise explained that, since the Gospel preaches a new and spiritual life, which is obedience toward God, it preaches about the same works. Therefore, let us now compare the law of nature to the Decalogue, even though I have practically done so already. For since I have shown the order of the commandments, no one can fail to see that nature itself prescribes to us both this order and the laws themselves. Nevertheless, we shall add a brief comparison.

THE LAW OF NATURE

The law of nature is the knowledge of the divine Law—a knowledge which has been placed into man's nature. There is nothing better or more beautiful in all creation, nor is there any trace of God more immanent than that God has impressed His likeness and the image of His own wisdom on the minds of men.

I have said that this knowledge has been placed into nature, which should be understood in this way. As a certain lamp has been divinely placed into the eyes, so a certain knowledge or a certain lamp has been inserted into human minds by which they recognize and judge certain things all by themselves. The philosophers call this lamp a "knowledge of first principles" (*noticia principiorum*). They call it "common sense" (κοινὰς ἔννοιας) and "preconception" (προλήψεις). And just as they teach concerning speculative principles that men, by nature, know and embrace them as certain, so one should also conclude concerning practical principles, that is, concerning the law of nature.

I have added, moreover, that the law of nature is the knowledge of the divine Law. Here it must be understood that, in this corrupt nature, the law of nature has been greatly obscured by the vice of origin. For man was created especially for the purpose of knowing God and furnishing perfect obedience toward God. Therefore, he had a firm knowledge of the Law concerning God, namely, that God is the Creator and Ruler of all creation, that He is good and righteous, that He does good to the righteous and punishes the unrighteous. This is the knowledge of the Law. And since it was a lamp that was divinely implanted in nature, the mind of man surely assented to it without any doubt, and all his powers were able to obey that knowledge perfectly. In addition, there was a second kind of knowledge, namely, that which was useful for fostering the society of the human race. This kind of knowledge was pure, for they understood that men were to love, to help, and to take care of one another without covetousness, since they were created to know God and to proclaim His glory in a certain society of life. For man's whole life was to be a certain philosophy of God and of His presence in the creation and preservation of things. There were to be exercises of faith and love. This is what the law of nature was supposed to be like up to that point.

But now it has been obscured. We are born with a very obscure knowledge of God, to whom, nonetheless, our minds do not assent with certainty, for they continually doubt whether God cares for human affairs, whether He does good to the righteous, whether He punishes the unrighteous. Although our natural preconception teaches us these things, nevertheless, since they are obscure, men do not assent to them. They are likewise dislodged from men's minds for other reasons which oppose their natural knowledge. They see things going well for the ungodly; they see that the greatest and most noble men are oppressed through injustice; therefore they argue that human affairs are neglected by God. They see how much wickedness and trouble there is in the world; therefore they argue that there would be a better administration and management of the world, if it were divinely ruled. Such arguments lead human minds astray so that they do not assent to the law of nature. The knowledge concerning the society of the human race, although it has been obscured, remains, nevertheless, in the things that instruct about the external duties that are necessary for preserving life. The philosophers gather these things together, too. Even though these things are a small part of the law of nature, it must be understood that the law of nature was once a far greater and brighter light and a very certain knowledge about God. It is evident, moreover, that even the minds of the greatest men are full of errors and doubts about God—whether He cares for us, why He permits good men to be afflicted, whether He punishes the wicked, where these horrible calamities come from. Mankind's weak nature is challenged by all these things, and philosophy surely does not explain them.

Finally, one cannot even imagine what perfect obedience toward God is, and for that reason philosophy omits the chief part of the law of nature, although the causes have also been impressed on the very nature of man, demonstrating that men should acknowledge God, that they should obey Him, etc. But philosophy does not investigate these causes sufficiently, nor does it retain those which it has sought out on account of that infinite doubt which inheres in the minds of men. Instead, it seeks the causes of certain duties which are helpful for morality and civil society. And since the laws of nature are principles and conclusions that have arisen from first principles by necessary consequence, let us understand the philosophers' opinions, which have specific descriptions, to be the laws of nature. And since the descriptions produce an order, we, too, shall, for the most part, follow their order in recounting the laws of nature.

Catalogue

Although the first law about God has been obscured in the minds of men, certain traces still remain. For since men are born with some knowledge of God, nature itself commands them to acknowledge God, and that natural reason, that is, conscience, speaks loudly in every man, testifying that there is a God, that He is the Creator of all of nature, that He does good to the righteousness and punishes the unrighteous. It further testifies that this God, who is the Creator of all things, must be obeyed and called upon. The terrors of conscience themselves which arise in men testify that God threatens punishment on the unrighteous. It is clear that these traces of the first law, in whatever condition they are found, still exist, as Paul also teaches in Romans 1 and 2. Therefore, some philosophers, too, gather the weightiest reasons for this opinion about God, as did Cicero in *De natura deorum*, or Xenophon. This is also where the sayings of the poets and of the lawmakers come from, which either arose from this natural law (or knowledge) or were surely drawn from the holy fathers who understood the law rightly. It seems that these opinions were spread from the fathers to their descendants. They survive in Phocylides and Hesiod, each of whom affirms that God does good to the righteous and punishes the unrighteous. In Romans 1, where Paul accuses the Gentiles, he starts out by citing this law of nature, which requires acknowledging and glorifying God, that is, fearing Him and trusting in Him. It is, therefore, this first law of nature which we see reflected in the First Commandment of the Decalogue, which God revealed, both in order that the law of nature, once obscured by the vice of origin but now renewed by the divine voice, might shine forth more brightly; and in order that the testimony of God's Word might stand out which says that this natural knowledge is the Law of God; and that the saints might be confirmed by the Word of God, lest, in this natural weakness, some false persuasion should lead them astray from the natural judgment.

To the Second Commandment pertain the opinions and laws about the sanctity of oaths, about the penalties for perjury and the punishment of those who curse God. For natural reason also judges these things, inasmuch as these conclusions flow from the former law.

To the Third Commandment pertain the opinions and laws about preserving and defending ceremonies. For nature, too, teaches that ceremonies are to be observed and preserved, so that we may teach others about the religion, having illuminated it with these examples and signs. Therefore, when the Athenians swore an oath and put it down in writing between citizens, these were the words: "I will fight for the sacred things, both alone and together with other citizens." This ceremony, too, referenced by Hesiod, is entirely in agreement with nature, that we should call upon God morning and evening, "both when you lie down and when the holy light of day appears."[23] Many sacred customs of this kind are found, even in the civil affairs of the heathen, which stem from this natural knowledge of God, even though the nations that are

---

23   Hesiod, *Erga kai hemerai*, line 339.

ignorant of the Gospel could not use the Law rightly. For since the Law always accuses, it leaves consciences doubting whether God is kindly disposed toward us, whether He wishes to hear. But since the Gospel teaches us that God is kindly disposed toward us gratis, it removes this doubt. God cannot be worshiped with doubt; He requires faith. This must be said, so that we understand what was lacking to those great men like Xenophon, Cicero and others. For they know the Law and the conditional promises of the Law. But since they do not know the promise of gratuitous reconciliation (that is, the Gospel), doubt inheres in them, whether God is kindly disposed toward them, whether God hears them.

I judge what was lacking to them on the basis of the Gospel, as I ought, for without a knowledge of Christ, there is no salvation. I am not declaring what God did with them, and it is meddlesome to ask. But these things I say in order that a distinction might be observed between the nature of the Gospel and that of the Law. For there are not a few men who impiously imagine that the Gospel is also natural knowledge, that it is the law of nature, and in this matter they go perilously astray. Paul calls the Gospel a "mystery hidden from the ages" [Colossians 1:26]. He calls it "wisdom, not of this world, nor of the rulers of this world" [1 Corinthians 2:6]. John says in chapter 1 of his Gospel, "No one has seen God at any time. The Son, who is in the bosom of the Father—He has revealed Him to us" [John 1:18]. The Gospel, then, is a sentence concerning the will of God which is unknown to reason. For we properly call "the Gospel" the promise that God is willing to forgive and justify for the sake of Christ. This sentence is so unknown to reason that reason, which has some knowledge of the Law, strongly disagrees with it. And, therefore, it thinks that we are declared righteous, not gratis, but if we satisfy the Law. It cannot imagine that the unworthy and those who do not satisfy the Law are pleasing to God. For this reason, there is a great struggle between the conscience and reason, on the one hand, and this very voice of the Gospel, on the other. Indeed, it is difficult for the conscience to be comforted by the voice of the Gospel in that struggle against the pernicious persuasion that is ingrained in nature.

These things had to be said above, lest the law of nature and the Gospel should be confused. Up to this point, I have recited the laws of nature which pertain to the first table. Now I shall recount the laws of the second table, which are clearer, to some degree, for they give instruction about civil morality, which reason is better able to judge.

Let there be a fourth law, then. Man naturally understands virtue, and he senses that a person should aspire to virtue for God's sake, not only for the sake of utility. Therefore, he understands that it goes against nature to cause injuries, to have promiscuous sexual relationships, and to practice other vices. This is why he has concluded that marriage must be contracted with definite laws; likewise, that injuries be forbidden, that civil life be fostered, which is necessary for teaching and helping men. He has determined that authorities must be established and obeyed. This law, then, corresponds to the Fourth Commandment. And the first societal virtue is obedience. The next law is that no one should do harm. For society cannot be preserved if no one is safe from injury. This law corresponds to the Fifth Commandment, "You shall not kill." Here also pertain the rest of the laws that are necessary for preserving society, namely, laws concerning kindness and gratitude, concerning justice, which punishes those who do harm. For natural reason understands that the harmful members must be removed in order to look after the body as a whole. Therefore penalties are set forth among the authorities so that, by fear of these, the wicked may be deterred from inflicting harm. The law of Talio is entirely consistent with nature, namely, that the punishment should match the crime, according to the verse which Aristotle cites from the laws of Rhadamanthus: "If each one should suffer what he himself has done, then justice would be done."[24]

---

24   Aristotle, *Nicomachean Ethics*, Book 5, ch. 5.

To the Sixth Commandment pertains what I have already said about marriage. For reason understands that promiscuous sexual activity goes against nature. It understands that illicit sexual intercourse and disgraceful adulteries must also be punished. Likewise, reason understands that it agrees very much with man's nature to practice modesty and moderation in pleasures.

To the Seventh Commandment pertains the distribution of property. For since, given the selfish ambitions of men, men are unable to enjoy property in common, therefore, reason sees that a distinction in ownership is necessary. A distinction of ownership, then, is derived from natural law. For natural law properly signifies the natural judgment of reason. The philosophers call this the law of nature. Even the lawyers often speak in this way. But they clearly mean the same thing when they say more frequently that a distinction of ownership is derived from the law of nations (*iuris gentium*). For to them, the law of nations means a common understanding among men, that is, a common judgment of reason. Moreover, when they say that all things are common by the law of nature, they create degrees of natural law, for they understand that property, insofar as it pertains to its own nature, could be held in common if the selfish desires of men did not disrupt their society. They add, therefore, the second degree of the law of nature, which corresponds to the nature of man as he now is. This is what they call the law of nations.

The philosophers explain these things much more skillfully. For since the law of nature is the entire natural judgment, it includes many things that are supreme precepts, governing all laws, while other laws are inferior, yielding to the superior laws. The immutable judgment, therefore, is one thing; the use of property is another. The latter varies according to a variety of circumstances. Therefore, when they say that the law of nature is immutable, it should be understood concerning the entire judgment of nature, not concerning the use of those things which are, by their own nature, indifferent. Furthermore, reason does not only judge simply that property should be held in common; no, it judges where common possession is to be granted and where it should not be granted. Thus it is the use of property that is changed, not the judgment of nature. Indeed, since reason already pronounces that a distinction of ownership in such a nature is necessary, that law is now immutable. From these things it can be understood that a distinction of ownership is truly and properly derived from natural law.

In addition, since many and various things are needed in this life, there remains a common act of sharing that is done according to reason and by mutual agreement. This, too, is derived from natural law. That is, natural reason teaches us to enter into agreements in such a way that there is compensation for it, and that both parties are compensated equally.

But let us send these things back to the philosophers. We must firmly denounce the foolishness of those who imagine that in the Gospel the distinction of ownership is either forbidden or reproached. For they do injury to the Gospel who are willing to support fanatical and seditious opinions of this kind with the authority of the Gospel. For the Gospel teaches about eternal life and the righteousness of the Spirit. It does not destroy bodily life, nor does it abolish the judgment of nature which says that bodily life must be preserved, nor does it condemn civil life or domestic life, etc. Therefore, the voices must be rejected, not only of Plato, who praises common ownership against the judgment of reason, but also of the theologians who think that this Platonic common ownership is either commended or commanded in the Gospel.

To the Eighth Commandment pertain testimony and the honesty behind contracts. All men agree that lying is greatly opposed to man's nature and is highly destructive to the human race in countless ways. Therefore, it can easily be understood that honesty is derived from the law of nature, that it exists in contracts, in testimonies, in judgments, etc. Indeed, these are the chief laws of the second table. For we legally discharge our whole civil and domestic life—magistrates, civil offenses, prohibition, marriage, distinction of ownership, good faith in contracts and testimonies. These are the chief matters in civil life, and they include all decent morality. For from this natural judgment have arisen the laws concerning decent morality in the state. Indeed, the form of society is loveliest where the laws do not depart from that right judgment of nature, as Aristotle elegantly says, that "there is one form of society which is truly beautiful," namely, that which is according to nature.

But since we have accommodated the laws of nature to the Decalogue, the comparison itself demonstrates that the law of nature is contained in the Decalogue, and indeed set forth in the most appropriate order, with certain laws being revealed even more clearly. Therefore, we normally use the name "Decalogue" for the moral law. Now, the law of nature, as all agree, pertains to men of all nations. The moral law, then, is the same for all times and for all nations. The fact that God again pronounced this law of nature with His own voice confirms us in the knowledge that these works truly please Him. From this we should also learn that the laws of nature are truly divine, wherefore those who violate them commit mortal sin. There is also great dignity in philosophy and its decrees which explain this law. When they seek the causes which have been set in nature, they demonstrate that the will of God is written in nature. Therefore, one must reverently consider this kind of philosophy, which has reliable proofs, as well as the decrees of the teachers which are consistent with those proofs.

THE USE OF DIVINE LAW

It remains for us to discuss the use of the divine Law. Here we shall be rather brief, since this topic was treated above where we discussed how the Law is possible, that is, how it is possible for the Law to be obeyed. Here, right at the beginning, the reader must again be warned that God's Law requires perfect obedience of human nature. Furthermore, since human nature cannot provide this perfect obedience, it follows that men are not pronounced righteous before God on account of the Law, for sin always remains in the nature. Therefore, Paul removes justification from the Law in this corrupt nature. I wanted to issue this warning briefly now concerning the uses of the divine Law, lest justification be attributed to it. For later this topic will have to be treated thoroughly.

What, then, are the functions of the Law in this corrupt nature? Above I listed three. The first is civil, namely, that it should coerce all men by means of a certain discipline. Paul speaks about this function when he says, "The Law is made for the unrighteous" [1 Timothy 1:9]; that is, God wants the wicked also to be coerced not to commit external crimes. And, for the purpose of this discipline, He has ordained magistrates, law, doctrine, penalties, human calamities. To this pertains also that saying of Paul, "The Law is a schoolmaster toward Christ" [Galatians 3:24]. Discipline is highly praised here in that he calls it a "schoolmaster toward Christ." For instruction, good training, and discipline are conducive to hearing and learning the Gospel. These high praises should incite temperate men of good character not to spurn discipline. I already stated above that no one should imagine that such discipline merits the forgiveness of sins.

The second and proper function of the divine Law is also the chief function: to show sins, to accuse, to terrify, and to condemn consciences. Concerning this office, Paul says the most, as, for example, when he says, "Through the law is the knowledge of sin" [Romans 3:20]. Likewise, "The Law works wrath" [Romans 4:15]. Again, "Through the Law sin is made exceedingly guilty" [Romans 7:13]. And again, "The sting of death is sin, and the power of sin is the Law" [1 Corinthians 15:56]. These and similar sentences proclaim that consciences are terrified by the Law, for it always accuses us, and it not only censures deeds, but it also reveals and condemns our natural weakness, ignorance of God, contempt for God, and similar attitudes. And although men without the knowledge of gratuitous mercy attempt most vigorously to appease the wrath of God by means of the Law, they accomplish nothing except to doubt more and more and to despair. We see an example in Saul, who, since he seeks salvation through sacrifices and good works without faith, can find no rest, but doubts and despairs.

Furthermore, the Law does not have this use among secure men. As Paul says, "I lived at one time without the Law" [Romans 7:9], that is, I was a secure hypocrite. But afterward I became terrified and acknowledge my weakness and my sins. The Law had this use in David when, reproached by the prophet on account of his adultery, he became terrified. Then contrition, as they call it in repentance, can be clearly understood, if we recognize it as true terrors of this kind. But men must be taught about the reason why these terrors are instilled in us, namely, not that we should perish, but that we should acknowledge our need for mercy and the benefit of Christ. So also Paul says, "God confined all under sin, so that He might have mercy on all" [Galatians 3:22]. There is enormous comfort in this sentence. To be confined under sin means that we are accused, not so that we may perish, but in order that we may seek mercy. And in order that we may know that such great comfort pertains to us all individually, the universal particle is added: "He confined *all*, that He might have mercy on *all*."

The third function of the Law in those who are righteous by faith is that it should both teach them about good works, showing which works are pleasing to God, and demand certain works in which they are to show obedience toward God. For although we are free from the Law insofar as justification is concerned, the Law remains, nevertheless, insofar as obedience is concerned. For the justified must necessarily obey God, and indeed they begin, in some part, to do the Law. That beginning of obedience is pleasing for the very reason that the persons are pleasing for Christ's sake.

Let it be enough here to have given these instructions about the use or functions of the Law. For when we speak about justification, it will again be necessary to address the second use of the Law. The third use will be repeated under the topic of works, and again under the abrogation of the Law.

THE DIFFERENCE BETWEEN COMMANDMENTS AND COUNSELS

Some people have imagined that there are in the Gospel counsels concerning not seeking revenge, poverty, virginity. Indeed, they think that such things are taught in the Gospel to the end that these works should merit reconciliation more than other works. They further imagine that perfection consists in these works. But these notions are full of errors and superstitions. There is but one Law of God, and it contains nothing but commandments. Indeed, Christ's sermon in Matthew 5 is the interpretation of the Law. For Christ preaches as He does in order to demonstrate that perfect obedience is required in the Law. For this reason, when He forbids hatred, covetousness, and the desire for revenge, He is not introducing new counsels, but interpreting the very Law of God and giving commandments. "The Law," as Paul says, "is spiritual" [Romans 7:14], encompassing spiritual motives. For although we are unable to satisfy those commandments, they must, nevertheless, be learned, in order that we may know that we are in need of mercy, and that we may partially perform them. The words of Christ clearly testify that these are commandments, for they add eternal punishment. "He who is angry with his brother will be subject to judgment, etc." [Matthew 5:22]. Likewise, "Everyone who looks at a woman to lust after her has already committed adultery in his heart, etc." [Matthew 5:28].

The passages about vengeance are also commandments. For they forbid private vengeance, that is, the desire for vengeance and such vengeance as takes place without the authority of the magistrate. They do not, however, take away the public vengeance which is exercised by the magistrate. For since it is clear that the magistrates are not abolished by the Gospel, but are much more confirmed by it, as Paul testifies in Romans 13, those statements of Christ must necessarily be forbidding only private vengeance. Therefore, both are commands—the one instructing the magistrate to practice vengeance, according to the Law; the other forbidding them to practice private vengeance. See, then, how absurd it is when they say that the statements about vengeance are counsels! For if it were a counsel, as they themselves want to understand it, it would be permissible to take up arms privately and practice vengeance. Thus the world would be full of rioting and there would be no need of magistrates. On the other hand, if the magistrate thinks he is being given counsel not to exercise vengeance, he will not punish criminals; he will neglect his office, or certainly will not act in good conscience. For good works should have God's commands, so that we know that they please God and that we undertake them with trust in the divine command. And so it happens that many among the magistrates have been badly tortured by their conscience, since they doubt whether this type of life is pleasing to God. Therefore, this absurd and wicked opinion must be rejected which teaches that the passages about vengeance are mere counsels.

A distinction must prudently be made between public and private vengeance, so that the magistrates know that they must necessarily carry out their office, and that they know that the administration of their office is pleasing to God. Then, that we may all learn privately that we are required to endure injuries. For God says, "It is mine to avenge, and I will repay" [Romans 12:19]. Just as the praise properly belongs to God for wisdom, justice, and strength, so praise is owed to Him as the Judge for vengeance. Indeed, divine vengeance is public, for it is divinely ordained.

But let us learn in private matters to yield to God the glory of carrying out vengeance, and let us accustom ourselves with the highest zeal and with the greatest effort to a life of patience, to ignoring and enduring injuries. Such passages about vengeance commend and command this private virtue. Yes, we see the image of it in Christ. Therefore, let us set before ourselves both the commands and the examples of Christ's patience, and let us fiercely repress the burning desire for vengeance in this feeble nature.

This virtue is a form of worship which God deems most acceptable, and it is necessary for the concord of the Church and for preserving society. For both in the Church and in all earthly realms, the greatest tumults have arisen for no other reason than from a desire for vengeance. This madness is found especially among ambitious men of talent. Therefore, let us learn that the greatest things are commanded when Christ preaches about vengeance. Let us not seek to elude these most holy commands with that frigid fabrication about counsels.

Surely our explanation in this matter is useful, for the spiritual life as well as the civil, for it fortifies the tranquility of the commonwealth. For Christ also stresses the same thing on many occasions with His apostles, teaching them not to take vengeance, that He might remove from them the false persuasion which they had about Christ's kingdom. For they thought that they would subdue the Gentiles and take charge of the kingdoms of the world. Christ calls them back from this error when He forbids vengeance to them as private citizens who were not governing magistrates.

It is a common saying: Natural law allows a person to use violence to fend off violence. There are not a few who reject that saying as being at odds with the Gospel. But I have often said that the law of nature and civil ordinances are not abolished by the Gospel. Therefore, the Gospel is not at odds with this. It is a matter of natural law to fend off violence with violence, as long as it is understood correctly. For it should be applied to public vengeance, that is, to the office of the magistrate. The magistrate fends off violence with violence when he fends off robbery with arms and warfare. For that saying does not permit private citizens to incite riots, but to fend off violence with violence according to the manner and order prescribed by the magistrate. For that same order comes from the law of nature, namely, that there should be magistrates. Why would there be a need for magistrates if each of us took vengeance privately?

Let these admonitions about vengeance suffice. Let them be clearly understood as commandments of God, and let us understand that civil ordinances are neither abolished nor condemned by the Gospel. We will say more about magistrates and their offices under their own topic.

POVERTY

Now concerning poverty. The Gospel neither commands nor counsels anyone to part with one's possessions or to transfer one's property to a common purse. Indeed, since it approves of civil ordinances, it also approves, at the same time, of the distribution of possessions and property. So let the godly understand that they hold their possessions by divine ordinance, and that holding such property is pleasing to God. In addition, the Gospel commands us to help the needy generously, and it promises immense rewards, both bodily and spiritual, for this generosity. As Christ says, "Give and it will be given to you" [Luke 6:38]. 2 Corinthians 9, "Those who sow sparingly will reap sparingly." Let us, then, follow the elegant command of Solomon given in Proverbs 5, "Drink water from your own fountains, and drink the streams of your own well. May your fountains spring forth abroad and may your banks flow into the streets. But you alone should be lord of them, not the strangers with you, for he will be blessed by your fountains." This is a wonderful passage due to the sweetness of its allegory in which the good side of domestic life is painted most beautifully, for it commands us to hold onto our possessions and to enjoy our own things, not to steal it from someone else. And it admirably extols private property when it says, "You alone should be lord of these things, not the foreigners with you." And yet he wants streams to spring forth abroad from our fountains, that is, that each one should be generous toward the needy from the fruits of his own estate or from his own fortunes, but in such a way that he retains his estate and is not reduced to begging. Paul also commands us to be generous in such a way that we ourselves do not become needy, and that lazy people do not abuse our generosity, etc.

This is the Gospel's simple and genuine understanding in this matter. Moreover, if any passages are cited in favor of a Platonic commune, it is necessary first to compare such passages with others that approve of private property. Then the principal matter of the Gospel must be considered, namely, that it teaches about eternal things, about an inner eternal righteousness and eternal life which does not pertain to the bodily life. Therefore, it does not abolish the Law and civil affairs, which regulate and uphold our bodies. Using first principles of this kind, it is easy to address the interpretation of the passages in which there is some question.

Moreover, many testimonies confirm private property, for it is permissible to have wealth, as Christ testifies in the Gospel. Likewise Paul in 1 Timothy 6. And in 1 Corinthians 7, he grants that purchases will take place, etc. Likewise the godly can be kings. But kingdoms cannot be maintained without wealth. However, there is no need of a long discussion of this matter, since the things which come from the law of nature are not mutable, nor can the ordinance concerning the distinction of ownership be changed. For natural reason teaches that such a distinction is necessary in this state of the human race. For although any given family can use its possessions in common, that group of people, nevertheless, has its own possessions and keeps other people away from those possessions. The magistrate defends the holdings of the monasteries and determines that they belong to the monks. Therefore, those who deny that they have any possessions are merely playing a game of empty words. For the very ordinance of nature cannot be changed.

Furthermore, poverty should not be understood as beggary, for beggary among the idle and physically capable is a sin, as Paul teaches in his epistle to the Thessalonians: "He who does not work, let him not eat" [2 Thessalonians 3:10].

From all these things, it follows that it is neither a counsel nor a command to part with one's resources or to hand over one's possessions to the community. Indeed, the Gospel teaches us much more to use the civil ordinance of the distinction of ownership.

The fact is that Evangelical poverty is spiritual. That is, the Gospel teaches us to hold onto the resources which we have by the kindness of God without avarice, without pride. In other words, without trust in riches and without impiety. This means that, when our wealth is at stake in the confession of the Gospel, we should prefer to lose our wealth rather than to reject the Gospel. Evangelical poverty also includes patience when our wealth is stripped away from us or when it perishes by some happenstance, lest, at such a time, out of a desire for fortunes, we become angry with God or commit some sin against God's commandments. Instead, we are to bear that injury or happenstance for God's sake with a calm spirit. Thus, although they had great riches, Abraham, David, Job, and many others were poor in spirit. For they held their possessions without avarice, without pride, and without impiety, and they also were patient when they lost their resources.

Here it must be observed that there are two ways of parting with our resources. The one happens by our own choice, without the command of God and apart from our vocation, as when a rich man willingly leaves his patrimony without anyone forcing him to do it. Such abandonment of resources is not praised in the Gospel. Indeed, it is a mistake to carry out such an abandonment as a form of worshiping God, as Christ testifies, "In vain do they worship Me with the commandments of men" [Matthew 15:9]. There is another abandonment of resources that has the commandment of God and vocation, as when tyrants force a person either to lose his resources or to abandon the Gospel. Here Christ praises the abandonment of resources when He says, "Whoever leaves behind field, house, etc., for the sake of the Gospel" [Mark 10:29]. He adds "for the sake of the Gospel," that is, for the confession of the Gospel. And He only praises such abandonment when one is called to it, as is evident from His words, for He also gives orders to abandon parents, spouse, children, and even one's own life. Therefore, as He does not praise those who desert spouse and children or who take their life by their own hand, so He does not praise those who abandon their patrimonies without the commandment of God, etc.

CHASTITY

The Scriptures forbid fornication, adultery, and similar wantonness with the most severe statements. Chastity, however, pertains not only to virgins, but also to spouses. For marriage itself is a divine ordinance, and all who fail to restrain themselves have the command to use marriage. As Paul says, "On account of fornication, each one should have his own wife" [1 Corinthians 7:2]. Indeed, he commends the use of marriage with an honorable title when he adds, "Let the husband render due benevolence to his wife" [1 Corinthians 7:3]. Chastity, then, is not only virginity, but also the controlled behavior of spouses.

This must be mentioned at the outset so that we remember that the ordinance of God must be used in a holy way, while the fanatical spirits must be condemned who deny that marriage is conceded to Christians. There were many such people long ago, like Tacianus and Hierax. But although the monks do not want to be seen as condemning marriage, they greatly disparage it, teaching that virginity is preferable and that it exemplifies perfection and cleanness, as if marriage were something unclean. They have not lightly troubled the consciences of the unlearned.

Let us understand, first of all, that virginity is not commanded. Secondly, it must be granted that Paul gives advice about preserving virginity. But here one must judge sensibly. For Paul does not think that anyone earns justification more with virginity than with marriage; both spouses and virgins should know that they are righteous through mercy, that is, that they are acceptable for Christ's sake, not for the worthiness of marriage or virginity. It is, therefore, a vain confidence of the monks who imagine that they merit the forgiveness of sins and justification more than the rest of men because of their celibacy. They go much further astray for thinking that such celibacy is evangelical perfection. For many husbands (such as Abraham, Isaac, David, and Isaiah) were more perfect that most virgins. For evangelical perfection is spiritual, that is, it consists in acknowledging more and more our weakness, being terrified by it, and, on the other hand, being raised up by faith. Perfection—if it is to be called that—dwells in such exercises.

No, Paul praises and recommends virginity for a practical reason, namely, that we may be more unencumbered in learning, teaching, and attending to the ecclesiastical ministries. For these reasons, Christ also praises the celibate when He says, "Those who have emasculated themselves for the sake of the Gospel" [Matthew 19:12], that is, for the sake of learning and teaching it. For it is true what Paul says: "A celibate man cares for the things which are of the Lord, in order to please the Lord" [1 Corinthians 7:32]. And in fact, it is not only domestic concerns, but other things that turn one's gaze much more away from the troubles of the Church and interrupt the studies of those who learn and those who teach. Therefore, if those who are called to ecclesiastical ministries are affected by the troubles of the Church, if they weigh in their heart the magnitude of their own burden, if they think about how difficult it is to explain dogmas and to govern the Church, these concerns and distresses will easily dislodge any thoughts of marriage from them.

But the world judges wrongly. It views celibacy superstitiously, as a special form of divine worship and as an extraordinary work which makes one more deserving of the forgiveness of sins and justification, while it remains unconcerned about studies or about the miseries faced by the Church. Thus it embraces celibacy, not because of its usefulness to others or for the sake of studies, but as a matter of superstition. But it would make more sense to praise virginity for the sake of studies or because of its usefulness to others. And the governance of the churches is a very great matter and by far the most difficult affair of all. For the doctrine itself is difficult and challenges students to an extraordinary degree, and the explanation of it is also full of difficulty. The mind that is occupied with domestic thoughts can hardly sustain these labors.

Therefore, Paul encourages virginity in such a way that he first admonishes us not to do anything indecent; then, that we may be able to serve the Lord unceasingly. For first he requires that we not do anything indecent, that is, that if anyone cannot control himself, it is better to take a wife, lest he become the perpetrator of some shameful deed. Then, if a person can control himself, he should pursue celibacy to this end, that he may serve the Lord unceasingly, that is, that he may spend more time in learning and teaching, in caring for and thinking about the troubles of the Church, and also in prayer—more than others who are involved in multiple activities. But since not all are equally suited to celibacy, he prudently warns us not to do anything indecent.

From these things, it is clear that marriage is commended, and yet the counsel concerning virginity is given. It is clear likewise to what end virginity is praised, namely, not to merit the forgiveness of sins or justification, but because it is a good work and useful for studies, prayer, and serving the Church. Therefore, the celibate should test their strength and diligently endeavor to live purely. That virtue also has its rewards. Meanwhile, idleness and comfortable living entice not a few men who are endowed with the gift. Therefore, self-control must be summoned and the mind applied to studies. But those who fall into lust contrary to the commandments of God will also remember themselves, that they will pay the penalty to God, and that often, because of them, whole cities are punished, as the history of Sodom testifies. Likewise God said that He would wipe out the Canaanites on account of their errant lusts. This is also said to be the cause of the flood. And Paul indicates in Ephesians 4 that the penalties of lust are blindness and madness, or carnal security, where he writes, "Who, since they grieved no more, gave themselves over to unchastity" [Ephesians 4:19]. For here he attributes numbness or madness to those who are unchaste, for which reason they think little of the divine threats and of all divine matters, and thus they run to their destruction. Hosea said the same thing, "Fornication, wine and drunkenness bear the heart away" [Hosea 4:11].

THE GOSPEL

The word "gospel" (*Euangelium*) is found among the most ancient Greek authors. In Homer's writings it signifies a reward which is given to the one who announces happy things. In the *Odyssey*, Book XIV, it says, "Let me have good news" (εὐαγγέλιον δέ μοι ἔστω). And in Aristophanes and Isocrates, "to sacrifice good news" (εὐαγγέλια θύειν) refers to a sacrifice that was made when things that had turned out fortunately and well were announced. The apostles used the term for the announcement itself of the benefit. Indeed, a new word was needed so that there might be a more obvious distinction between the Law and this new doctrine.

First, then, we must consider what the difference is between the Law and the Gospel. We are not inventing here any idle or cunning distinctions beyond those which are necessary. For it is certainly necessary that the commandments be distinguished from the forgiveness of sins—that the commandments be distinguished from the promises—and likewise, that the gratuitous promise be distinguished from the promises which are not gratuitous. Therefore, the Law (as said above) is a doctrine which requires perfect obedience. It does not forgive sins for free. It does not pronounce people righteous, that is, acceptable to God, unless the Law is satisfied. And although it includes promises, nevertheless, these are conditioned on the Law's fulfillment. The Gospel, on the other hand, although it preaches about repentance and good works, contains the promise of the benefit of Christ, which is the proper and chief doctrine of the Gospel and must be separated from the Law. For the Gospel forgives sins and pronounces us righteous, even though we do not satisfy the Law. We will explain shortly how these things agree with one another—that the Gospel preaches equally about repentance and the Law, and yet the promise is gratuitous. For first the reader must be warned to observe the distinction in the promises, since the Law, too, includes promises.

It must be understood that there are two kinds of promises in the divine Scriptures. Some are added to the Law and include the condition of the Law, that is, they are fulfilled because a person has kept the Law. Such are the promises of the Law. The Law teaches that God is good and merciful, but only to those who are without sin. Human reason teaches the same thing, for reason has some knowledge of the Law. Here each one should examine himself, for he will discover that he naturally judges God to be merciful, but only to the worthy, that is, to those who are without sin. But no one can pretend that he pleases God, since everyone is unworthy and unclean. Thus the Law and the promises of the Law, since they are conditional, leave consciences in doubt.

Then there is the promise which is proper to the Gospel. It does not include the condition of the Law as a cause, that is, it does not make promises on the condition of the Law being fulfilled, but gratis, because of Christ. This is the promise of the forgiveness of sins, or reconciliation, or justification, about which the Gospel chiefly preaches. For in order that these benefits might be certain, they do not depend on the condition of fulfilling the Law. For if it were to be understood that we only have the forgiveness of sins when we have first satisfied the Law, we would have to give up hope on the forgiveness of sins. Therefore, forgiveness and reconciliation or justification are given gratis, that is, not because of our worthiness. And yet there had to be a victim in our stead. Therefore, Christ was given to us and made a sacrifice, in order that, for His sake, we may know for certain that we are pleasing to the Father.

Therefore, this evangelical promise of reconciliation is unlike the promises of the Law, for it promises gratis, for Christ's sake. For this reason, Paul diligently and frequently emphasizes this little word (*particulam*) for us, as in Romans 4: "Therefore it is gratis, by faith, that the promise may be sure."[25] For this little word, "gratis for Christ's sake" (*gratis propter Christum*), makes the distinction between the Law and the Gospel. For if we fail to notice this little word about the gratuitous promise, doubt remains in our minds and the Gospel is transformed into the Law. This renders our consciences no more certain of the forgiveness of sins or justification than does the Law or the natural judgment of reason. Our adversaries, too, render consciences uncertain, for, although they loudly proclaim that they teach the Gospel, nevertheless, since they do not teach about the gratuitous reconciliation, they leave

---

25   Melanchthon substitutes the adverb *gratis* for the Vulgate's *secundum gratiam*, "according to grace," to emphasize the free-of-charge meaning of the word "grace," thus removing any doubt about the meaning. Therefore, as mentioned above in the Translator's Note, I have consistently rendered it with the same word, "gratis," which has come down to us in the English language with essentially the same meaning as the Latin.

consciences in doubt and teach the Law in place of the Gospel. Hesiod (that is, the natural judgment of reason) does the same thing. Therefore the mind and the eyes must be fixed on this little word, "gratis." For it is necessary to teach about the gratuitous promise so that doubt may be removed from men's consciences, so that they may have a sure comfort in the face of real terrors. For in these terrors it can easily be judged how this gratuitous promise is needed and how this doctrine must certainly be brought back into this struggle.

But it must be understood that the promise must be accepted by faith. Paul teaches this in Romans 4. And John says, "He who does not believe God makes Him a liar, etc." [1 John 5:10]. Consequently, the little word "gratis" does not exclude faith; it excludes, rather, the condition of our worthiness and transfers the cause of the benefit from us to Christ. Therefore, it also does not exclude our obedience; it only transfers the cause of the benefit from the worthiness of our obedience to Christ, so that the benefit may be certain. Therefore, the Gospel preaches about repentance, but in order that reconciliation may be certain, it teaches that sins are forgiven and that we are pleasing to God, not for the sake of the worthiness of our repentance or our renewal. This is a much-needed comfort for godly consciences. And from this it can be judged how these things agree with one another when we say that the Gospel preaches about repentance, and yet it promises reconciliation gratis. But we will say more about this comparison shortly.

Christ, as the Author of the Gospel, defines the Gospel in the last chapter of Luke when He commands His disciples to teach repentance and the forgiveness of sins in His name. The Gospel, then, is the preaching of repentance and the promise—which reason does not naturally comprehend but is divinely revealed—in which God promises that He forgives sins for the sake of Christ His Son and pronounces us righteous, that is, acceptable, and gives the Holy Spirit and eternal life, if only we believe, that is, if only we trust that these things certainly happen to us for Christ's sake. And these things He promises gratis, that they may be certain. This is the definition of the Gospel in which, by means of three members, we have summed up the proper benefits of the Gospel, namely, that sins are forgiven gratis for Christ's sake; that we are pronounced righteous gratis, that is, we are reconciled or accepted; and that we are heirs of eternal life. We will explain these three members a little later. Here you do well simply to remember that these are the proper benefits of the Gospel which are otherwise comprehended in the single word "justification."

WHY THE PROMISE OF THE GOSPEL IS NEEDED

After human nature was overwhelmed with sin and death on account of Adam's fall, there remains some knowledge of the Law. Nevertheless, since sin remains in man's nature, consciences cannot be sure that God is willing to forgive if they never hear anything but the Law. For the Law does not teach that sins are forgiven gratis. We know, moreover, that we are not without sin, and we know it all the more when our minds are utterly terrified by the judgment of God. There is a need, then, for gratuitous forgiveness. Therefore God has revealed, in mercy, that He is willing to forgive us and to restore to us eternal life. And He has provided the victim for us—His Son—that we might know that these things are given to us for the sake of the Son, not because of our worthiness or merits. This Gospel was promised and revealed immediately after Adam's fall, lest that first Church be lacking in consolation.

It is one and the same Gospel by which all the saints since the beginning of the world have been saved at all times—Adam, Noah, Abraham, Jacob, the prophets, the apostles. Therefore, we should not imagine that the fathers were saved by the law of nature, the Jews by the law of Moses, and we by some law of our own. Indeed, there is one moral law of all ages, of all nations, as we said above. But neither the fathers, nor the Jews, nor the Gentiles, nor we are saved because we satisfy the Law, for no one satisfies the Law. No, the Law leaves consciences in doubt. This is the difference between the fathers and Xenophon, Cicero, and similar great men: they all know the Law, but they do not all know the Gospel. Xenophon, Cicero, and similar men doubted whether God cared about them, whether they had a propitious God, whether they were heard by God. For although they knew the Law, they saw, nevertheless, that they were not innocent. The Law, moreover, teaches that God is propitious toward those who are without sin. They did not know the Gospel of the gratuitous forgiveness of sins. But Abraham, Jacob, and similar men, since they knew the Gospel, were convinced that their sins were forgiven them, that they had a propitious God, that God cared about them, that they were heard by God, even though they were unworthy. Therefore it is written, "Abraham believed God, and it was account to him for righteousness" [Genesis 15:6]. There is one Law, and it is known to all nations and ages by nature. There is also one Gospel, but it is not known by nature; it is divinely revealed. Therefore Paul calls it a "mystery which has been hidden" [Colossians 1:26]. And John says, "The Son, who is in the Father's bosom—He has declared Him to us" [John 1:18]. But all these things will be clearer when we speak a little later about grace and about justification.

But since we asserted that the fathers had the same Gospel, we must explore how the Gospel was initially revealed. I will cite a few passages to which similar passages in the reading of the prophets should be applied. For the Gospel was revealed more and more clearly, and it will be evident that the prophets predicted this gratuitous reconciliation.

The promise about Christ and the benefits of Christ was first revealed to Adam immediately after the fall, so that, when he encountered the wrath of God and death, he might have a consolation by which he might know that God was and would again be propitious, that death might someday be abolished. For these two benefits are clearly set forth by that first promise, which seems somewhat obscure, and yet to Adam it was not so at that time. "I will place enmity between you and the woman, and between your seed and her seed. He will crush your head, and you will strike his heel" [Genesis 3:15]. This is a wonderful declaration, and while it may appear ridiculous and fictional to the ungodly, the godly see that the greatest things are signified in these brief words. Right away in the beginning, the punishment for sin is described; namely, that because of sin, the devil would harass the human race with cruel tyranny, that is, with sin and death, even as the history of the world testifies, all of which is depicted for Adam in this whole terrible sermon. Then a brief description is added of the kingdom of Christ: the seed of the woman would crush the head, that is, the kingdom of the serpent. That is, He would destroy sin and death. Adam is raised up by this consolation. He acknowledges that he has a kindly-disposed God, even though he is unworthy and unclean. He sees what he has lost, but he awaits that seed by which the lost righteousness and eternal life are to be restored. By means of this trust in mercy, he is pleasing to God. And as for the antithesis of the holy seed, that the devil would strike his heel, he understands that both Christ and the saints are to be afflicted in this life, and yet will overcome the kingdom of the devil.

This promise is renewed afterward to Abraham: "In your seed all nations will be blessed" [Genesis 22:18]. This means that all nations have already been cursed, that is, that God is angry with all nations and that they have been oppressed by sin and death, but that through Abraham's seed they would again be freed from these ills. Indeed, this is how the apostles themselves interpret this promise, as is evident from Paul and from Acts. What is more, in the same story of Abraham is added the picture of justification. God comforts Abraham and says, "Do not be afraid. I am your Guardian" [Genesis 15:1]. He then adds the promise about the seed. Abraham believes this word. That is, although he sees and acknowledges that he is unclean and unworthy, nevertheless he is convinced that he has a favorable God on account of His mercy and the promised seed, and he is thus pronounced righteous. This example teaches us that reconciliation is obtained by the promise and faith. Moreover, faith depends not on our worthiness, but only on the mercy of God.

Many sermons and examples of the forgiveness of sins follow little by little, but the clearest statements are in the Psalms and Prophets. In them, the Gospel is clearly set forth in several places. In the Psalms, the psalmist asks for the forgiveness of sins for mercy's sake, not for the sake of his own worthiness or merits. For example, "Enter not into judgment with Your servant, for in Your sight no one living will be justified" [Psalm 143:2]. This seeking of mercy and confessing of sin is certainly not the preaching of the Law. Indeed, the Law condemns all men in order that we may all know that sins are remitted to us gratis. Likewise, "If You mark iniquities, O Lord, who shall stand?" [Psalm 130:3]. Again, "I said, I will confess against me my unrighteousness, and You forgive the wickedness of my heart" [Psalm 32:5]. Likewise, he describes Christ the Priest, "You are a priest forever" [Psalm 110:4]. He testifies, therefore, that this Priest will appease God and will restore eternal righteousness and eternal life, for He is called an eternal priest.

Similar passages in the Psalms should be applied to this understanding of gratuitous forgiveness. For then these most pleasant songs will become sweet to us and will afford us a firm consolation. For if we judge that those promises depend on our worthiness when the Psalms command us to rejoice or to trust in mercy, then our consciences will always cry out in protest that we are unworthy, that these promises have nothing to do with the unworthy. Therefore, against this very doubt the mind must be reassured; we must know that all those words commanding us to rejoice have been set forth that they may cure that very doubt that has arisen from our unworthiness. If we conclude that reconciliation is promised to us gratis, then faith will be certain and we will truly rejoice in mercy and give thanks to God. But such is the infirmity and anguish of the human mind, that it cannot grasp the magnitude of this mercy. And so we are oppressed by the opinion and judgment of the Law so that we cannot be persuaded of the Gospel, that mercy is being offered, both to all and gratis. Therefore, faith must constantly wrestle with this infirmity of ours, so that we reassure ourselves and learn to trust God and truly to call upon Him and worship Him.

In the book of Isaiah there are many sermons about Christ, the forgiveness of sins, and eternal life. In chapter 53, he clearly testifies that the forgiveness of sins is promised, and that it is promised on account of Christ, not on account of our worthiness. "The Lord has laid on Him the iniquities of us all" [Isaiah 53:6]. And lest the Jews imagine that they merited the forgiveness of sins by means of their Levitical offerings, he testifies that another offering remains which will truly destroy sin. "He will make His soul an offering for sins" [Isaiah 53:10]. He likewise condemns all men: "We have all gone astray" [Isaiah 53:6]. He says this so that we understand that we obtain the benefits of Christ for the sake of mercy, not for the sake of our own worthiness. Finally, he adds the clearest testimony of all: "By knowledge of Him He will justify many" [Isaiah 53:11]. This must certainly be understood to mean that we are declared righteous if we acknowledge Christ, that is, if we acknowledge that God is propitious toward us for Christ's sake. Therefore, we will not be forced to doubt on account of our unworthiness, nor should anyone conclude that we are righteous on account of the Law.

But I will refrain from offering more testimonies. I have listed these as examples, so that those who read in the Scriptures may take note which passages properly preach about the Law and which ones properly preach about the Gospel, and that they may observe the difference between the Law and the promise of the Gospel. For these are the two chief topics and headings of Scripture to which all parts of Scripture should be prudently traced back.

Thus far we have defined the Gospel, and we have demonstrated the difference between the Law and the Gospel. But all these things will be clearer when we speak about justification and about faith and works.

For now, only one little word must be added, namely this: Just as it is necessary to know that the Gospel is a gratuitous promise, so also it is necessary to know that the Gospel is a universal promise. That is, reconciliation is offered and promised to all men. It is necessary to maintain this universality against the pernicious ideas about predestination, lest we argue that this promise pertains to a few others, but not to ourselves. For there is no doubt that this notion assails the minds of all men, and from it many useless arguments have arisen among the writers concerning predestination. However, we declare that the promise of the Gospel is universal. For just as the preaching of repentance is universal, so also the preaching of the forgiveness of sins is universal.

To this end, let us gather the universal statements about the Gospel which are found throughout the Scriptures. John 3, "God so loved the world that He gave His only-begotten Son, that everyone who believes in Him should not perish" [John 3:16]. Likewise in Paul's writings, "He has concluded all men under sin that He might have mercy on all men" [Romans 11:32].

It is enough for now that we have reviewed these things. For we will have to say more later on about this universality when we speak about predestination. But not all men obtain the things promised by the Gospel because not all believe. For although the Gospel promises gratis, nevertheless it requires faith, for the promise must be accepted by faith. Indeed, the little word "gratis" does not exclude faith; it excludes the condition of our worthiness, as said above. It requires us to accept the promise. This cannot be done in any other way than by faith.

GRACE AND JUSTIFICATION

This topic contains the sum of the Gospel, for it shows the proper benefit of Christ. Indeed, it sets forth a firm consolation for pious minds and teaches what the true forms of divine worship are. It is easy for the pious to judge how great the power is of such things, how necessary is this knowledge for the Church. Therefore, it was to be hoped that this topic would have been explained clearly and distinctly in the Church without interruption. But there exists a tragic variety of opinions and judgments on this topic. Some utterly dismiss this doctrine, although it contains much-needed comfort. Others spread mist over it, having imported foreign discussions about predestination and other irrelevant matters. In the words of Aristotle, "Peripheral matters are given more attention than the matters themselves."[26] In short, the essential matters are buried under many ambiguities. This sophistry leads consciences into doubt, and it also disturbs the Church. Therefore, I shall recite the Pauline interpretation simply and in good faith, and I shall not quarrel with anyone at this time. For I hope that, when I have explained this interpretation, I shall leave the wise and fair readers the more content when they see that what I am saying is not at all absurd or perplexing. Then they will see that these things are clearly and plainly set forth in the Holy Scriptures. Finally, they will see that these are not idle and useless musings, but the most serious doctrine which has a useful purpose in the life and exercises of the godly, which instructs and comforts pious minds.

Therefore, not only does the authority of the apostles and fathers defend us, but the universal Church of all times also proves this interpretation. That is to say, the experience of the godly testifies that there is set forth in this interpretation, not idle vanities, but necessary, true, and firm consolations. Indeed, it also illustrates the benefits of Christ

---

26   Aristotle, *Nicomachean Ethics*, Book 1, ch. 7.

and demonstrates the true forms of divine worship, which are also proper for Christians. Moreover, what other theater do we seek but the Church; that is, the consensus of the godly, the learned, and the experts? If this consensus is favorable toward us, then let us not pay much attention to the unfair or even slanderous judgments of the unlearned or the ungodly.

To reiterate the case: The Gospel, as I have said, teaches chiefly about repentance and the forgiveness of sins for Christ's sake. Therefore, this is how I speak about justification in the simplest way. The Gospel reproves sins and teaches that we need Christ the Mediator, for whose sake the forgiveness of sins and reconciliation are given us. Consequently, it is necessary, when speaking about justification, to speak of the forgiveness of sins. Indeed, there are certainly some ridiculous people who have had much to say about justification, but have failed to mention the forgiveness of sins, as if it had nothing to do with the matter at hand. Furthermore, we will explain in its place how God moves the hearts of infants and sanctifies them when they are offered to Him through Baptism.

For now, we are speaking about adults, who must be taught on the basis of the Gospel and who should be convinced about the will of God on the basis of the Word. The mind, terrified by the recognition of sins, should be convinced that sins are forgiven to a person gratis, for Christ's sake, through mercy, not on account of the worthiness of his contrition, love, or other works. When the mind is thus encouraged by faith, the forgiveness of sins and reconciliation are given. For if we had to conclude that we only had the forgiveness of sins when our contrition or love were sufficient, our spirit would be driven to despair. Therefore, that we may have a firm and certain consolation, the matter depends, not on the condition of our worthiness, but only on the mercy promised for Christ's sake. If we are willing to consider the Scriptures and the exercises of the Church, then there is certainly nothing absurd, nothing perplexing about these things. Yes, in this way, merit is removed from works in the forgiveness of sins, not because we do nothing, but because the forgiveness of sins is a gift, that it may be certain.

It still remains for us to gather the testimonies that support this interpretation, that we obtain the forgiveness of sins and reconciliation for Christ's sake by faith, not because of the worthiness of our works. But first we shall set forth the meaning of the terms in this matter.

"Justification" means "the forgiveness of sins and reconciliation," that is, the acceptance of a person to eternal life. For in Hebrew, "to justify" is a forensic term, so to speak. The Roman people justified Scipio, who was accused by the tribunes. That is, they absolved him or pronounced him righteous. Paul, therefore, took up the word "justify" from the custom of the Hebrew language to mean "acceptance," that is, reconciliation and the forgiveness of sins. When God forgives sins, He, at the same time, gives us the Holy Spirit who produces new powers in the godly. Indeed, I gladly and publicly confess that in the godly there must exist, not only faith, but also other fruits of the Spirit (as we shall explain later). But we should not conclude, on that account, that our worthiness or cleanness is a cause of the forgiveness of sins.

"Faith," in this matter, in Paul's writings, undoubtedly means "trust in the mercy promised for Christ's sake." Although certain unlearned sycophants madly cry out in protest and deny that faith means trust in mercy, nevertheless, I do not hesitate to appeal to all learned and good men. That learned man, van Campen,[27] although he disagrees with certain things in this discussion of ours, wisely sees that "faith," in Paul's writings, should be understood as trust in mercy. Indeed, he completely approves of this interpretation of mine. We do not, of course, exclude the knowledge of the history about Christ, as some people slanderously accuse us of doing. For when we speak of trust in the mercy promised

---

27   Jan van Campen (1491–1538), also known as Campensis, a noteworthy Hebrew scholar at the University of Louvain and the University of Cracow.

for Christ's sake, we certainly include all the articles of faith, and we refer the history of Christ to that article which recalls the benefit of Christ: the forgiveness of sins. Therefore, this trust includes the knowledge about Christ the Son of God and the condition or action of the will by which it wants and accepts the promise of Christ, and thus it rests on Christ. But I will omit further technicalities.

That faith means trust in mercy is attested both by the examples in which faith is mentioned and by Paul's own argument. For Paul combines the promise of grace with faith and requires faith which grasps the promise. This faith, again, is trust in mercy. And in the entire discussion, he rejects trust in one's own worthiness and, on the other hand, requires faith in the benefit of another, namely, Christ. Now, if Paul had understood that men are righteous (that is, acceptable to God or reconciled) on account of their own cleanness or the worthiness of their qualities or works, then he certainly would have taught trust in one's own worthiness. But he clearly says, "Boasting is excluded" [Romans 3:27]. Likewise, he cites the Psalm, "Blessed are those whose iniquities are forgiven" [Romans 4:7]. And he contends that we are pronounced righteous in this way: if we believe that sins are forgiven to us. Now this faith which is convinced that sins are forgiven is that trust of which we are speaking. Likewise, when he says, "Having been justified by faith, we have peace" [Romans 5:1], he declares that he is not speaking about some idle knowledge, but about faith which encourages and comforts the spirit. For he contrasts this sentence with the Law, of which he says, "The Law works wrath" [Romans 4:15], that is, it accuses and terrifies the conscience.

But what need is there to produce arguments in a matter that is already clear? For it is clear that faith means trust in the mercy promised for Christ's sake. This article of the forgiveness of sins must be firmly believed, while the conventional opinion must be rejected which commands us to doubt whether we have the forgiveness of sins or not.

Therefore, faith corresponds to mercy, as to an object. Consequently, when it is said that we are justified by faith, this figure of speech can better be understood if we change the word "faith" into the corresponding word "mercy." We are justified through the mercy promised for Christ's sake. But this mercy must be apprehended by faith. For this is what Paul is driving at, that men are reconciled by trust in the benefit of another, not for the sake of their own worthiness, either of their qualities or of their works. This is the genuine and simple meaning of Paul.

And although this trust (as I shall explain later) should be accompanied by our obedience and all kinds of virtues, I am not pleased with the idea of those who now employ a dangerous misuse of this teaching in order that they may appear to be useful interpreters. Their interpretation is that we are justified by faith—that is, by the whole doctrine of the religion. In other words, by the Law. This interpretation is improper, and it obscures Paul's meaning. Aristo of Chios[28] is also said to have regularly argued that all virtues are really a single virtue which he himself called "soundness" (ὑγίεια). Thus these people imagine that faith, in Paul's writings, means the whole chorus of virtues. Then, having lost the primary meaning of Paul, they return to the doctrine of the Law and magnificently bluster about it as they pretend that men are righteous on account of their own worthiness, on account of their keeping of the Law. They fail to see, therefore, that Paul speaks so passionately about trust in mercy because even the best men are far from perfection. Let this suffice concerning the phrase, "We are justified by faith."

"Grace" means "the gratuitous acceptance or mercy promised for Christ's sake." Paul adds, "the gift by grace" [Romans 5:15]. This is what he calls the giving of the Holy Spirit and eternal life. And while grace also signifies the aid of the Holy Spirit or a divine action, as Augustine often interprets grace, nevertheless, one must take care here lest, having abandoned Paul's meaning, we slip into the doctrine of the Law. This is

---

28   A Stoic philosopher who lived in the third century B.C.

what happened to the Scholastics who, when they say that a man is justified by grace, say nothing there about trust in mercy, but imagine that a man is pronounced righteous on account of his own worthiness and renewal, or on account of his cleanness, without trust in mercy.

There is an exclusive little word in the term "grace," namely, that the forgiveness of sins and reconciliation are given gratis. This exclusive little word does not exclude our repentance and good works; it only excludes the condition of worthiness and shifts the whole matter of the benefit of Christ to the realm of mercy, that it may be certain. Contrition should certainly exist in Peter and in David. But that their consciences may be rendered peaceful, they should be convinced that their sins are surely forgiven them, not on account of the worthiness of their contrition or other works, but gratis, through mercy, for Christ's sake.

There is nothing absurd in this exclusive interpretation. Indeed, it is necessary. For in true terrors, the mind is not unaware that God is good or that He is merciful. But what it wonders is whether He forgives sins to the unworthy; whether He forgives sins gratis. It finds no work that it can set against the wrath of God, that it might appease God's wrath. It acknowledges its own unworthiness. It recognizes that it is guilty. The main point (*epitasis*) of the struggle, then, is whether it is certain that the forgiveness of sins is given gratis to the unworthy.

Therefore, the Gospel sets forth a firm consolation to consciences in this struggle and teaches that the promise is gratuitous. It testifies that sins are remitted gratis for Christ's sake, and thus it truly teaches us to use Christ as Mediator and High Priest. It insists that this Mediator be set against the wrath of God. It insists that we be convinced that, on account of this High Priest, the Father is favorable and propitious toward us.

The monks have buried this comfort. They insist that one must doubt whether the forgiveness of sins takes place, and they have shifted the benefit of Christ over to the works of men. They have taught that the forgiveness of sins takes place on account of the worthiness of the works. Thus, at the same time, they have obscured the benefit of Christ and tortured pious minds. Indeed, based on this opinion, they have invented new forms of worship and monkery.

Therefore, it is necessary in the Church that this comfort should exist, that the glory of Christ may become clearer, that pious minds may be fortified against despair, and that the true forms of the worship of God may be understood.

Moreover, I shall add testimonies from which the whole matter may become more perspicuous. Again, the following must be carefully observed in these testimonies, that when justification is named, it includes both the forgiveness of sins and the acceptance of a person, or, reconciliation. It is helpful to keep these two understandings in view so that we may ever regard them in this great infirmity of ours and awaken faith and fortify it with such testimonies throughout our whole life, in all perils and in every invocation. God requires this worship, this work, above all things. This worship brings true honor to Christ, when we use Christ as Mediator and High Priest. For those do not use Christ as Mediator who do not understand faith in this way and imagine that they satisfy the Law, not acknowledging their own infirmity. Or, if they acknowledge it, they live in doubt, which produces either despair or contempt of God. For such a life without this trust in mercy does not please God. Indeed, those who live in this way, since they are unable to expect or ask anything from God, are just like those who are without God. But I will recite the testimonies.

Romans 3, "All have sinned and lack the glory of God, and are justified freely by His grace, through the redemption in Christ Jesus, whom God set forth as a Propitiator through faith in His blood." This sentence, where he says, "they are justified," includes at the same time the forgiveness of sins and justification. And he expressly says, "whom He set forth as a Propitiator through faith," that he may signify that the application is needed; namely, that we apprehend Christ as Mediator by faith. This faith, as we have said, is trust. And since he requires this trust, he rejects doubt. He also adds the exclusive little word, "gratis by His grace," that is, by mercy, that we may understand that we are pleasing to Him, not on account of the worthiness of our works, but for Christ's sake. And that this may be even clearer, he speaks first about our uncleanness, that we are all guilty and lack the glory of God, that is, that glory or righteousness which God approves.

Then, in the fourth chapter, Paul himself gathers arguments in favor of his own understanding, of which we will recite two here.

"Abraham believed God, and it was imputed to him for righteousness" [Romans 4:3]. Here the Scripture expressly affirms that Abraham was pronounced righteous because he believed, that is, because he was convinced that he had a propitious God, not on account of his own worthiness, but through the mercy promised by God Himself. And Paul himself adds this interpretation of the exclusive statement, "Not to the one who works, but to the one who believes in Him who justifies the ungodly, his faith is imputed for righteousness" [Romans 4:5]. Thus he contrasts faith, that is, trust in mercy, with our own worthiness.

Here again, I advise the pious reader to consider how rich, how necessary is this comfort, to have this conviction, that God is certainly willing to forgive sins, although you do not bring Him your merits. Likewise, that He has instructed you to believe yourself forgiven, that He requires this worship. Also, that He approves of this beginning of obedience, although it is far from the perfection of the Law, because the person has already been reconciled by faith in Christ. If a person either despises or rejects these things, he has no idea what true repentance or true piety are.

The final argument from Romans 4 is taken up from the sources of the topic, namely, from the cause of the promise, and it chiefly confirms the exclusive statement in this way:

If the promise of reconciliation depended on the condition of the Law as a cause, it would become uncertain. But this promise must be certain for our consciences. Therefore, it is necessary that the forgiveness of sins and reconciliation be promised gratis and accepted by faith, not on account of our worthiness.

Paul proves the major premise, since the Law works wrath. That is, since no one satisfies the Law, the Law accuses all men. Therefore, it would be necessary for consciences to doubt concerning justification—indeed, to despair!—if it were to be understood that we are not pronounced righteous except after we have satisfied the Law. Here let each one consult his own conscience and ask whether he satisfies the Law. Even hypocrites, although they do not see that they are accused by the Law, realize in moments of true terrors of conscience that they will not be able to set their works against the judgment of God. It is necessary, therefore, to maintain this understanding of gratuitous reconciliation. As Paul says, "Therefore it is by faith, gratis, that the promise may be firm" [Romans 4:16].

But some cry out in protest that we are interpreting Paul uncivilly and distorting his statements and applying them to moral commandments, when he is only removing justification from ceremonies! Surely such sophistry must be removed above all from the doctrine of the religion! Indeed, if anyone hates sophistry with a passion, it is I. Therefore, I shall attempt properly and simply to state the meaning of Paul. It is a fact that Paul often affirms that no one satisfies the moral Law, that this weak nature of man is under sin. Therefore, he cannot set his own righteousness or cleanness against the judgment of God. And therefore Paul says, "Through Christ we have access to God" [Ephesians 2:18]. And Christ says, "If the Son sets you free, you will be free indeed" [John

8:36]. Again, "I am the Vine, you are the branches, etc." [John 15:5]. Likewise, "He gave them power to become sons of God, to those who believe in His name, etc." [John 1:12].

This, then, is what Paul is driving at. He teaches that sins are forgiven us and that we are justified—that is, reconciled—for Christ's sake, not on account of the worthiness of ceremonial or moral works, seeing that this weak nature does not even satisfy the moral Law, although afterwards a beginning of obedience is required and is pleasing to God in those who have been reconciled. Paul himself also testifies that this is his meaning when he says of the Law, "Through the Law, sin is made abundantly sinful" [Romans 7:13]. That is, since the Law accuses and condemns sin, guilt is acknowledged, and it both terrifies and kills the mind. If we were to judge according to the Law, then we would only have a propitious God if we satisfied the Law. In that case, our minds would never be at peace, since the Law always accuses. Indeed, to emphasize this understanding he cites the moral Law, "You shall not covet." Likewise, the little word "gratis" excludes not only ceremonies, but also morality from the cause of reconciliation. Indeed, Paul presses this little word that he may render men's consciences certain. But the certainty of consciences cannot be maintained if one is forced to conclude that we obtain the forgiveness of sins on account of our fulfillment of the moral precepts, since no one satisfies the moral Law. From these things, it is clear that Paul is not speaking about ceremonies only, but also about the moral Law.

Nor is it sophistry to interpret Paul in this way, as I have said thus far, especially since there is nothing at all absurd or perplexing about these things. Rather, it would be sophistry to mutilate Paul's meaning by plucking something out of his argument, thus removing gratuitous forgiveness, removing the certain comfort of men's consciences. Indeed, it would be to affix a childish interpretation to Paul's meaning, as if faith signified only a knowledge of history, as if the conscience, in its agony, should be convinced that it has the forgiveness of sins, that it has a propitious God, on account of fulfilling the Law, on account of its own worthiness. It is not difficult to judge how wrong these things are. Let us understand, then, that Paul is speaking, not only about ceremonies, but also about the moral Law in his statements, "It was impossible for the Law to justify, because it was made weak by the flesh" [Romans :3]. Likewise, "From the works of the Law no flesh will be justified" [Galatians 2:16].

I will also add a passage from Ephesians. "You have been saved gratis through faith, and this not from yourselves; it is the gift of God, not of works, lest anyone should boast" [Ephesians 2:8–9]. He presses the same understanding with many words, so that trust may not rely on our worthiness, but on mercy.

Romans 5, "Having been justified by faith, we have peace." Here he attributes two things to faith: that we are justified by faith, and that faith puts consciences at peace. Therefore, Paul does not understand faith to be idle knowledge, but something that struggles against terrors in the struggle of the conscience. The same thing is taught in this passage: "With the heart one believes for righteousness" [Romans 10:10]. For this trust in mercy is effective in the heart. It acknowledges that God is favorably disposed, and thus it comforts the heart and justifies. This, then, is our understanding of justification: Although our repentance or contrition is necessary, nonetheless we obtain justification, that is, the forgiveness of sins and reconciliation, not on account of the worthiness of our repentance, but by faith, for Christ's sake, gratis.

That these things may be even clearer, I shall further add that, when hearts are encouraged in this way by faith, they receive the Holy Spirit, as Paul teaches in Galatians 3: "That we may receive the promise of the Spirit through faith." We are not, then, speaking about some idle knowledge. The unlearned err when they imagine that the forgiveness of sins happens thus in idle moments, without a true impulse of the mind, without a struggle, without trust that comforts the mind. And since, as I shall explain later on, the Holy Spirit brings new life and new impulses along with that comfort, this renewal is called "regeneration," and new obedience should follow, as I shall explain shortly.

And here, lest pious minds be troubled by labyrinthine discussions about predestination or about free will, I shall briefly advise that one should not bring in here a discussion of predestination. Rather, it should be maintained that the promise of grace is universal. Just as the preaching of repentance pertains to all, so God offers the promise to all, as the very words of Christ testify, "Come to Me, all!" [Matthew 11:28]. And Paul says, "The same Lord of all, rich toward all" [Romans 10:12]. Likewise, "God wants all men to be saved" [1 Timothy 2:4]. But I shall gather more testimonies in the proper place.

A person should not judge about the will of God differently than the Gospel judges. The command which instructs us to believe certainly pertains to all. So also the promise pertains to all. Therefore, let us not disagree with God's command, but let us believe, and let everyone individually include himself in the universal promise, and let them know that they truly obtain the benefit of Christ if they believe the promise. Concerning free will, we said above that it should begin with the Word; we should not disagree with the Word. We are doing something when we resist despair and when we encourage and console ourselves with the promise of Christ. When we do this, God is efficacious through the Word and aids us. For the certainty should be retained that we truly obtain the benefits of Christ when we believe. For since these things are done by faith, we should retain the Word of God, nor should explanations be sought apart from the Word of God. Indeed, as I said earlier, merit is removed in the forgiveness of sins, not because we do nothing, but because the forgiveness of sins is a gift, that it may be certain.

Now I ask the prudent read to consider carefully the things I have said, that the forgiveness of sins is given gratis for Christ's sake to those who repent, that it is offered to all, that the command is that all should believe, that we must retain the certainty that we truly obtain the benefits of Christ when we believe and console ourselves with the promise. If the reader truly considers these things, he will understand that they are by no means complex or perplexing or sophistical, but clear and explicit and useful for piety and practical for the life and exercises of the godly. On the other hand, I do not wish to recite in this place the labyrinthine arguments and the many perplexing statements of those who disagree with us.

GOOD WORKS

Since I have explained reconciliation and faith, I should also add my understanding of the doctrine of good works and our obedience. I shall, therefore, speak plainly and clearly. Our obedience, that is, the righteousness of a good conscience, or of the works which God prescribes to us, should necessarily follow reconciliation. For Christ teaches about repentance in the Gospel, and Paul says, "We are debtors, that we may not live according to the flesh" [Romans 8:12]. And Christ says, "If you want to enter life, keep the commandments" [Matthew 19:17]. Indeed, we are justified for this purpose, that we may live a new and spiritual life, which is obedience toward God, according to that saying, "I will put My Law into their hearts" [Jeremiah 31:33]. And in Ephesians it says, "We are His work, created for good works" [Ephesians 2:10]. The acceptance to eternal life, or the gift of eternal life, is linked to justification, that is, to the forgiveness of sins and reconciliation, which happens by faith, according to that saying, "Those whom He justifies, the same He also glorifies" [Romans 8:30]. Therefore, eternal life is not given on account of the worthiness of our works, but gratis, for Christ's sake. And yet good works are necessary for eternal life in that they should necessarily follow reconciliation. Therefore, Paul says, "Woe to me, if I do not teach the Gospel" [1 Corinthians 9:16]. Likewise, "Those who do such things will not inherit the kingdom of God" [Galatians 5:21].

Not only external, civil works are required, but also spiritual impulses: the fear of God, trust, invocation, love, and similar attitudes. Those who do not understand the doctrine of faith cannot teach anything at all about these primary forms of divine worship, for they insist that we must doubt. Therefore they cast aside the exercises of faith and invocation, according to that saying, "How will they call upon Him if they do not believe?" [Romans 10:14]. For that doubt, as I said above, produces either despair or contempt. Now, those who despair or have contempt for God do not call upon God. Therefore, such people are hypocrites. Although they boast that they are teachers of good works, nevertheless they neither understand nor teach the primary works of the saints and the primary forms of divine worship. For it is not sufficient to teach external, civil works; faith itself, which gives glory to Christ, is the primary form of divine worship. In addition, invocation should be made in connection with the belief that God is willing to forgive us and to hear us. Indeed, this faith should guide all our actions.

But it is not sufficient to teach that our obedience is necessary. One must also explain how it is pleasing God, since it is true that no one satisfies the Law. We have many adversaries in this whole topic. For the godly ask, "How is our obedience pleasing to God, since no one satisfies the Law? How shall we be saved, since we perceive that sin still dwells in us?" These questions must be answered. It must be shown how this incipient and imperfect obedience is pleasing to God, lest they fall into despair or confide in their own cleanness, shifting the glory of Christ to their own works.

One can read many things about this topic throughout Augustine's writings. And Jerome has a long discussion of it *In Attico*. This, however, is the first thing Christians should be taught: that this obedience in those who are justified is imperfect; it does not satisfy the Law, as far as the obedience itself is concerned. Paul testifies clearly to this when he says, "I see another Law in my members, opposing the Law of my mind" [Romans 7:23]. Also, "The flesh lusts against the Spirit" [Galatians 5:17]. Likewise in 1 John 1, "If we say that we have no sin, we deceive ourselves, etc." And Psalm 143, "Do not enter into judgment with Your servant, for no one living will be justified in Your sight." And Psalm 130, "If You, Lord, should mark iniquities, who will stand?" For covetousness remains in the saints, as we all know, and is, by its very nature, sin and worthy of death. Nor is it idle, but it constantly produces wicked emotions. Indeed, the saints confess these sins and pray, "Forgive us our debts." How often do the saints doubt that God cares for them? How many times does their faith waver? Who fears God as much as he ought? Who loves God ardently enough? Who endures hardship with sufficient patience? Meanwhile, who is not inflamed with hatred and other passions? Who satisfies his own vocation? How many saints murmur when they see the wicked and tyrants flourishing and enjoying all the luxuries of life, possessing kingdoms, wealth, and glory, while they themselves are assailed with calamities of every kind? These vices should not be minimized; they are by their nature truly sins. But they are forgiven to believers. Therefore, those people are mad who imagine that the saints satisfy the Law and are without sin. Indeed, what is even more monstrous, they imagine that external works not commanded by God are more perfect than the works of the Decalogue!

Therefore, in order that we may respond to pious questioners, I shall briefly explain how an incipient and imperfect obedience is pleasing to God. This obedience is indeed necessary, and it is pleasing to God, but only in those who have been reconciled. It is righteousness, not because it satisfies the Law, but because the persons are already pleasing. This is what the godly will conclude in order that a sure comfort may be maintained: The person is reconciled and accepted to eternal life for Christ's sake, only through mercy. Afterwards, that incipient obedience is also pleasing to God, because the person is pleasing on account of something else, namely, for Christ's sake. For that incipient obedience cannot be set against God's judgment, but Christ the Mediator must be held fast, for whose sake the Father is favorably disposed toward us. This is what Paul teaches when he says, "There is now no condemnation for those who walk in Christ" [Romans 8:1]. He does not say that they are without sin, but that they are not condemned, because they have already been made God's children for Christ's sake. Likewise, "You are not under Law, but under grace" [Romans 6:14]. That is, although you do not satisfy the Law, it still does not accuse you, because you are now sons. And in Galatians, "Christ redeemed us from the curse of the Law" [Galatians 3:13]. In other words, the Law does not accuse us now that we have been reconciled by faith; we have a propitious God.

Now just think how splendid is the benefit, how immense is His mercy, how great is His love toward us, that God still approves of these small deeds and of this obedience that is tainted in so many ways. Indeed, He even extols it with the most distinguished praises and rewards, as I shall explain shortly. To this pertains the saying of Paul, "We establish the Law through faith" [Romans 3:31], as if to say, since no one satisfies the Law, those who are not reconciled by faith, even though they perform certain works of the Law, cannot please God, for they are always accused by the Law and remain in doubt and despair. No, then only is the obedience pleasing, although it is imperfect: after we have first been reconciled by faith. Faith, then, does not destroy the Law; rather, it causes the Law to be pleasing.

Furthermore, love and true obedience of the heart cannot even be furnished unless the heart first receives comfort and believes that its sins are forgiven. It is necessary, therefore, for the reconciliation of the person to occur first, and this reconciliation takes place, as I have said, by faith, which does not rely on our own worthiness, but only on mercy. But after this, the subsequent obedience is also pleasing because we are in Christ.

It will go a long way toward clarity if you distinguish the person from the work. Although David has good works, he also has the remnants of sin, and therefore he cannot be convinced that he is pleasing to God on account of those good works. He must first be convinced that his person is pleasing through mercy. Only then are his good works pleasing. Paul says the same thing. "I am not aware of anything against myself, but in this I am not justified" [1 Corinthians 4:4], as if to say, although I have the righteousness of a good conscience, I still do not set this against the judgment of God; instead, I set Christ the Mediator against it. So when David says, "No one living will be justified before you" [Psalm 143:2], he teaches that justification is to be sought through mercy, not on account of our worthiness. So then, when we reassure ourselves by faith and are convinced that our person is pleasing to God through mercy and that the infirmity of our nature is forgiven us, then the incipient obedience is also pleasing. For such faith cannot rely on our worthiness. Thus both should be held fast at the same time: Christ the Mediator and the recognition of our unworthiness.

From all these things it is clear that our obedience, or the righteousness of a good conscience, is necessary and pleasing to God, not because it is perfect, but because the persons have already been reconciled by faith and have the forgiveness of their infirmity. What is more, after we both acknowledge our infirmity in this way and apprehend reconciliation by faith, then the worthiness of works is not to be diminished. For Scripture also ascribes the greatest honor and praise to this righteousness of works in the saints.

First, the necessity must be considered. For faith must grow in us by means of regular exercises—in invocation, repentance, and perils. Thus the spiritual renewal grows, of which Paul says, "Desiring to be clothed, we will thus not be found naked" [2 Corinthians 5:3]. And although the person has the forgiveness of sins through mercy for Christ's sake and is righteous, that is, acceptable, as I have said, nevertheless this righteousness of works should also necessarily follow. For it is God's mandate that we furnish this obedience, because Christ clearly commands, "Repent!" [Mark 1:15]. And if anyone here argues that these things are done without further mandate in those who have been renewed, then let him at least find some amusement at my expense by means of the precise arguments I am making. I cannot see why I ought to shrink back from this word "commandment," since Christ also says, "It is My command" [John 15:12]. And Paul says, "We are debtors" [Romans 8:12]. Besides this, the necessity is so great that Paul clearly says about adulterers, fornicators, murderers, etc., "Those who do such things will not inherit the kingdom of God" [Galatians 5:21]. Finally, faith is not able to exist together with a bad conscience, for faith is the confidence that God is favorably disposed toward us. A bad conscience judges the opposite. Likewise, those who do not repent, but indulge in wicked desires, do not retain faith. For faith seeks the forgiveness of sins; it does not delight in sins. Nor does the Holy Spirit remain in those who give in to wicked motives, according to that saying of John, "He who does sin is of the devil" [1 John 3:8]. These many cases of necessity concur and should rightly sharpen in us our diligence for doing good works, in order that we may retain the benefit of God. As Peter teaches, "Take care to make your calling and election sure," that is, to persevere in your calling and sanctification.

In the second place, not only should necessity be considered, but the worthiness of good works should also invite us. For although in this great infirmity of ours we surely should not think too highly of ourselves, nevertheless our vocation should be magnified. Although our virtues and good deeds are by no means sufficiently motivated or clean, they still pertain to the glory of Christ, and great, therefore, is their worthiness. And that we may know that they are truly pleasing to God, He extols them with honorable titles. They are called "sacrifices," that is, the proper and true honors with which God is delighted. Peter says that we are a "holy priesthood, destined to offer spiritual sacrifices, which are also pleasing to God through Jesus Christ" [1 Peter 2:5]. How pleasing it must be, how much encouragement toward virtue should fill the godly father of the family to know that God thinks so highly of his diligence in feeding, raising and teaching his offspring that He even counts it a true and spiritual sacrifice! How much comfort there is for those who undergo perils or are tortured for the sake of the Gospel, to understand that these works are true and laudable sacrifices! The godly young man will learn with greater zeal if he thinks that this labor is a most pleasing sacrifice to God. Let everyone think of his vocation in this way. Christ says, "Let your light shine before men, that your Father who is in heaven may be glorified" [Matthew 5:16]. Here He not only encourages us to perform all our deeds in order that our examples may benefit others, but He also extols our duties by calling them "light" and by saying that through them the glory of God becomes brighter.

In addition, since the gifts of the Holy Spirit have been bestowed, it would be an ungrateful and wicked spirit who failed to acknowledge the Giver. In the book of Isaiah, the godly are called a "planting of the Lord for glorifying Him" [Isaiah 61:3]. This, too, is high praise for gifts and good works, that the Church is blessed by the Holy Spirit with various gifts for this purpose, that the glory of God may be spread and published more broadly. Why, good works are even Sacraments, that is, signs of God's will. "Forgive, and you will be forgiven" [Luke 6:37], says Christ. Here He does not mean that we are forgiven on account of our act of forgiving, for the conscience could never be at rest if we had to conclude that we are only forgiven when we have forgiven others purely enough. And yet Christ commands us to forgive and intends it to be a sign and Sacrament by which we are to be reminded of divine forgiveness. It is helpful to remember these and many other things about the worthiness of good works, that we may think highly, not of ourselves, but of the vocation itself, and that there may be kindled in us a zeal for acting rightly for the sake of God's glory, when we consider that we are members of Christ and that our moral behavior pertains to God's glory.

Thirdly, we must understand that rewards have also been set forth for good works. In other words, good works merit bodily and spiritual rewards. Although many rewards are given to the saints in this life, nevertheless, since the Church is also subjected to the cross, the principal rewards are given after this life. As Christ says, "Great is your reward in heaven" [Matthew 5:12]. Paul says, "Godliness has promises for the present life and for the one to come" [1 Timothy 4:8]. That is, God blesses us even in this life with many rewards according to His own counsel, caring for us and defending us. For although the Church is subjected to the cross, nevertheless, since it must also be preserved in the world, God aids the godly with many bodily benefits also in this life. Then the principal rewards are given after this life. The same understanding is reflected in these words, "Seek first the kingdom of God, and the rest will be added to you" [Matthew 6:33]. And in Mark 10, "He will receive a hundredfold now in this time, with persecutions, and in the coming age, eternal life." Paul prays for the Corinthians that God would give them an increase of spiritual gifts for the alms they had gathered. And Augustine rightly says, "Love deserves to be enlarged by love." There are many clear testimonies in the Scriptures. Here, however, it must be understood that we are speaking about the good works of the righteous. For first the forgiveness of sins, reconciliation, and the acceptance to eternal life must be accepted by faith. And these are given through mercy, for Christ's sake, that they may remain certain.

But when the Scriptures say in several places, "He will render to each one according to his works," it is a phrase that has been taken up from the Law, and it clearly means nothing else than that He will render the things He promised to the righteous, and He will render punishment to the unrighteous. For God approves the works of no one but the righteous. First, then, the person is justified before God, through mercy alone, which the person accepts by faith. This is the simplest and mildest interpretation of this phrase. For if anyone presses the phrase "according to his works" and contends that eternal life is given on account of the worthiness of our works, then absurdity follows. For since no one satisfies the Law, it follows that all will perish. Therefore, the appropriate interpretation must be added. As it has already been said repeatedly, the reward should be attributed to works in such a way that the forgiveness of sins is not made uncertain, or the benefit of Christ transferred to the worthiness of our works. The person is justified before God gratis, by faith which relies only on mercy. After that, the good works are pleasing to God and earn their reward.

THE PROMISES OF THE LAW

Above I noted that there are two kinds of promises. There is one that promises reconciliation gratis. This is the proper promise of the Gospel. There are others that promise rewards for good works, such as, "Give and it will be given to you" [Luke 6:38]. The latter I call "legal promises," wherever they are found in the Scriptures, because, although the Law of Moses, and the promise of the Palestinian land and the Jewish civil society do not pertain at all to us, nevertheless, just as the moral Law applies to all people, so the general promises added to the moral Law apply to all. For example, "Honor your father and your mother, that you may live long in the land" [Exodus 20:12]. Therefore, I call them legal promises, since they were added to the moral Law and apply to all people.

But since no one satisfies the Law, the legal promises would be useless unless we already knew from the Gospel that the reconciled are pronounced righteous, just as if they had satisfied the Law. Thus good works are judged to be a fulfilling of the Law, and they earn rewards when they are done by those who have already obtained the forgiveness of sins and reconciliation by faith.

One might easily conclude that we are rather cold toward doing good because we imagine that our works and exercises are unworthy of rewards, or that perils and labors are surely undertaken in vain. Such is the perversity of the human mind; it believes neither the Gospel nor the legal promises. If we were absolutely convinced that God would give us peace and other good things when we pray, for the sake of our good deeds, then we would be more zealous for doing what is right. Therefore, let us diligently impress on ourselves and on the Church that our labors are not undertaken in vain, but that we will obtain great rewards by our good deeds. In this way, God commands faith to be exercised, and He has added promises to works for this reason, that we may exercise faith on such occasions, that we think to give alms because this service pleases God. And that although we seem to store up less for ourselves, God will preserve our resources, giving us peace and other public goods. If we did not have such things, even our private resources would utterly perish.

These are the things I have said ought to be kept in mind with regard to legal promises: We should know that they are not useless, even though we do not satisfy the Law, but that obedience in those who have been reconciled is a sort of fulfillment of the Law. We should also remember that faith is to be awakened, exercised, and confirmed in these works.

I have set forth the reasons which ought to stir us up to doing good: the necessity, the worthiness of good works, the rewards, the exercise of faith. To these reasons that primary reason must be joined, that, although obedience is imperfect, nevertheless it is pleasing in those who have been reconciled. In addition, we are aided and protected by the Holy Spirit, lest the devil lead us astray into pernicious errors or disgrace. This is what is meant by what is written, "I will not leave you as orphans" [John 14:18]. No human speech can utter just how great this benefit is, how widely it extends, how pleasant it should be to us. Over the last several years, we have seen the Anabaptists practically driven mad, as by some spell, maintaining openly godless, absurd, and seditious opinions so tenaciously that not only will they not permit themselves to be rescued from such opinions, but they also most arrogantly despise those who warn them. Thus they have brought terrible ruin upon themselves in many areas. Here let us consider how great is the benefit of God, that we are kept safe, lest, deceived by the devil, we should embrace these or similar errors. For human wisdom, without the Holy Spirit, cannot sufficiently guard against the awful traps set by the devil. Therefore, may these reasons also stir us up to do good: the Law can now be kept, to some degree; the incipient obedience is pleasing; and God promises to grant us His aid.

On the other hand, let us consider how harmful evil works are. First, they earn God's wrath and eternal condemnation. Furthermore, they are a disgrace to the Gospel and glory of God, as the prophet says, "Because of you the name of God is blasphemed among the Gentiles" [Romans 2:24]. Thus God is offended in many ways. Thirdly, evil works result in punishments here and now, such as the tyranny of the devil, who holds the ungodly in his power and drives them into errors and shameful behavior of every kind. For example, after Saul broke out in hatred for David, he became so enraged that he even butchered the priests with the utmost cruelty, although they were innocent men. Bodily punishments also follow—wars and other calamities. Fourthly, all spiritual exercises are impeded; faith is extinguished in those who indulge their passions. Finally and most horrendous of all, sins merit a hardening and are punished with sins, as Paul indicates in Romans 1. These reasons should be carefully weighed, that we may drive carnal security from our minds and learn to fear God's wrath, and also stir ourselves up to do good works.

It should also be added briefly which works are required of Christians and what the true forms of divine worship are; namely, the works which God commands us to do, as Paul teaches when he says, "The summary of the Law is love from a pure heart, a good conscience, and faith that is not feigned" [1 Timothy 1:5]. Moreover, they can aptly be included in the Decalogue.

To the First Commandment belong repentance (or fear) and faith (or trust in the mercy promised for Christ's sake). This faith should not be considered a frivolous or cold work; it is a momentous impulse by which, in true contrition (that is, in genuine terrors), hearts are encouraged as they overcome the terrors of sin and receive comfort and a new, spiritual life. In addition, this trust must continually be exercised in invocation, in all perils and troubles. We must ask God to have mercy on us and to sanctify, rule, guide, and aid us. Thus the exercises of this faith extend broadly throughout one's whole life. This trust, in turn, produces Love for God, for since we have acknowledged the magnitude of God's mercy, we now also begin to love Him and to be convinced that God cares for us and hears us, etc. Also belonging to the First Commandment is obedience in afflictions, that is, patience, of which we will speak in its place.

To the Second Commandment belong invocation, thanksgiving, confession of the doctrine, and the preaching of God's Word, if one's vocation demands it.

To the Third, the preservation of the public ceremonies, which are divinely ordained, as well as reverence toward the ministry.

To the Fourth, the duties of civil life, obedience, diligence in attending to one's vocation.

To the Fifth, love for one's neighbor, justice, and kindness toward our neighbors.

To the Sixth, chastity, faithfulness to one's spouse, temperance and sobriety.

To the Seventh, justice in contracts and the use of one's resources, generosity in works of charity.

To the Eighth, truthfulness in one's entire life, hating deceitfulness and lies.

But we explained the Decalogue more amply above. If that is rightly understood, it can easily be judged which works God demands.

I have spoken very simply and without sophistry about justification, faith, and the fulfilling of the Law; that is, good works. Nor do I see how anything can possibly offend good men in the interpretation I have expressed, since there is nothing absurd, nothing perplexing about it; since it is not new but has clearly been handed down in the Holy Scriptures and is in agreement with the ecclesiastical writers; and finally, since it is useful for piety and outlines a form of piety that is highly beneficial. It shows the true exercises of faith. It teaches us about our infirmity. It highlights the benefit of Christ. It teaches plainly and simply about the forgiveness of sins, and it sets forth a solid comfort for consciences. It shows what the true forms of divine worship are and how the incipient obedience is pleasing to God. Finally, it shows the reason why some people shrink back so fiercely from this interpretation, in which we say this in summary: Repentance is necessary, and yet the forgiveness of sins, that it may be certain, takes place, not on account of the worthiness of our works, but by trust in Christ. We do not remove good works; we simply transfer the cause of the forgiveness of sins to Christ. And I do not mix in here anything absurd concerning free will or predestination. I am demonstrating that the doctrine of faith is presented for this reason, not to disturb consciences, but in order to set forth a genuine, godly, and firm comfort, and also that we may retain throughout this whole life the godly and spiritual exercises of faith. Can anyone find anything disagreeable in such things?

The Scholastic teachers say nothing at all about this faith or trust by which we obtain the forgiveness of sins. Indeed, they even insist that we doubt. But they diminish too much the uncleanness and corruption of human nature. Therefore, they imagine that men are able to be without sin and that they are righteous by their own fulfilling of the Law. This darkness surely obscures the doctrine of faith, for it leaves people unable to comprehend how desperately mercy is needed, since they diminish too much the uncleanness of nature and since confidence in one's own purity is encouraged. I know that such Platonic or Stoic notions are highly praised, that in man is to be summed up the perfection of all virtues, and who-knows-what other equanimity (*apatheia*) and things of this kind. When these things are explained in such a way that the pure doctrine of faith is buried, or when nothing at all is said about faith, they have no place in life.

Rebuttal

It is not difficult to reconcile the different sayings that are cited against the interpretation which I have given of faith. I despise not only slanderous and cunning interpretations in the causes of religion, but also arguments that are unnecessarily precise. Indeed, it is sufficiently clear that I am doing this with great zeal in order that, as far as I am able, I may extricate the majority of the controversies from those involved disputations and from sophistry. Therefore, I shall respond simply to all the sayings which are cited about the Law or the righteousness of good works.

I admit that our obedience, that is, the righteousness of good works, is necessary. But it is not pleasing to God except in those who are reconciled, that is, in those who are righteous. For no one satisfies the Law. Therefore we must first obtain the forgiveness of sins by faith and become children of God. Such faith relies, not on our worthiness, but only on the mercy promised for Christ's sake. Afterwards, our obedience is also pleasing.

This is the simple and plain response, taken up from the very sources of the matter. It has not been cunningly invented. For it is understood that everyone needs the forgiveness of sins. Then, since no one satisfies the Law, a certain equitable leniency (*epieikeia*) must surely be added to the sayings about the Law. Therefore, Paul says, "Christ is the end of the

Law" [Romans 10:4]. That is, the Law is of no benefit without Christ, wherefore the Gospel concerning trust in Christ must be added to the Law. Nor should those be tolerated who imagine that a man is righteous by his own fulfilling of the Law, while they say nothing at all about trust in mercy. Therefore, I will briefly touch on several passages.

"'If you want to enter life, keep the commandments, etc.' [Matthew 19:17]. Therefore, eternal life is given on account of the Law, or on account of observing the commandments." I respond: Since no one satisfies the Law and no one is without sin, all would perish if they could not be saved without fulfilling the Law. This absurdity follows logically from this saying, if a person tries to retain its strict meaning, without any interpretation. It is necessary, therefore, to add an interpretation: Obedience toward the Law is necessary, but the Gospel about Christ must be added to the Law. First we must become children of God through mercy, for Christ's sake. Then our obedience ought to follow. And since our obedience is imperfect, the person is pronounced righteous, that is, acceptable, on account of something else, namely, on account of Christ. For if we had to conclude that we are pleasing to God on account of this fulfilling of the Law, then the conscience would be rendered uncertain. Therefore, something else must be set forth first, on account of which we are convinced that God is favorably disposed toward us. And since the person is now pleasing on account of Christ, this incipient obedience is also pleasing.

James says, "You see, therefore, that a man is justified on the basis of works and not on the basis of faith alone" [James 2:24]. Indeed, James seems to have expressly made this statement for the purpose of correcting Paul's sayings, in order to emend the exclusive little word of which we spoke above. Now, for my part, I am not looking for a fight; I am accustomed to dealing with adversaries who are not entirely hostile. Therefore, I gladly express my agreement with James, as long as neither absurd opinions nor foreign concepts are affixed to him.

There is no need to search long and hard for the correct interpretation. Let us look at the words themselves. If James understands faith as a knowledge of history—as he says, "The demons believe" [James 2:19]—then there is no controversy. Indeed, that whole sermon of James is speaking of the righteousness of works, not of the forgiveness of sins, not of that struggle of conscience of which David says, "No one living will be justified in Your sight" [Psalm 143:2]. For Paul understands faith as trust in mercy, by which the forgiveness of sins is to be received and by which the conscience is to be freed from the terrors of sin. This confidence cannot be ascribed to the devil. If, then, James understands faith to be something different than Paul does, they do not disagree with one another. For just as James requires good works along with the knowledge of history or one's profession of it, so also Paul, among other good works, requires a knowledge of history or the profession of the articles of faith. Meanwhile, it is a separate discussion, how we obtain the forgiveness of sins, whether for the sake of the worthiness of our works or through mercy. This is the simple and genuine response. But I will add yet another for those who wish to be difficult.

Even if he were speaking about faith according to Paul's custom, I grant, nonetheless, that, as I have often said, both types of righteousness are necessary: the righteousness of faith and that of works. But this latter, namely, the righteousness of good works, is not the righteousness that can be set against the judgment of God, nor is it pleasing except in those who are reconciled. First, then, we obtain the forgiveness of sins and the person becomes righteous, that is, acceptable, through mercy, for Christ's sake, by faith, not for the sake of the worthiness of the subsequent obedience. But afterwards, the subsequent obedience is righteousness, that is, it pleases God. No inconsistency results if the saying is accepted in this way: We are justified by faith and works, that is, both types of righteousness are required. But if anyone pretends that the faith which is mentioned in Paul or in Genesis does no good toward the forgiveness of sins except for the sake of the worthiness of works, then one must consider what great inconsistency results. For the forgiveness of sins would become uncertain; consciences would have no solid comfort. A faith which relies on our own worthiness would be entirely overturned, since it is made uncertain. It is easy for the learned to judge from the phrase what the word "to be justified" means. For here in James it does not mean "to obtain the forgiveness of sins or reconciliation." It means that "we are justified," that is, "having faith and works, we have both of the righteousnesses that are required." However, Paul openly speaks of the forgiveness of sins and understands justification to be the forgiveness of sins and reconciliation, or that acceptance in which a person is acceptable before God. This, moreover, takes place through mercy.

I hope that this abundantly satisfies good men concerning the passage in James, especially since I am holding properly to the words themselves. Those who pretend that we obtain the forgiveness of sins for the sake of the worthiness of works, and that faith does no good except on account of the worthiness of works, are attaching foreign concepts to James. Indeed, they are corrupting the word "faith." For faith, that it may be certain, should only rely on mercy. What kind of torture would it be for the conscience if it must conclude that we only have the forgiveness of sins when we have works that are worthy of such a great benefit? This notion drives consciences to despair, buries the glory of Christ, and destroys faith. Therefore, it is not to be associated with James. But let us hold to the simple words, as I have said, without these absurd opinions.

I have sufficiently interpreted many other sayings elsewhere. "If I have faith, but have not love, I am nothing" [1 Corinthians 13:2]. Here Paul teaches that love, that is, our obedience, is necessary. I have also said the same thing many times. But Paul does not say that sins are forgiven on account of our love.

"Forgive, and you will be forgiven" [Luke 6:37] is a sermon on repentance. The first part teaches about repentance; the second offers the forgiveness of sins. The idea that the forgiveness of sins takes place on account of the worthiness of our forgiving should not be tacked onto this. For Christ does not say this as in the passage, "Cease to do evil," and it follows afterward, "Though your sins be as scarlet, etc., they shall be washed clean again" [Isaiah 1:16, 18]. Here and in similar passages it should not be immediately added that sins are forgiven on account of our contrition. But it should be understood that the promise must be accepted by faith. It is good, however, that the promise has been added to our work in these passages, not that it depends on the worthiness of our work, but that our work is a sign and a sort of sacrament which teaches us about the will of God, as Baptism, too, is a sign which teaches us that we are surely forgiven. When we forgive others, our work teaches us in such a way that we keep in view the attached promise and are convinced that our sins, too, are forgiven.

The same judgment should be made concerning similar passages which are sermons of repentance, such as, "Redeem your sins with righteousness and with benefits toward the poor, and there will be healing for your offenses" [Daniel 4:27]. The first part teaches about repentance. "Redeem your sins with righteousness and with benefits toward the poor," that is, "Come to your senses! Become righteous! Acknowledge God! Believe! Then administer your kingdom in such a way that you use your power for the salvation of men, not for their harm." The king is admonished, not only about alms, but about acknowledging God, about faith, and then about his vocation, that is, about exercising righteousness and kindness in his rule. These two virtues should especially be cultivated by the highest kings. "You shall redeem sins," that is, you shall see to it that the accusation is removed, then the guilt, then the punishment, since forgiveness is promised to the converted, not on account of the worthiness of repentance, but through mercy, if they grasp it by faith. And yet repentance is necessary. The second part is the promise, "There will be healing, etc.," which surely ought to be accepted by faith. And that it may be certain, it should not depend on the condition of our worthiness.

The passage in Tobit ("Alms deliver a person from death" [Tobit 4:10]) and similar passages mean that alms merit enormous benefits, that we may be defended by God in great peril. Such sayings are celebrations of good works, which should certainly be praised, but not in such a way that the benefit of Christ is obscured. We obtain the forgiveness of guilt by trusting in Christ.

Furthermore, it should be understood that good works do merit the forgiveness or mitigation of temporal punishments, as will be discussed in its place. This benefit should not be considered lightly, that the most difficult storms of life are governed, that troubles, wars, famine, the plundering of the civil estate, and other evils are all mitigated. Good works surely merit the mitigation of such things. The passages of Scripture often address this benefit. As Isaiah says in chapter 58, "Break bread for the hungry, and the Lord will always give you peace." This passage can also be applied: "Love covers a multitude of sins" [1 Peter 4:8], that is, it merits a mitigation of punishments.

An objection is also made concerning reward. "Eternal life is called a reward. Therefore, it is owed for works and is not given gratis." Similarly, "Works are worthy of eternal life as a reward that is owed." Before I respond to this argument, I must first admonish the reader to consult his own conscience in this argument. For never will any experienced conscience affirm that his own good deeds are worthy of eternal life or that eternal life is owed to him on account of the worthiness of his works. Therefore, those who raise this objection act unwisely, since the judgment of all men's consciences cries out against their argument. David attests that the conscience cries out in protest when he says, "Do not enter into judgment with Your servant, for no one living will be justified in Your sight" [Psalm 143:2]. And Christ says, "When you have done everything, say, 'We are unprofitable servants'" [Luke 17:10]. Therefore, if anyone insists that the conscience, which is anxious concerning the hope of eternal life, should take into account its own good deeds, and its own cleanness, and the worthiness of its own merit, and that it should hope for eternal life on this account, he is by no means setting forth a firm comfort for the spirit that wrestles with despair. Here the mind must surely be taught to know with certainty that both justification and simultaneously the gift of eternal life take place by trusting in mercy. Therefore Paul says, "Eternal life is the gift of God" [Romans 6:23]. Indeed, Hezekiah confesses his sins, "You have cast all my sins behind Your back" [Isaiah 38:17]. And David says, "Blessed is the man to whom the Lord will not impute sin" [Psalm 32:2]. Surely sin can be imputed to all men. Therefore, mercy must be sought, and one must be convinced that God justifies or accepts us in such a way that He remits sins. This very justification always brings with it both new life and obedience. Paul says that the victory over death happens by trusting in Christ, not on account of our worthiness, when he says, "The sting of death is sin, and the power of sin is the Law. But thanks be to God, who has given us the victory through our Lord Jesus Christ" [1 Corinthians 15:56–57]. Surely the Law would always accuse us, etc., if we were to measure our worthiness. And in John 6, "This is the will of My Father who sent Me, that everyone who sees the Son and believes in Him should have eternal life." John 3, "He who believes in the Son has eternal life." These comforts must be set forth to the spirit that is battling despair, and eternal life must be expected for Christ's sake, not for the sake of our own worthiness.

Why, then, is it called a reward? Not even here shall I reply artfully. Even though eternal life is called a reward or is said to be owed to the righteous, this should not be understood as if it were owed on account of the worthiness of our works, but on account of the promise which, of course, is made not on account of the Law or the worthiness of our works, but for Christ's sake, to those who lay hold of mercy by faith. Therefore, when eternal life is called a reward, it is a figure of speech taken up from the Law. For the Law is accustomed to speaking about righteousness as if it were speaking about our worthiness, and it promises a reward for it. It also speaks of faith as if it were a work or merit. And yet it must be understood from the Gospel that justification and the gift of eternal life are granted through mercy, by faith, for Christ's sake, not for the sake of the worthiness of our works. Then, when Scripture promises a reward for works, it must be understood that, although eternal life is granted for a different reason, nevertheless, since it also compensates afflictions and good deeds, for this reason it is rightly called a reward.

For surely our works are not the price of so great a gift. And yet the gift itself is a kind of compensation, just as the inheritance falls to the son of a family for another reason, and yet it compensates his duties. It is not fitting to interpret the word "reward" so stringently that it transfers the benefit of Christ to our works; so that consciences are driven to despair, judging that they do not have enough works; or so that hypocrites place a hollow trust in their merits, imagining that they have worthy works, that they are without sin, that they have satisfied the Law—indeed, that they have even done more than enough, so that they can sell their superfluous merits to others. Once these inept opinions have been repudiated, it is easy to see where the word "reward" fits in. For as we have said, works deserve their rewards.

> We are righteous by faith;
> Faith is a work;
> Therefore, we are righteous by works.

I respond to the major premise: We are righteous by faith, not because it is a work or quality in us, but because it accepts mercy. And that the matter may be made even clearer, let the sentence be changed into the correlative statement. We are righteous by faith, that is, we are pronounced righteous through mercy; this must be accepted by faith. The minor premise is true; faith is a work. But just as other works or other virtues are imperfect, like love, patience, or chastity, so faith is imperfect. Therefore, we are not righteous because of the worthiness of faith, but because it accepts mercy. For faith is the instrument by which the mercy promised for Christ's sake is grasped. By this mercy, as Paul says, we have been perfected.

> Righteousness is obedience toward the whole Law;
> Good works are obedience toward the Law;
> Therefore, good works are righteousness.

First the minor premise must be negated, for good works are not perfect obedience toward the Law, since, as Paul says, the carnal nature is unable to obey the Law of God perfectly. However, they would be righteousness and they would justify if we obeyed the Law perfectly. Then I reply to the major premise: The righteousness of the Law is obedience toward the whole Law, but since we do not furnish this, the Gospel brings gratuitous justification. It signifies, then, the imputation of righteousness by which we are acceptable through mercy, not on account of the worthiness of our virtues. This is how righteousness should be understood in Paul and, often, in others. Indeed, it should be carefully noted where Scripture is speaking about the righteousness of the Law and where it is speaking about this imputation. The term from the fifth book of *Ethics* fits well with the righteousness of the Law where universal righteousness signifies obedience toward all laws. In addition, good works or virtues in those who have been reconciled are considered to be a certain fulfillment of the Law, as has been said. The term "righteousness" from the fifth book of *Ethics* agrees with these.

> Righteousness is in the will;
> Faith is not in the will;
> Therefore, faith does not justify.

I reply: The major premise is true concerning the righteousness of the Law, which signifies our obedience, our virtues, and qualities in the will. But when we speak of the righteousness of faith, righteousness signifies the imputation of righteousness or the acceptance by which God accepts us through mercy, not on account of our qualities or worthiness. But there is need of faith which grasps the acceptance which is set forth in the promise. And this faith is not merely knowledge, but also to want and to accept the promised mercy, just as trust is in other respects an impulse or a condition of the will by which we accept or expect the help that is offered. I have demonstrated above that faith signifies this kind of trust.

> Works against the Law are sins;
> Therefore, good works are righteousness.
> The consequence is evident from the nature of contrary things;
> Therefore, good works justify.

I reply: The consequence would be valid, if we satisfied the Law, for then good works would be righteousness and would justify. But since men do not satisfy the Law, nor are they without sin, it is necessary to seek something else, namely, mercy, by which we are to be pronounced righteous.

> The forgiveness of sins depends on the condition of repentance;
> Therefore, the forgiveness of sins is conditional.

I approve the antecedent, since actual sin cannot possibly be forgiven unless a change of action occurs.

> Therefore, the change of action is at least a partial cause of justification and is partially meritorious.

I reply: The consequence must be denied, for since we are speaking of a condition, we understand the condition of our worthiness. Furthermore, we grant that the promise contains the condition of repentance, and that a change of actual sin is necessary. But we subtract worthiness from this change, in order that certainty may remain. For even though we lay aside the external work, the attitude still remains in the mind.

Therefore, since wicked actions never entirely cease, the promise would become uncertain if it depended on the worthiness of that change. Furthermore, sins are forgiven even if covetousness and wicked attitudes still inhere and remain in men. Therefore, the need for gratuitous forgiveness can easily be grasped.

Secondly, that abandonment of sin is full of despair, fear, and death. Therefore, it is neither righteousness nor payment. Paul also removes justification from the Law, since the Law works wrath. Therefore, it is clear that justification cannot be attributed to contrition, since contrition itself would become eternal death if we weren't free from those terrors after having been encouraged by faith. Now, if the forgiveness of sins depended on the worthiness of contrition, the conscience would be pushed further and further into death, since it sees that no pain, no matter how great, is a price worthy of the forgiveness of sins.

These things must be diligently considered, so that we understand that contrition is required, and yet the worthiness must be transferred to something else. We must likewise consider the nature of Law and of works. For if the chief work of the Law (namely, to condemn sin and to be angry at sin) does not justify but brings death, it is a great testimony that men are neither justified nor vivified by the Law, but that there is need of the comfort which faith brings. And yet, where there is faith, that contrition and mortification become a sacrifice and are pleasing to God. Therefore, throughout one's entire life repentance should increase and faith should be exercised, as it reassures terrified minds and drives us to call upon God in every danger and trouble.

For invocation cannot exist if we think that we are rejected, that we are not heard, etc., as Paul says, "How will they call upon Him, if they do not believe?" [Romans 10:14]. This doctrine of faith, then, nourishes the true forms of divine worship and the chief works. Those who despise this doctrine, even though they boast that they are teachers of good works, nevertheless fail to understand these proper works of Christians.

They turn the eyes and minds of men away from the sight of them to external works alone, which, although necessary, are far inferior to the invocation of God. Let us exercise faith, then, in invocation, in all the dangers and troubles of life. Let us ask God to sanctify, guide, and preserve us. There we will learn by experience that we need this comfort, that God is surely favorably disposed toward us through mercy, that He hears us, although we are unworthy. As David says in the Psalm, "If You, O Lord, should mark iniquities, who will stand? For with You there is propitiation, wherefore You will be feared. My soul has waited upon His Word; my soul has hoped in the Lord" [Psalm 130:3–5]. That is, I acknowledge that I am unclean, and yet I take courage and I trust that You are propitious toward me on account of the promised propitiation. Let us also take courage by this faith and remember that this prayer pertains to those who repent, not to those who indulge securely in their corrupt desires. Let us chant this very Psalm to God daily. Let pious minds comfort themselves with such music and take courage, that they may learn to render true acts of worship to God.

In this way, too, those sayings in the Psalms about mercy and those which command us to rejoice, to trust, and to hope will finally be understood and become truly sweet when we keep in view this doctrine of Paul. For all those sayings are discarded by the minds of men if they think that mercy is only promised to the worthy and to those who have earned it, for we are unworthy of such a great benefit. Therefore, let us learn from Paul that the forgiveness of sins is promised gratis, and thus let us understand that the Psalms preach about gratuitous mercy. Indeed, these sentences which command us to rejoice, to trust, and to hope, are preached to the very people who feel that they are unworthy. They command them to rejoice in order to banish despair and to teach that gratuitous mercy has been promised.

These things must be considered when we encounter those sayings in the Psalms. "Let the nations rejoice and be glad, for You judge the peoples rightly and You direct the nations on the earth" [Psalm 67:4]. That is, since You truly reign, You have given the Gospel; You care for us; You forgive sins to believers; You hear those who call upon You, although they are weak and unworthy. On the other hand, those who do not believe, You punish and destroy. And Psalm 41, "Why are you troubled, O my soul? Hope in God, for I will yet confess to Him." He indicates that he is terrified because he feels that he is unworthy. And yet he reassures his spirit, being convinced that God is favorably disposed toward him.

When these sayings are understood in this way, they bring tremendous comfort to those who repent. For these alone are able to judge where this doctrine of faith is to be used and how much power it has; namely, in the struggle of the conscience as it deals with God in calling upon Him. But I will gather no further examples, for they are obvious to the godly in their daily prayers, in which faith must surely be continually stirred up and confirmed in all the perils of life, for God requires this act of worship above all. But those who bury this doctrine of faith or try to erase it have no understanding of such worship whatsoever. Men who are partly inept, partly evil, cry out that we are dissenting from the Church. They kindle the wrath of princes against us. But I hope that godly readers will point out that I am both maintaining and elucidating the genuine understanding of the Church, and that it is rather our adversaries who dissent from the ancient and purer Church; that those who, when they teach about the forgiveness of sins, make no mention at all of faith, that is, trust in Christ, are the ones abandoning the flock. Indeed, they insist that we must doubt concerning the forgiveness of sins. Then they add that forgiveness is granted on account of the worthiness of our works, and yet one is always to doubt whether it has been granted. And they imagine that men are able to satisfy the Law and to be without sin. But let the judgment be left to the Church, that is, to the godly and learned. I, for my part, have attempted to demonstrate "the holy and righteous judgment."

THE DIFFERENCE BETWEEN MORTAL AND VENIAL SIN

Mortal sin, that is, sin worthy of eternal death, should generally be understood, not merely to be a certain deed, but also the disease that infects a person's nature. This disease is called the sin of origin: to be devoid of the fear of God; to doubt whether God cares about human affairs or takes care of us or hears us, etc.; not to trust that God is willing to forgive, willing to save; and also covetousness. Therefore, the ungodly, that is, those who do not grasp the forgiveness of sins by trust in Christ, have mortal sins and are condemned, even if they do not exhibit actions that are externally disgraceful. Many passages testify to this. John 3, "He who does not believe has been judged already, for he does not believe in the name of the only-begotten Son of God." Likewise, "He who believes in the Son has eternal life, but he who does not believe in the Son will not see life, but the wrath of God remains on him." But let us speak of the justified.

The division of sin into the categories of mortal and venial is ancient, but it is explained in various ways. We will summarize it as follows. First, in connection with that disease of nature; that is, covetousness or the vice of origin which remains in all people. This disease is mortal sin according to its own nature, but it is forgiven to those who grasp the forgiveness of sins by faith. "There is now no condemnation for those who walk in Christ Jesus" [Romans 8:1]. Secondly, this disease is not idle, but gives birth to desires and wicked impulses even in the saints. Paul admits that such impulses exist in the saints when he says, "The flesh lusts against the Spirit" [Galatians 5:17]. Likewise, "If by the Spirit you put to death the deeds of the flesh, you will live" [Romans 8:13]. But the disease itself should not be minimized in such a way that these impulses are considered to be trivial vices; they are also, by their nature, mortal sins. For these are not trivial sins—to doubt whether God cares for us or hears us, to rage against God in our afflictions, to distrust God, to trust in temporal things; likewise, to burn with illicit love, hatred, etc. Impulses of this kind, since they are forgiven to the saints, become venial sins, that is, sins that have been forgiven. For the saints do not approve of such impulses but fight against them. Faith still exists in such people. Therefore, they are still pronounced righteous. I will not introduce here the Stoic distinction concerning primary motives and assent. For there is so much weakness in human nature that the assent is suppressed before the motives are sufficiently understood. It is necessary to understand that the righteous should fight against those motives. Paul teaches all these things in that passage, "There is now no condemnation for those who walk in Christ Jesus" [Romans 8:1].

But there is another category of deeds which are of such a kind that those who commit them fall out of God's grace, cease to be accounted righteous, and are condemned, unless they repent. These deeds are called mortal sins. Although it is difficult to establish with great precision the degree of this category, and one must take care that the fearful not be driven to despair and that those who are secure not be further hardened, nevertheless, a certain degree of Law must surely be maintained. Indeed, Paul establishes this degree when he says, "Let love be from a pure heart and a good conscience and faith unfeigned" [1 Timothy 1:5]. For he requires a good conscience, and a conscience should certainly be ruled by the Word of God. Therefore, in this category of deeds, it is a mortal sin to approve or to do something against conscience, that is, not to fight against ungodly opinions, unbelief, and wicked impulses. Likewise, it is a mortal sin to commit externally shameful deeds contrary to God's commandments. For we are now speaking about the deeds by which, when a man commits them, he ceases to be pronounced righteous. We are not speaking now about the natural disease, nor about sins of ignorance, which I include as part of the natural disease. Paul speaks of these deeds when he says, "If you live according to the flesh, you will die" [Romans 8:13]. Likewise in 1 Corinthians 6, "Make no mistake. Neither fornicators nor idolaters nor adulterers nor the effeminate nor homosexual practitioners nor thieves nor cheaters nor drunkards nor revilers nor plunderers will inherit the kingdom of God." In Ephesians 5, "Know that no fornicator or impure or greedy man, who is an idolater, has an inheritance in the kingdom of Christ and of God. Let no one deceive you with vain words, for on account of these things the wrath of God comes upon the disobedient." Galatians 5, "The works of the flesh are manifest: adultery, fornication, uncleanness, sexual impurity, idolatry, sorcery, hatred, contentions, rivalries, discord, divisions, jealousy, murder, drunkenness, carousing, and similar things. I declare to you concerning these things that those who practice such things will not inherit the kingdom of God."

The apostle also preaches the Gospel and requires repentance. But it is contrary to repentance to act against the conscience. Nor can faith exist in the one who acts against conscience. For faith is the confidence that we are pleasing to God. This confidence must necessarily be discarded when the mind approves or does something which it knows to be displeasing to God. As Paul also says, "He who eats while doubting is condemned, for he does not act from faith. And whatever is not of faith is sin" [Romans 14:23]. In other words, when the conscience feels that it is displeasing to God, it has already cast faith away. Therefore, it is also a sin when the conscience determines that it is displeasing God.

This degree in deeds, then, must be upheld: It is mortal sin to act against conscience, that is, to approve something or to do some work which the conscience determines to be displeasing to God. Therefore, as noted above, Paul requires love from a good conscience. And he instructs Timothy to fight the good fight, having faith and a good conscience. In 2 Corinthians 1 he says, "This is our boast, the testimony of our conscience." To the Galatians, "Let each one examine his own work.

Thus he will have a boast in himself" [Galatians 6:4], that is, a good conscience. It is necessary for the righteous to have this boast; namely, that, as those who repent, they do not persevere in those things in which they determine that they have acted against the will of God. As it is written, "I do not desire the death of the sinner, but that he be converted and live" [Ezekiel 33:11]. Likewise, "If I say to the ungodly, 'You will surely die!', and he repents of his sin and does justice and righteousness, etc., he will surely live" [Ezekiel 33:14–15].

Therefore, it is necessary for the righteous to have this boast of a good conscience. And yet they must understand that this very obedience which they furnish is not perfect but is full of vice. Therefore, when it comes to God's judgment, let them not trust in the worthiness of their works, but let them trust that their person is righteous, that is, acceptable for Christ's sake, just as Paul also requires a good conscience, and yet transfers justification to something else when he says, "I am not conscious of anything against me, but in this I am not justified" [1 Corinthians 4:4]. So also John says, "In this we know that we are of the truth and have peaceful and quiet hearts before Him" [1 John 3:19]. Here he requires a good conscience. We truly love when we love in such a way that our conscience does not condemn us before God. Then he adds concerning justification, "But even if our heart condemns us, God is greater than our heart" [1 John 3:20]. That is, even if we feel that our love is not sufficiently pure before God, that we do not satisfy the Law, nevertheless, he says, trust in the mercy of God must be retained, for He has pronounced us righteous and is greater than our weakness. Therefore, he adds again, "If our heart does not condemn us, we have confidence toward God" [1 John 3:21]. It is of the utmost importance to ponder and meditate on these things, that we may keep Paul's words: "Do not grieve the Holy Spirit of God which whom we were sealed for the day of redemption" [Ephesians 4:30]. In other words, let us not reject the benefit of Christ and so perish.

Furthermore, to this category of mortal sin pertain also the sins of omission and feigned ignorance. For this pretense itself is against the conscience, as when a person is unwilling to learn the Gospel, or to understand his duty, or otherwise acts negligently. Therefore Paul says, "Woe to me if I do not preach the Gospel!" [1 Corinthians 9:16]. Such sins even now are committed by many people who neglect hearing and learning the Gospel, although they know the command, "Hear Him!" [Luke 9:35]. Such also was the ignorance of the Jews who persecuted Christ, of which Christ says, "If you were blind, you would not have sin. Now you say that you can see, etc." [John 9:41]. Thus the idolatries of the nations, etc., are mortal sins. But I already explained at the beginning of this section about the sins of those who are entirely without the knowledge of Christ. For in such people, both the disease of nature and all their wicked impulses are mortal sins.

PREDESTINATION

With regard to predestination, one must judge, neither from reason, nor from the Law, but from the Gospel. In addition, one must not seek a different cause of predestination than of justification. If a person establishes these two principles from the outset, he will easily disentangle himself from many questions. For if we are only to make a judgment from the Gospel, and if predestination is to be discussed together with justification, then there will be one simple path. Just as we begin with the Word when inquiring about justification, so we must also begin with the Word, that is, the Gospel, when inquiring about predestination. On the other hand, all the temptations concerning election and all the debates of the writers concerning the same arise partly from human reason without the Word of God, and partly from the Law. Men imagine that the cause of election is our worthiness or merits, since reason and the Law judge this to be so. Therefore, practically all the more recent Scholastic teachers are carried away into this way of thinking, since they only teach the righteousness of the Law. But we shall remember that the Gospel must be kept in focus.

Now, there are two things which must be considered in the promise of the Gospel; namely, that it promises righteousness gratis, and that the promise is universal. For these two things challenge the human mind. Sometimes we dispute our worthiness, concluding that we were not elected, because we are unworthy. At other times, we dispute the particularity, concluding that even if we were worthy, nevertheless God elected certain ones of His own with whom He was more contented, and thus we deny that salvation is something we should hope for, since perhaps we are not in that number. Both notions must be repudiated, and it is of great benefit to be diligent in fortifying godly minds against them. Therefore, we should neither focus on our worthiness nor should we turn a universal promise into a particular one. But let us each include ourselves in that universal promise. When we are distressed, then, concerning election, or when we dispute it, let us not begin with our own ideas or with the Law, but let us begin with the promise of the Gospel. If a person seeks a cause of election outside the Gospel, he cannot help but go astray. Therefore, let us not allow ourselves to be torn away from the Gospel, and let us drive our other ideas far away from us.

Therefore, since the promise is gratuitous, it is rightly stated that mercy is the cause of election. Consequently, since the promise is universal, if anyone wishes to turn the universal promise into a particular one, he will simply render the promise uncertain and will take faith away. Now, while it must be concluded that the promise is truly universal insofar as it pertains to the will of God, just as we say *a posteriore* in justification that there is a certain cause in the one who accepts it—namely, not his worthiness, but the fact that he grasps the promise with which the Holy Spirit is effective, as Paul says, "Faith comes from hearing" [Romans 10:17]—so also let us judge *a posteriore* concerning election. There is no doubt that the elect are those who grasp mercy by faith and who do not cast off that confidence at the end. All these things arise from this principal source: that we are not to judge the will of God outside of and apart from the Word, which is exactly what they do who seek the cause of election without directing consciences to the promise of the Gospel.

I will not be distracted by someone who wants to look into other more obscure things in this matter. Even if such things have some truth in them, they are still useless and confusing and only end up disturbing consciences and leading them away from the sight of the Gospel. Indeed, no temptation drives men's minds more tenaciously and stands more opposed to the faith than the idea that makes the promise particular. Therefore, the weakness of our souls must be assuaged; unbelief is not to be strengthened. Let each one, therefore, gather for himself testimonies which show that the promise is universal. Such are the following passages:

Romans 3, "The righteousness of God through faith in Jesus Christ, which is toward all and upon all."

John 3, "That everyone who believes in Him should not perish but have eternal life."

Romans 10, "The same Lord of all is rich toward all who call upon Him, etc."

Passages such as these bring the sweetest comfort, especially when we also set forth for ourselves that other little word; namely, that the benefit is gratuitous. To this pertain also the following passages:

"God wants all men to be saved" [1 Timothy 2:4]. Likewise, "With God there is no respect of persons" [Romans 2:11]. These things must be considered so that we do not confirm our natural unbelief by attributing partiality to God. In addition, this, too, should be noted, that evil comes from us, wherefore we must take care not to indulge willingly our natural unbelief or to fight against the promise or depart from the promise while seeking other causes of election apart from the Word of God. Therefore, for as harsh as Augustine is, nonetheless he writes thus in *De Praedestinatione et gratia*: "God helps those who take up the responsibility of their calling with suitable piety and who, as much as is in a man, keep the good gifts of God within themselves, etc." Therefore, even if some people argue more subtly in this matter, for me it is sufficient to collect those things which are certain to benefit consciences. For in the present struggle, the conscience should certainly be summoned back to the promise and consider this above all, that the promise is both gratuitous and universal.

Nor do the things which I have said oppose the words of Christ, "No one comes to Me unless the Father draws him" [John 6:44]. For we should begin with the Word. Therefore, when we grasp the Word, God is at once effective through the Word, according to that saying, "The Gospel is the power for salvation to everyone who believes, etc." [Romans 1:16]; and the saying of Paul, "It is not of the one who wills nor of the one who runs, but of God who is merciful" [Romans 9:16]. He does not make the promise particular but teaches that mercy is the cause of election, as we also said above. Indeed, that whole sermon of Paul was prepared about election, not to disturb minds, but to comfort them. He firmly sets forth the necessary comfort, removing the merit and worthiness of the righteousness of the Law. Therefore he says, "It is not of the one who wills nor of the one who runs." What is more desirable than an election which depends, not on the worthiness of our righteousness, but on mercy, that it may be certain? Consequently, this comfort was also necessary, speaking about the effect of election, namely, that there is a certain Church of the elect which believes the Word of God, lest we be deceived and think that that multitude is the Church of God which, on account of the righteousness of the Law, arrogates to itself the title even while persecuting the Gospel. Paul does this in order to remove the title

"Church" from the Jews, which they were arrogating to themselves on account of the righteousness of the Law. Therefore, he contrasts it with another Church—the Church of the elect—and says that the other Church is hardened, speaking of the punishment for their persecution. He says in Ephesians 1, "He elected us in Christ" [Ephesians 1:4], in order to teach that the cause of election is not our worthiness, but Christ, lest we contemplate election apart from Christ and the Gospel; in order that we should seek the cause of election in the benefit and promise of Christ. So also Romans 8, "Those whom He predestined, the same He also called; those whom He called, the same He also justified." Here he comforts the saints, that they may know that there exists a definite Church of the elect and that the Gospel will be effective, etc. Then he adds the calling, in order to show that all this is being accomplished through the Word and that the call pertains to election.

Let it suffice to have taught briefly about predestination. We have already spoken above about the cause of evil and about contingency.

THE DIFFERENCE BETWEEN THE OLD AND THE NEW TESTAMENT

We said above about the Law and the Gospel that, although the Law of Moses pertained to a certain people and a certain time, the law of nature is common to all nations and pertains to all times, because it is written in nature. The Gospel (that is, the promise of reconciliation for Christ's sake) also pertains to all times. And although it is not a part of natural knowledge, nevertheless the promise was revealed to the fathers from the beginning. Now, if we assert that the Old Testament is properly the Law of Moses, that is, the whole Commonwealth (*politia*) under Moses, it is easy to distinguish the Old Testament from the New. The Old Testament (that is, the Law of Moses) contained the

Law and the promises about the Commonwealth of the people of Israel. For a testament signifies either contracts or promises or an arrangement. And those Mosaic laws were handed down for this purpose, not because the people were righteous before God on account of them, but in order that they might distinguish the Israelites from the rest of the nations until the time of Christ's public appearance. For God wanted to separate this people from the other nations in order that there might be a defined group of people among whom the Christ should be born and among whom the promises should be preserved, that the firm testimonies concerning the Word of God might continue to exist. For this reason, the people were led out of Egypt with such great miracles, and for this reason new miracles were subsequently done among that people, namely, that there might be a firm testimony that that people had the Word of God and the promise concerning the salvation of the human race. Therefore, although the Israelites did not merit the forgiveness of sins and justification—that is, reconciliation before God—on account of these laws, God subjected them to these laws which were to be observed as a form of discipline by which the flesh should be restrained, etc. As Paul says, "The Law is a schoolmaster" [Galatians 3:24]. And yet those ceremonies were also types for the godly and signs of the coming Christ. But the Israelites obtained the forgiveness of sins and were justified before God, not by those observations of the Law, but by trusting in the mercy of God promised for the sake of the coming Christ, just as also the saints in the New Testament. Nor was there any difference between the testaments with regard to the forgiveness of sins and reconciliation. For both the saints of the Old Testament and those of the New are justified by faith in Christ, not by the Law.

These things are abundantly discussed in Galatians and Hebrews, where Paul removes justification from the Law and transfers it to Christ. Let us now consider how greatly this doctrine offended the Jews, who had the opposite opinion about the Law; namely, that they obtained the forgiveness of sins and justification before God on account of their acts of worship and the works of the Law. Indeed, by trusting in their own righteousness and acts of worship, they heaped up sacrifices—just as many in the Church also thought that the Mass and other ecclesiastical ordinances merited the forgiveness of sins and justification, and by this opinion they heaped up the very same kinds of ordinances. Yes, they even cite the example of the Mosaic Law in defense of their traditions. For a poor imitation of the Law deceives them. They mistakenly twist this imitation of the Law into a means of justification and falsely apply it to our works. Just as now the ungodly rage when anyone seeks to remove justification from the Mass and other ecclesiastical ordinances, so the Jews raged against the prophets and apostles when they taught that men are not pronounced righteous on account of ceremonies and other works of the Law. Indeed, this comparison of Pharisaical opinions is useful, first of all, that we may consider the sources from which the false opinions about ecclesiastical rites originated; and also, that we who live and struggle for a similar cause may take comfort in the example of the prophets and apostles.

But here someone will ask whether the sacrifices for sins merited the forgiveness of sins. I reply: It is clearly written in the Epistle to the Hebrews that sins could not be abolished with the blood of bulls and calves, etc. Consequently, it is clear that hearts cannot be made alive nor can death be conquered by any external rites. Therefore, those sacrifices did not merit the forgiveness of sins before God. But they did merit the forgiveness of sins in a civil sense, that is, before the Church, namely, that they should continue to be part of the people, or rather, should not be excluded from the commonwealth of Moses.

Furthermore, for the godly and believing, all those forms of worship in the Law, although they were righteousnesses, that is, good works, were first and foremost signs of the coming Christ. Having been instructed by such things, the godly exercised and confirmed their faith, even as David alludes to Christ when he says, "You will sprinkle me with hyssop, O Lord, and I will be clean" [Psalm 51:7]. Thus they were signs of confession.

There were also eucharistic sacrifices, that is, works by which they gave thanks to God, by which they professed to call upon that God who had given them His Word and who was watching over them, etc. Indeed, to the godly consciences it was a great source of comfort to exercise their faith in such ordinances which they knew to be pleasing to God, since they were instituted by Him, just as also now it is helpful for consciences to know which works God requires, etc. For since human traditions have been invented without God's mandate, how can they be true forms of worship, since the conscience cannot be sure that such worship forms are pleasing to God?

The New Testament is God's promise to give justification and eternal life for the sake of Christ. And since this promise, that is, the Gospel about Christ, pertains to all ages, the New Testament should not be understood as if it did not pertain to the fathers. No, it is called the New Testament because it is a new and different covenant than the covenant of the Law. It is a different promise. For the Law held the promise of a kingdom for Israel. But the Gospel holds a promise of eternal things, namely, of the abolition of death, the renewal of human nature, and the gift of new righteousness and eternal life for Christ's sake. It forgives sins in such a way that, at the same time, it makes hearts alive and renews them by the Holy Spirit. Since, then, the New Testament brings righteousness and eternal life, there are required in the New Testament spiritual acts of worship of the mind. As Christ says, "The true worshipers will worship the Father in Spirit and truth" [John 4:23], that is, not with external observances, but with true and spiritual movements of the heart, with faith, hope, love, patience, etc. This is how Paul distinguishes the Old and New Testament in 2 Corinthians 3 and Romans 8, "You have received the Spirit of the adoption of sons, in whom we cry out, 'Abba, Father.'" And Jeremiah 31, "Behold, I shall make a new covenant, etc. After those days I shall place My Law in their entrails, and in their heart I shall write it, etc." [Jeremiah 31:31, 33].

Here, together with the forgiveness of sins, He promises the Holy Spirit, who will work the new and true knowledge of God and a new obedience in the heart. Therefore it says in Romans 14, "The kingdom of God is not food and drink, but righteousness, peace, and life in the Holy Spirit." And Philippians 3, "Our citizenship is in heaven." In other words, the Gospel does not establish a worldly civil society, but is a new, heavenly life. But while we live in the body, the Gospel permits us to use the customs and laws of all nations, like food, and drink, and the other necessities of life, for the benefit of this bodily life. Therefore, Abraham, David, and other such men, since they were pleasing to God by faith and had the Holy Spirit, belonged to the New Testament, and yet for a time, while they lived in the body, they used their own rites and laws. So also now the people of the New Testament are not the ungodly, but those who are pleasing to God by faith and have the Holy Spirit. And while they live in this body, they should use the present customs and laws. That other spiritual life of theirs does not keep their body from using food, drink, civil customs and laws. In addition, although the New Testament preaches the Gospel about righteousness and eternal life and about spiritual acts of worship, the law of nature and discipline remain in the world, whereby the rest of men who do not belong to the New Testament should be both curbed and trained so that they may be taught and led to acknowledge Christ.

THE SPIRIT AND THE LETTER

This topic is born from the one above, for this is how Paul distinguishes the Old Testament from the New in 2 Corinthians 3. He calls the Old Testament "the letter and the ministration of death." On the other hand, he calls the New Testament or the Gospel "the ministration of the Spirit and of life." Now "the Spirit" signifies both the Holy Spirit and the spiritual movements which the Holy Spirit stirs up in hearts, as Paul testifies in 2 Corinthians 3, "We are being transformed from glory into glory by the Spirit of the Lord." But "the letter" signifies all the thoughts and observations and "good intentions," as they call them—the efforts of reason—without the Holy Spirit, that is, without true fear and true trust in Christ. For the letter is opposed to the living and true movements of the heart, and thus it is called the letter, because it is a doctrine, or an imitation which we have come to practice by doctrine and discipline.

The Law, then, is the letter when we imitate it with good intentions or externally moral behavior apart from the Holy Spirit; that is, without true fear and without true faith. In and of itself, the Law is the very ministration of death, either because it only brings about a discipline which does not deliver from eternal death, or because, when it truly accuses, it kills consciences. For it does not promise the forgiveness of sins gratis, nor does it bring the Holy Spirit, etc.

Furthermore, the Gospel is also the letter when it is not grasped by the spirit, that is, when we do not truly fear or truly believe God. But the Gospel is the ministration of the Spirit and life when the forgiveness of sins is grasped by faith, when hearts are delivered from terrors, when they receive the Holy Spirit and new impulses that are in agreement with God's Law. For the Gospel promises the forgiveness of sins gratis, together with the Holy Spirit and eternal life.

Therefore, the interpretation of Origen must be repudiated. He understands the letter to be the history, or the ceremonies, or the literal sense. But he understands the Spirit to be the allegorical interpretation. Indeed, the allegories themselves of ceremonies and of the histories in and of themselves are nothing but letter, that is, doctrine. And when Paul says that "the Law is spiritual," it should not be understood that the

Law is allegorical, but that the Law is not merely an external and civil discipline, but requires spiritual impulses, namely, true fear of God, true trust, true love, etc. It was not the ceremonies that kept David and the rest of the saints from keeping the Law spiritually. For the ceremonies do not exclude the Holy Spirit. Indeed, they are signs by which faith should be exercised. Nor does it matter that the signs are dissimilar. The fathers had their own signs—circumcision and other ceremonies. We have the signs passed down to us. But it is the same Holy Spirit, and the trust in mercy which exists among the saints should be similar, even if the signs vary with the times.

Let it be sufficient to have given this instruction about the words "letter and Spirit," that we may understand that the letter does not only pertain to the time of the Mosaic Law, but to men of all ages who are to be ruled by discipline. On the other hand, the Spirit also pertains to the saints of all ages, just as we said above concerning the Law and the Gospel. For it should be understood that the letter, that is, the practice and imitation of the Decalogue which human reason produces, does not justify before God, but that this discipline is still necessary, as stated repeatedly above.

CHRISTIAN FREEDOM

This topic is related to the ones above and illustrates the difference between the Old and the New Testament. The knowledge of Christian freedom is essential, since it shows in what things Christian righteousness properly consists, and what we should conclude about ceremonies, concerning which infinite dissensions have arisen in every age. Likewise, it shows the dignity of civil affairs. Moreover, it is necessary that there be a firm doctrine in the Church concerning such things. For the sake of teaching, we shall delineate four degrees of Christian freedom.

The first degree of Christian freedom is that the forgiveness of sins and the imputation of righteousness are given, not on account of the Law, but gratis, on account of Christ. This is the chief degree. It is a spiritual freedom and has nothing at all to do with the external or civil life, but only pertains to the struggle of the conscience in God's judgment, in which this comfort is needed. Christ speaks of this level when He says, "If the Son sets you free, you will be free indeed" [John 8:36].

The second degree is the gift of the Holy Spirit, by whom believers are made alive and ruled, and are also defended against the devil's cruelty. This degree belongs to the one above and should not be separated from it. But for the sake of teaching I am making a distinction so that by such enumeration the variety of Christ's benefits may be viewed more clearly, and that we may learn to use both benefits. In the fearful struggles of the conscience, the first degree should be kept in view. In the other perils of life, the second degree should teach us to take courage and to ask to be ruled and defended by the Holy Spirit. Paul speaks of this second degree in 2 Corinthians 3, "Where the Spirit of the Lord is, there is freedom." Likewise, "I will not leave you orphans" [John 14:18].

But here it is of the utmost importance to teach concerning the first degree, so that we know how to understand freedom, that is, the abrogation of the Law. First of all, the freedom, or the abrogation of the Law, of which we are speaking in these two degrees has nothing at all to do with those who do not repent, for these are under the Law; that is, they are accused and condemned by the moral Law. No, it only pertains to those who grasp the benefit of Christ by faith. And concerning these, the distinction must be upheld that to be free from the Law is not to be free from obedience to the moral Law, but to be free from the curse of the Law. That is to say, although we do not satisfy the Law, we already have the forgiveness of sins and the imputation of righteousness on account of something else, namely, on account of Christ, just as if we had satisfied the Law. It is with this understanding that Paul says,

"You are not under the Law, but under grace" [Romans 6:14], that is, you are surely already pleasing to God through grace, that is, through mercy, not on account of the fulfillment of the Law. For no one satisfies the Law. Likewise to the Galatians, "Christ has redeemed us from the curse of the Law, having been made a curse for us" [Galatians 3:13], that is, since no one satisfies the Law, the Law used to accuse and condemn everyone. Now it does not accuse or condemn those who have been reconciled through Christ. This, then, is the benefit of freedom, that consciences can have a firm consolation when they understand that the forgiveness of sins is granted gratis and that the righteous are pleasing to God through mercy, even though the remnants of sin still remain in them and they do not satisfy the Law. Therefore, the whole Law has been abrogated in such a way that we have been freed from the curse of the whole Law; and something else has been set forth for the purpose of seeking justification, in order that justification may be certain. But the moral Law still remains, so far as obedience is concerned, for the Gospel certainly subjects us to obedience toward God. As to how this obedience is pleasing, it has been stated repeatedly above. I shall explain shortly why it is necessary to retain the moral Law, so far as obedience is concerned, and on the other hand, why it is permissible to omit the ceremonies and judicial laws of Moses.

Augustine treats this subject at length. "The righteous are free from the Law, because, having received the Holy Spirit, they perform voluntarily the things required by the Law." This sentence seems to be speaking only about the second degree of freedom. It does not speak clearly about the first degree, of which it is very important for consciences to be taught; namely, that this is freedom—the forgiveness of sins—is granted gratis and that the righteous are pleasing to God even though they do not satisfy the Law. After that, it is (in my judgment) quite helpful to speak about lawful obedience: that the Law remains, so far as obedience is concerned.

This is also how the passage from Paul should be taken, "The Law is good if a person uses it lawfully, knowing that the Law is not given for the righteous, but for the unrighteous" [1 Timothy 1:8–9], that is, all the duties of the Law pertain to the unrighteous. The Law accuses and condemns the unrighteous. Likewise, by the Law the unrighteous are to be restrained. But the righteous are free from the Law; that is, they are not accused or condemned by the Law, for they are righteous, that is, acceptable, on account of something else. Since they are righteous, they already obey the Law and are restrained, nor are new chains needed to burden their conscience, as happened in the Church and among the monks, where their consciences were immediately burdened with new chains and there was no end to making the Law stricter. The authority of Gregory was cited, "It is the nature of a good mind to fear guilt where there is no guilt." And yet, meanwhile, men were not taught to know that they were righteous by faith, but were left with a doubtful and despairing conscience. Paul intended to forbid this tormenting of consciences when he said, "The Law is not given for the righteous." In other words, since the Law does not accuse or condemn the righteous, neither should the righteous be burdened by new chains of laws, etc., since he already does the Law.

The third degree of freedom is that the Gospel frees us from the ceremonies and the so-called judicial laws of Moses. This degree pertains in a certain way to one's outward life, but it has its cause in the above degrees. For the Gospel does not require Levitical ceremonies, since it teaches that we obtain the forgiveness of sins gratis and that we are pronounced righteous through mercy for Christ's sake, not on account of any of our works or acts of worship. This is why Paul so vehemently contends that Levitical ceremonies should not be thought of as necessary, lest the Gospel about faith be obscured, that is, lest the benefit of Christ be transferred to the Levitical worship rites or similar things, etc. This is the great and noble reason why he contends so vehemently concerning freedom, concerning the abrogation of the Law, namely, that a firm consolation of consciences may be retained, teaching that sins are forgiven gratis, etc.

Furthermore, it must be understood concerning the judicial laws of Moses that they are not required in the Gospel, because the Gospel teaches about an eternal and spiritual righteousness, while also permitting us in this corporal life to use the laws of all the nations in which we live, just as it permits us to use the architecture and medicine of all nations, or the periods of day and night. Men must necessarily be taught about this degree of freedom, for we see that great tumults have frequently arisen from those who, being unaware of this freedom, have tried to bring the Law of Moses back onto the stage.

But someone will ask: Since the Gospel abrogates the Law of Moses, should the abrogation be understood about the whole Law, especially since the Decalogue is the most difficult part of the Law? Indeed, the remaining parts, namely, the ceremonies and the forensic laws, seem more like delightful displays than burdens! To this I reply: The abrogation of the Law should principally be understood concerning the abrogation of the right which the Law had to accuse and condemn all men. So, then, for the believer the whole Law has been abrogated—the Decalogue and the remaining parts of the Law—in such a way that something other than the Law has been set forth for seeking the forgiveness of sins and justification; and that the Law does not condemn believers, even though they do not satisfy the Law. We have already explained above how this should be understood. Freedom or abrogation concerning the whole Law should chiefly be understood in this way. For it is sufficiently clear that the works of the Law are not even done perfectly by the saints, for the remnants of sin are in them. The Gospel, then, frees the conscience from that horrible burden; namely, from the terrors and from the death which the Decalogue instills. For when Paul says that we are freed from the curse of the Law, he is surely speaking about the whole Law, and especially about the Decalogue, which accuses and curses more than the other parts of the Law.

But someone will say: If the whole Law has been abrogated, why is it permissible to omit the ceremonies and the judicial laws, but not permissible to omit the works of the Decalogue? I reply: The ceremonies and the judicial laws of Moses are external, bodily ordinances which belonged to a certain nation, given for a limited time, and came to an end after the revelation of the Gospel, as written in the Epistle to the Hebrews. Since the Gospel preaches about spiritual and eternal life, it does not require those external Mosaic ordinances, for they pertain to bodily life. And yet, since it brings a new and spiritual life, it requires obedience toward God; it preaches repentance; it condemns the wicked nature; it restrains covetousness. Therefore, it requires the spiritual works which are taught in the Decalogue. For there remains in man's nature a natural knowledge of the Decalogue or the moral Laws which teach us about this obedience. Therefore, it would be foolish to understand the abrogation of the Decalogue as if it could be omitted just like the ceremonies, since it has been written in our minds. Furthermore, insofar as the Decalogue condemns us, the Gospel about the abrogation of the curse should be set against our natural judgment, as we said above.

Until now we have still been speaking about the spiritual life. But it should also be understood concerning the external, bodily life that, although the Gospel does not require a Mosaic commonwealth, nevertheless, just as it does not abolish arithmetic or rhetoric, neither does it abolish the Law of nature, that is, our natural judgment concerning morality and civil life. For it does not corrupt nature, but rather heals and restores it. Therefore, it retains the Law of nature, that is, the honorable ordinances concerning marriage, the distinction of ownership, magistrates, courts. For if this natural judgment were erased, nature itself would be removed.

Accordingly, one can understand how foolishly they judge who dream that in the Gospel a certain Platonic sharing of possessions is taught, or a monastic abdication of property. For the Gospel does not establish a new bodily society, but in this outward life it wants us to use natural judgment, and it places us under the governing magistrates, even commanding us to obey them for conscience' sake. Indeed, here the authority of the laws of nature and of the magistrates must be magnified, first, lest we assume for ourselves a freedom to refuse due obedience or to undermine public discipline, as some people despise all honorable customs under the pretext of this freedom. They do not keep the laws about degrees of kinship, although natural reason forbids the marriage of relatives in the closer degrees. Then, lest we bind ourselves to the Mosaic state because of some superstition, the Christian judge should divide inheritances and judge cases according to the laws of his nation, for each one should be obedient to his own magistrates. Therefore, he should not change the order of the courts or the penalties instituted by the magistrates. Therefore, it is permissible to punish the thief with the accustomed penalties, even if the Law of Moses imposes a different punishment. Thus in the matter of tithes and other payments and contracts we are not bound by the authority of the Mosaic Law; we should comply with the current laws and submit to the regular magistrates.

Therefore, it is helpful to understand rightly this degree of freedom, not only for the sake of the public peace, but also to fortify consciences. For it teaches that it is a godly and holy work to obey the current laws, even if they have been made by heathens, just as Joseph, Daniel, and other such men did a godly and holy work when they administered the laws of the heathen nations. For we already have God's command to submit to the laws of the governing magistrates in this civil life. Indeed, they do a great disservice to the Gospel who pretend that the Gospel is a new doctrine that has to do with changing political affairs, the marketplace, possessions, courts, and similar things.

The fourth degree teaches what we are to think about the ecclesiastical ceremonies which the bishops or other men have instituted. Consciences must be educated about these things. For traditions breed many dangers, unless this freedom is understood, as we shall discuss shortly.

Now this is the sum of this degree. Since in this bodily life certain rites are needed, according to the times and places in which one lives, the Gospel permits such ordinances to be made in the Church to this end: that all things in the Church may be done in an orderly fashion and without confusion. Therefore, certain days are established so that the people may know when they should come together. Certain readings are instituted, as in the schools, so that men may be taught more beneficially. These are bodily ends, for they serve the purpose of tranquility and convenience. The Gospel permits ordinances to be made for these purposes, as Paul says, "Let all things be done in the Church decently and in an orderly fashion" [1 Corinthians 14:40].

But in addition, the Gospel teaches two things about traditions. First, it forbids us to conclude that any traditions established by men are acts of worship or worthy deeds that merit the forgiveness of sins or justification. As Christ attests, "In vain they worship me with the commands of men" [Matthew 15:9]. Secondly, it also teaches that it is not a sin to omit traditions, except in the case of offense. Thus it removes from them the notion of justification and necessity. The testimonies are found in Paul's writings, as in Colossians, "Let no one judge you in food, drink, festival day, etc." [Colossians 2:16]. For he is speaking about Levitical laws and about human traditions. And when he says, "Let no one judge you," he means, "Let no one condemn you for neglecting these rites." And in Galatians, "Stand in the freedom with which Christ has called you, lest you be subjected again to a yoke of slavery" [Galatians 5:1].

In order to understand why this doctrine concerning freedom is needed, we shall recount the harmful things that ensue if this doctrine concerning freedom is not found in the Church.

First, the righteousness of faith is obscured when the benefit of Christ is transferred to traditions; that is, when men think that they merit the forgiveness of sins and that they are pronounced righteous because of such observances, or when they think that faith is useless without such observances. From this persuasion, consciences fall into despair and lose the true knowledge of faith and of Christ.

Second, the unlearned imagine that such outward observances are acts of worship and even perfection itself—fasting and similar things—when, in fact, the true acts of worship and Christian perfection are fear, faith, love, and the works of one's vocation, etc.

Third, the concord of the churches is torn apart, for when these rites are considered necessary, contentions arise, since every church tenaciously defends its own rites, as happened over the date of Easter.

Fourth, one must also take into account the godly consciences, which will never be at rest if they think that these rites are necessary. For who has ever observed all traditions? Therefore, [Jean] Gerson long ago sought an equitable leniency (*epieikeia*) with regard to such traditions in order to assuage godly consciences. Indeed, the enormous number of summaries which collect and interpret traditions testifies how great the torment of consciences has been. The Church was so oppressed by these debates that, but for a very few, no one had time to touch on the Scriptures or to learn better things. From this, then, it can easily be understood that this doctrine of freedom is necessary for the Church, in order that these dangers and detriments may be avoided.

Paul calls the human traditions about foods, celibacy, and similar things "doctrines of demons" [1 Timothy 4:1], thereby signifying that there is great danger in them. Therefore, we must see to it that those dangers are understood. Now, since this bodily life cannot be entirely devoid of traditions, wisdom must be applied as to how far they are to be approved and how far they are to be rejected as doctrines of demons.

For they are doctrines of demons when they are set forth as forms of worship and as worthy deeds that merit the forgiveness of sins, or when they become torments for the conscience, as if they were necessary for righteousness, or as if faith were useless without them, or when they are regarded as Christian perfection. When these opinions are attached to traditions, they are doctrines of demons, even though they otherwise deal with matters of adiaphora. They are likewise doctrines of demons when they command such things as cannot be observed without sin, such as the law concerning celibacy, etc. Therefore, since there is so much danger associated with traditions, it is necessary in the Church for the doctrine about this degree of freedom to be taught, so that one may be able to judge rightly concerning traditions whenever there is a need for them, as we have said, for the sake of external tranquility.

Still others have sought an equitable leniency (*epieikeia*) for traditions. But this doctrine of Paul is the most useful interpretation. It teaches that traditions should be considered, not as forms of worship, but as external matters and adiaphora. And it must be understood that they can be omitted without sin, except in the case of offense. This doctrine also retains at the same time the righteousness of faith, and it frees consciences from dangers. And yet it does not destroy good order, for it teaches that certain traditions should be kept in the public practice of the Church, to the extent that offenses can be avoided. Thus the Church has certain festivals—not that the observance of festivals is necessary according to the Jewish custom, but because fixed times are needed for teaching. This ordinance must be observed with an understanding of Christian freedom. But they sin who, either on account of a contempt for religion or teaching, do not observe the festivals, or who harm others by their own example. For freedom must be understood, but in practice, wisdom must be shown, lest we become a cause of offense to anyone.

Gerson and others followed this reasoning: Traditions can be omitted because the bishops do not have the right to burden the Church with traditions. But against this reasoning is set the command about obedience: Obedience is necessary, even if the authority abuses its own right. Likewise, "The scribes and Pharisees sit in Moses' seat. Whatever they say, etc." [Matthew 23:2]. When their sayings are magnified and the necessity for obedience is emphasized, the conscience becomes utterly terrified. Therefore, it is necessary to seek a firm reasoning which sufficiently fortifies consciences, lest they be oppressed by a false notion concerning traditions.

The chief argument, then, which can be made in objection to this must be refuted:

It is necessary to obey the authority;
Ecclesiastical authority has established traditions;
Therefore, traditions must necessarily be obeyed.

We must respond to the major premise, which is not true when the authority demands that we do or think wicked things, for then the rule must be upheld, "We must obey God rather than men" [Acts 5:29]. On the other hand, even if traditions speak of matters of adiaphora, they become wicked and doctrines of demons when they are set forth with the opinion that they are forms of worship which merit the forgiveness of sins, or that they are necessary for Christian righteousness. This reasoning must especially be kept in view so that the glory of Christ may be contrasted with the overemphasis on obedience. For when traditions are set forth in this way, the glory of Christ is obscured. For they transfer the benefit of Christ to the traditions. Moreover, a good many hypocrites defend traditions in this way, which is why it is necessary to dissent and to oppose it especially with solid teaching. Paul, by example, also declared freedom against the stern hypocrites. And Christ excuses the apostles when they violate the Pharisaical tradition (Matt. 15).

This first solution is entirely clear and plain. But the second one must also be upheld. The major premise is true concerning the kind of obedience which the Gospel requires. But the Gospel wants this freedom in traditions to be left to consciences. In these things which are of divine right, the conscience should necessarily obey the pastors. In traditions, it should obey to the extent that it avoids causing offense. But the conscience is free and should understand that freedom in these matters cannot be altered or abolished by any human authority, according to the saying of Paul, "Let no one judge you in food, drink, etc." [Colossians 2:16]. Likewise, "Stand in that freedom in which Christ called you and do not be subjected again to a yoke of slavery" [Galatians 5:1]. Therefore, even when we keep human traditions, the notion of necessity must not be added; they should be kept as the customary form of vestments is kept.

These two solutions must be carefully considered. For they are taken from the very fount and source of the matter and should clearly teach the conscience what to conclude about traditions. The first solution removes the honor of justification from traditions; the second removes the notion of necessity. It is good for consciences to know these things, and yet we do well to remember that good order is to be preserved, for which there is a need for ceremonies, fixed places and times. To destroy this good order is the work of barbarians; it is foreign to civilized and humane society.

I have spoken about traditions and about this fourth degree of freedom. We shall also assert below that one must think reverently about the canonical ordinances and ecclesiastical authority on account of the most holy ministry.

Furthermore, concerning the ceremonies instituted by Christ (that is, the Sacraments), it must be understood that they must be observed, since they have God's command. And yet evangelical freedom teaches that we are not justified by ceremonies without faith; likewise, that necessity excuses us, if we are impeded in such a way that we are unable to use those ceremonies, as when, in a certain situation, it were impossible for a person to be baptized. If such a person truly believed in Christ, he would be saved even without the ceremony, as Christ says, "The Son of Man is Lord even of the Sabbath" [Matthew 12:8]. Likewise, "In Christ you are complete" [Colossians 2:10]. Nor is the requirement of ceremonies greater in the Gospel than it was in the Law of Moses. For example, David used the sacred bread in a case of necessity. For although he knew that the ceremonies were to be observed as a form of external discipline, he also knew that he was righteous on account of something else, and that this external observance admitted a certain dispensation in a case of necessity. The godly have this excuse in the distant nations where they do not have access to men who can administer the pure Sacrament to them.

THE SACRAMENTS

God has frequently added to His external promises certain marks which are subject to the senses in order to instruct men and to preserve and prolong the memory of the Word to all their posterity. For the memory of things endures more sturdily when the eyes observe them being highlighted with fixed ceremonies, as in the theater. Thus circumcision was a wondrous ceremony that served to point to the promise of the Seed and to spread the memory of this promise to posterity. Therefore, whenever we speak about the Sacraments, we should not only consider the ceremonies, but immediately the mind must reach for the promise for whose purpose the sign was instituted. For properly speaking, a Sacrament is a sign of a divine promise instituted by God. Therefore, it depends on two things—the element and the Word—so that the memory of the promise may be visibly present. In order that the whole rationale of a Sacrament in general may be better understood, we will speak of its use and of its purpose.

First, then, the Pharisaical and monstrous opinion of the Scholastics must be condemned, for they have imagined that the men who use the Sacraments of the New Testament become righteous by the mere performance of the deed (*ex opere operato*). In fact, they even add, "without the good intention of those who use them." This Pharisaical persuasion should be eradicated from the Church, for it is properly at odds with the righteousness of faith. For they conclude that a man becomes righteous on account of the use of that ceremony, even if he does not believe—indeed, even if he adds no good intention of the heart, as long as he does not erect a barrier, lest he have an actual purpose to commit mortal sin.

On the other hand, there are some clever men who, wanting to appear unassuming in interpreting the ceremonies, say that the Sacraments are not signs of God's will toward us, but only marks of our profession, since there must be marks by which we may be distinguished from the rest of the nations, as the toga used to distinguish the Romans from the Greeks, or as the form of vestment distinguishes between monks. But this unassuming interpretation does not sufficiently explain the use of the Sacraments. For even though they are marks of profession and signs of confession, that is not their principal purpose, nor does it aid the conscience. We, for our part, seek the principal purpose and one that benefits consciences.

The third opinion is that of the Anabaptists, that the Sacraments are essentially allegories of good works, so that they understand circumcision to have been a sign of restraining covetous desires; or Baptism to be a sign of the afflictions—that Christians must go under the waves and pass through dangers of every kind, even as they are immersed in the waters. Thus they make the Lord's Supper into a mere signification of mutual goodwill, since banquets are considered by all nations to be signs of mutual goodwill. However, although these allegories of good works are not absurd, they do not yet speak to the principal use and purpose. For the Sacraments are signs, not only of love or works, but primarily of faith, and of the will of God toward us. For the Gospel does not only preach about works, but especially about the will of God toward us, and about faith. But the Anabaptists apply the signs of the Gospel only to one part, namely, to the works.

Fourth, the genuine understanding, then, is that the Sacraments of the New Testament were primarily instituted to be signs of God's will toward us, directed toward the eyes, that they may convince us to believe the promise that has been set forth in the Gospel. Thus we combine the Sacrament with the promise. Moreover, as the promise must be accepted by faith, so, too, in the use of the Sacrament faith should be present which is convinced that those genuine things which are set forth in the promise are indeed granted to us. This use benefits consciences as they deal with God. For Paul says that circumcision was "a seal of the righteousness of faith" [Romans 4:11, that is, testimonies added to the promises to the end that we should the more firmly believe. Likewise, so that we may grasp that the divine promises are properly applied to us when we see that the promise of God has been written, as it were, on our bodies by that immersion in water or by the taking of the body of the Lord.

Augustine aptly unites the Sacrament with the Word when he says, "The Sacrament is the visible Word." That is, just as the Word is a kind of mark which is received with the ears, so the Sacrament is a display or picture which is directed toward the eyes. So, then, just as the Word is a mark signifying something about God's will, and just as God is grasped by the Word when we believe, so also He is grasped by the Sacrament when we believe. Therefore, just as the Word is the instrument through which the Holy Spirit is effective, as Paul says, "The Gospel is the power of God for salvation to everyone who believes" [Romans 1:16], and, "Faith comes from hearing, etc." [Romans 10:17], so the Holy Spirit is effective through the Sacraments when they are received by faith. For they urge and move us to believe, just as the Word does. From these things it can be determined what the primary use and purpose of the Sacraments is and how they should be used to encourage and to comfort consciences as their purpose.

Both the apostles and the ecclesiastical writers teach this primary use. For Paul says of Baptism, "He saved us through the washing of regeneration" [Titus 3:5]. Therefore, God is effective through Baptism. And Peter most eloquently says, "Baptism is not only the external washing of dirt from the body, but a covenant of a good conscience toward God through the resurrection of Christ" [1 Peter 3:21]. That is, it is a covenant by which God testifies to us that He is favorable toward us on account of the risen Christ. And the conscience, in turn, trusts by means of this covenant that it has a favorable God, that is, that we are righteous on account of Christ. And in Acts, Peter says, "Let each one of you be baptized in the name of Jesus Christ for the forgiveness of sins" [Acts 2:38], where he affirms with certainty that Baptism is a testimony and sign of the forgiveness of sins and of the gift of the Holy Spirit. Therefore, the holy fathers, too, call the Sacraments signs of grace, that is, of God's will toward us, nor do they judge them to be merely marks of one's profession before men. It is profane to make the Sacraments into mere marks of one's profession before men without applying them to the use of consciences as they deal with God.

Furthermore, once we have the primary use and purpose, the remaining uses can also be added. For a thing usually has more than one purpose. They are signs of confession. And confession, as we know, is the chief form of divine worship. They are likewise allegories and symbols of good habits, as the holy fathers sometimes exhort us to mutual love in their sermons. For when we receive the body of the Lord at a common table, we are making a most holy covenant of mutual goodwill in which we all are made both members of Christ and one body among us. The holy fathers often used this argument, and gladly so.

THE NUMBER OF SACRAMENTS

There is no need to quarrel over the number of Sacraments. For if we call Sacraments, not only the ceremonies instituted in the Gospel, but also other things or works to which divine promises are added, many Sacraments can be numbered. Prayer will be a Sacrament. For it is a work that we do and has magnificent promises. "Whatever you ask the Father in My name, He will give you" [John 16:23]. Afflictions and alms will also be Sacraments, since they are works that have been commended with divine promises. For example, "Give and it will be given to you" [Luke 6:38]. Indeed, it would be beneficial to extol works of this kind with the title "Sacraments" so that, having been given a place of honor, they might be multiplied, and so that men who are admonished with this title might know that the promises are to be pursued and highly esteemed. In this way marriage, too, is a Sacrament, since it is an external thing that has been commended with the Word of God and promises. There is likewise a spiritual significance of marriage and the fellowship we have with Christ. The magistrate, too, will be a Sacrament in this way, for it is certainly a good work that has been commended with the Word of God and promises (Rom. 13). But none of these things which we have mentioned are ceremonies recently instituted in the Gospel.

Therefore, if we call "Sacraments" the ceremonies or rites instituted in the Gospel and properly pertaining to the chief promise which is particular to the Gospel, namely, concerning the forgiveness of sins, then it is easy to determine which things are Sacraments: Baptism, the Lord's Supper, and Absolution. For these rites were instituted in the Gospel and are used in order to signify this promise which is particular to the Gospel. For we are baptized in order that we may believe that our sins have been forgiven. So, too, the Lord's Supper and Absolution teach us to believe that our sins are surely forgiven us.

Confirmation and Extreme Unction are rites which were accepted by the fathers. But not even the Church requires them as necessary for salvation, for they do not have the command of God. Therefore, it is useful to distinguish these rites from those above, that we may know that they are not necessary. But Confirmation would have to be heartily approved, if it were used for the purpose of examining the youth and professing one's own faith.

Moreover, I am very pleased to have Ordination, as they call it, numbered among the Sacraments, as long as we understand by it both the ministry itself of the Gospel and the call to this ministry of teaching the Gospel and administering the Sacraments. For it is useful to commend the ministry of the Word with all diligence, and it is beneficial for men to know that the Holy Spirit is given through the ministry of the Word and through meditation on the Word, lest we seek other forms of enlightenment outside of the Word and apart from the Word, as the fanatical spirits do. The ministry of the Word has God's command, namely, that the Word should be both taught and heard. It also has tremendous promises attached to it. Romans 1, "The Gospel is the power of God for salvation to everyone who believes" [Romans 1:16]. Secondly, concerning Ordination, that is, the call to the ministry, it is beneficial to understand that God endorses those who have been called by the Church and wants to be present in their ministry. This benefit should be most agreeable to us and must be diligently praised and extolled. It would be most useful to number Ordination among the Sacraments in order to highlight the dignity of the ministry of the Word. But when others speak of Ordination without mentioning the ministry of the Gospel, they think that Ordination is the call to make sacrifices for the living and the dead. Then they add that there will be no forgiveness of sins in the Church if there is not a certain dependable sacrifice besides the sacrifice of Christ, and they pretend that by this sacrifice the priests are meriting the forgiveness of sins for others. These opinions arose from a certain unfortunate imitation; they improperly combined the New Testament with Levitical ceremonies. But we will have to speak further about the ministry and sacrifice a little later. For now, it is enough to have taught about the number of Sacraments.

BAPTISM

Baptism is the sign of the New Testament. This is shown by that very promise, "He who believes and is baptized will be saved" [Mark 16:16]. Therefore, when we are baptized, this promise is written, as it were, on our bodies. And since the signs are a type of allegory, this ceremony signifies repentance and the forgiveness of sins, or, as Paul calls it, regeneration. For immersion signifies that the Old Man, with his sin, was destined for death. And the coming up out of the water signifies that we who have now been washed clean await a new and eternal life and the righteousness acquired by Christ. The ceremony itself, then, as well as the promise, indicate the use. "He who believes and is baptized will be saved." Likewise the words which are used in Baptism, "I baptize you in the name of the Father, and of the Son, and of the Holy Spirit," that is, "With this sign I am making a covenant with you, and I testify that you have now been reconciled to God, that you are received by God, who is Father, Son, and Holy Spirit. The Father, moreover, receives you for the sake of the Son and promises you the Holy Spirit by whom He will vivify and sanctify you." Thus in the words themselves are included the broadest and most momentous promises and the sum of the Gospel. Therefore, this use of Baptism will last through one's whole life, so that we are convinced by this covenant that the forgiveness of sins and reconciliation have been set forth and given to us. For even when we fall away, the covenant into which we entered with God at one time is valid in those who repent, for the Gospel testifies that there is pardon for those who repent. Therefore, we will better understand the power and use of Baptism if, by constant meditation on this covenant, we exercise and strengthen our faith. Furthermore, the sign itself should not be repeated, for the repetition of the ceremony would profit nothing, and the sign which was received once is a continual mark and testimony, just as circumcision, performed once, was a continual testimony of the covenant, written on the body.

THE BAPTISM OF JOHN AND OF THE APOSTLES

Both Baptisms were a sign of the New Testament; there is no difference between the Baptism of John and that of the apostles, except that the Baptism of John testified to the Christ who would come, while the Baptism of the apostles testifies that Christ has already been manifested. Furthermore, both Baptisms are a ministry and require faith in Christ. By that faith, those who were baptized by John and those who were baptized by the apostles were equally sanctified and saved. Now, as for the saying of John, "I baptize with water for repentance, but the One who will come after me will baptize with the Holy Spirit and fire" [Matthew 3:11], he is making a distinction, not between the ministries or the ceremonies, but between the persons of the ministers and the person of Christ. For he testifies that Christ Himself is the Lord through whom Baptism is efficacious, who will give the Holy Spirit, who will give new and eternal life. John professes that he is the minister who merely uses the external sign and preaches the Word. Indeed, the external ministry of John is similar to that of the apostles and is equally valid in those who believe. Furthermore, this is true, that after the resurrection of Christ we have clearer testimonies that the Holy Spirit is given to the baptized, as the examples in the Book of Acts testify.

THE BAPTISM OF INFANTS

Paul commands us to test the spirits. And Christ teaches the rule, "From their fruits you will recognize them" [Matthew 7:16]. Indeed, wicked doctrines are the surest indications of a fanatical mind. Therefore, in judging those who condemn the Baptism of children, let us consider also what kind of marks they have. They have many wicked opinions, not only about Baptism, but also about other articles of Christian doctrine. They condemn many things in the civil realm, such as courts, oaths, the division of assets, etc. From this, it is sufficiently clear that they do not understand spiritual righteousness but imagine Christianity to be merely an external monasticism. Indeed, the Anabaptists born in recent years shamefully teach that a spouse should leave a spouse who is averse to the Anabaptist sect. And in other places they have already banished the legitimate magistrates through sedition. Likewise, they pretend that such a kingdom of Christ will exist on earth before the Last Day in which the saints will reign after all the wicked have been wiped out. These Jewish delusions are both seditious and wicked. Such marks must be carefully considered in order that the spirits may be tested. Therefore, since the Anabaptists embrace openly wicked opinions, they should be condemned and shunned.

In addition, they hold to many errors in the case of the Baptism of children. They deny original sin. This mark again indicates that they form judgments about sin and righteousness only according to a profane custom; they think that no sin exists except for actual sin. Therefore, since it is clear that the Anabaptists are driven by a fanatical spirit, let us not be moved by their authority so that we depart from the common consensus of the ancient Church about baptizing infants.

For the most ancient ecclesiastical writers approve of infant Baptism. Origen, commenting on Romans 6, writes this: "Therefore the Church has also received from the apostles the tradition of granting

Baptism to children. For they to whom the secrets of the divine mysteries were entrusted knew that there was a genuine filth of sin in all people which should be erased through water and the Spirit." These are Origen's words in which he testifies both that infants are baptized and that through Baptism they obtain the forgiveness of original sin. That is, they are reconciled to God.

Cyprian writes in the Council that a certain opinion was condemned which did not want to baptize infants before the eighth day. For the Synod decreed that infants were to be baptized; it was not necessary that the prescribed time of the eighth day be observed.

Augustine says of Baptism, *Contra Donatistas*, lib. 4: "Concerning the Baptism of children, which the whole Church supports and which was not instituted by councils but has always been upheld, it is most properly believed that it was handed down by none other than apostolic authority."

Likewise, "We can truthfully infer that the Sacrament of Baptism is valid in children based on the circumcision of the flesh which the former people received."

These and similar passages testify that the ancient Church approved the Baptism of infants. These passages must be noted, because there are not a few impostors who, in order to fool the illiterate, cite the fathers as if they disapprove of infant Baptism, although they do serious injury to the fathers. Secondly, this, too, should be observed: It is not safe to receive any dogma of which no testimony at all exists in the ancient Church.

But let us add still more reasons which prove that infants should be baptized. My reasoning is this:

> It is certain that the kingdom of God and the promise of the Gospel pertain to children;

There is, however, no salvation outside the Church, where there is neither Word nor Sacrament.

Therefore, children are to be grafted into the Church, and the sign is to be used which testifies that the promise pertains to them.

The major premise is certain, that the kingdom of Christ and the promise of the Gospel pertain to children. For Christ says, "Of such is the kingdom of heaven" [Matthew 19:14]. Likewise, "It is not the will before your Father who is in heaven that one of these little ones should perish" [Matthew 18:14]. Some would claim that Christ here promises nothing to children, but only wants us to imitate their simplicity. But these passages cannot be eluded with such sophistry; it is entirely inane. For clearly those passages are referring to those who are actually children according to age. And Christ says, "Their angels see the face of the Father" [Matthew 18:10]. He thus testifies that they are pleasing to God and that they are guarded by angels. How could this be said any more clearly? "It is not the will of God that one of these little ones should perish." This sentence sets forth the clear testimony of the Church concerning the salvation of children and should be most pleasant to us and diligently inculcated at the earliest age, so that this promise may be retained as long as possible. The law of circumcision also confirms the major premise, where God says, "I will be their God" [Genesis 17:8]. For God testifies that He favors those whom He commands to be circumcised, and He commands that infants be circumcised. But I think there is hardly anyone who would dare call the major premise into question. And yet, once the major premise is established, the remaining points can easily be defended.

Therefore, let us proceed to the minor premise. The minor premise is, "There is no salvation outside the Church, where the Word and the Sacraments are not." With this sentence, the adversaries can easily be refuted, for to us it is certain that there is salvation in the Church, while they cannot demonstrate that there is salvation outside the Church.

But all are agreed that there is no salvation outside the Church, for the Church is the kingdom of Christ in which Christ is efficacious through the Word and Sacraments, as Paul says in Ephesians 5, "Christ loved the Church and gave Himself for her, to sanctify her, cleansing her by the washing of water, etc." He does not describe the Church without the signs and without the Word. Therefore he says in another place, "One body and one Spirit, one Lord, one faith, one Baptism" [Ephesians 4:4–5]. All these things testify that those who belong to the Church have also been grafted into the Church by means of a certain external sign. The passage in Genesis concerning circumcision testifies to this same thing. "The male who is not circumcised in the flesh of his foreskin, that soul shall be erased from the people, for he has broken My covenant" [Genesis 17:14]. Here it clearly declares that he who does not have the sign is rejected by God. Moreover, circumcision was also a sign of the Church of God, just as Baptism now is. In summary, with regard to the minor premise, it is certain that children are saved in the Church. Therefore, let us conclude that the minor premise is sufficiently proven. The conclusion then follows: Children are to be baptized in order that, having received the sign, they may become members of the Church, and that God may bestow His promise on them. I think this argument satisfies noble and reasonable people.

To this point also pertains the declaration of Christ that sins are forgiven if the Church forgives them, according to the passage, "Whosoever sins you forgive, to them they shall be forgiven; and whosoever sins you retain, they shall be retained, etc." [John 20:23]. Therefore, it will also hold true for infants that sin is forgiven to them when the Church forgives them.

But our adversaries object, first, concerning faith: "Infants do not understand the Word; therefore they do not believe." They further contend that the Sacraments are of no benefit to them, because the Sacraments are of no benefit without faith. One must first oppose this argument with the example of the circumcised infants, who also did not understand the Word, and yet the covenant was valid, and they were pleasing to God Himself on account of the covenant. In addition, even though they do not understand the Word, one must admit from the above proposition that God is efficacious in them. For since it is certain that salvation and the kingdom of God belong to infants, it is also certain that God is efficacious in them, according to that passage, "Unless a person is born again of water and the Spirit" [John 3:5]. It is not our concern to investigate how God works in them. It is enough for us to maintain that salvation certainly applies to infants, from which it follows that God is efficacious in them.

They bring up another argument: "The Church should not institute anything as necessary for salvation without an express command of God. There is no command concerning the baptizing of infants. Therefore, they should not be baptized." I reply to the entire argument: First, the universal consensus of the Church of all times is the witness that this ordinance is apostolic in origin. Second, I reply to the minor premise: The minor premise must be denied. For the command is universal, "Baptize all nations" [Matthew 28:19]. Therefore, it includes children also.

Indeed, the Church has the finest and most weighty reasons for this interpretation. First, the Church knows that the promise of the Gospel also pertains to children. Likewise, it knows that salvation pertains only to children who are in the Church. Therefore, it judges that children must be grafted into the Church. Similarly, the Church knows that it has the command to forgive sins, and it knows that God forgives sins in this way: if the Church forgives them. Therefore, He bestows the forgiveness of sins on children also. In addition, the Church has the example of circumcision. If the infants at that time needed a sign in order to be grafted into the Church, then a sign is also needed now. For both signs signify the promise of grace, as Paul attests. These reasons have been drawn from the Scriptures. Therefore, the Church did not institute the Baptism of children by human authority, but uses it on the authority of the Scriptures.

If this response does not satisfy our adversaries, let us ask them, in turn, by what authority they disapprove the universal consensus of the Church and whether they think that children will be saved outside the Church. We have the general mandate of the Gospel. We also have most weighty arguments drawn from the Scriptures indicating that the general mandate also applies to children. For surely the benefit and promise of the Gospel apply to children. These things are sufficient for godly and reasonable men. Nor can our adversaries produce anything firmer than this, but they invent their opinion from their own minds, without the authority of Scripture or the Church.

Let us also add a third argument of the Anabaptists, although it is really so trivial it hardly needs to be mentioned: "Baptism is the covenant by which we promise the mortification of the flesh. Infants do not yet understand this, nor do they furnish it. Therefore, they are not to be baptized." The Monasterian Anabaptists make a great commotion over this argument. But the major premise was born of error, for they think that the Sacraments are merely signs of our own works or behavior; they do not understand that they are principally signs of God's will and promise toward us. The major premise, then, must be denied. For Baptism is principally a covenant of grace or of the divine promise toward us, by which He forgives us our sins. Infants, moreover, are in need of the forgiveness of the sin of origin, which we discussed sufficiently above. And in the ceremonies themselves, "I baptize you in the name of the Father, etc."—that is, I attest that you have now been reconciled to the God who is Father, Son, and Holy Spirit, etc.—no one says, "I baptize myself; my works are such and such, etc."

THE LORD'S SUPPER

There are various names for this Sacrament, but Paul calls it "the Lord's Supper" [1 Corinthians 11:20]. Later they called it the "Synaxis" because there was a common supper for the congregation in the Church. They also called it the "Eucharist," because this ceremony was instituted so that, when we use it, we may acknowledge the benefit of Christ; and that, having been admonished, we may be strengthened by faith and convinced that this Sacrament is being offered to us as a pledge which testifies that the forgiveness of sins is being given to us; and finally, that we may give thanks for such a great benefit.

Now, we said above that a Sacrament is a ceremony that has been added to a promise in which God offers us something. So also, this Supper is a Sacrament, for it should be understood that the ceremonies have been added to the entire sum of the Gospel, which is also enshrined in the very words, "This cup is the New Testament" [Luke 22:20], that is, the testimony of a new promise. The sum of the Gospel (or the promise) is also contained in these words, "This is My body, which is given for you." Likewise, "This is the blood which is shed for many for the forgiveness of sins." The main purpose, then, of this ceremony is to testify to us that the things promised in the Gospel are being offered; namely, the forgiveness of sins and justification for Christ's sake. For this is what we should see above all, that the Sacrament is a sign of grace, that this Supper is the sign of the New Testament. And what is the New Testament? Surely it is the promise of the forgiveness of sins and reconciliation for Christ's sake.

Secondly, this ceremony is beneficial in this way: when we add faith, that is, the faith by which we believe that the things promised are taking place; and when we are comforted and this spectacle is placed before our eyes and our minds, in order that it may urge us to believe and that faith may be awakened in us. For Christ testifies that His benefit applies to us when He bestows His body on us and joins us to Himself as members; no other bond can be closer than this. He likewise testifies that He will be efficacious in us, since He Himself is the Life and gives His blood in order to testify that He cleanses us. When we see these things happening in that most holy Supper, faith should be added. In this way, the use of the ceremony will be beneficial and will comfort and vivify the conscience. This use is individual; it applies equally to priests and to laymen, just as both groups have equal need of the forgiveness of sins and comfort. But the priests are ministers who offer the Sacrament to others. From these things, it is clear that the Lord's Supper is a Sacrament, for it is a sign that has been added to the promise of the Gospel. It is likewise clear what its principal purpose is, and that it does not profit simply on the basis of the work having been done, but that faith should be added in the use of it.

Let us also add something about preparation and who partakes of the Sacrament worthily. The Church long ago barred those who were guilty of manifest crimes from Communion, for this Sacrament should be used by those who repent. For here a testimony of the forgiveness of sins is set forth, whereby those who have terrified consciences should strengthen their faith after they have been admonished that those who repent are partaking worthily when they use the Sacrament. And yet they use it not relying on their own worthiness, but they believe that sins are forgiven to them gratis for Christ's sake, not on account of this work of partaking. But the partaking is a sign and pledge of that benefit. It is necessary to teach these things about the chief purpose, for others understand this ceremony to be only a sort of work in which we furnish something to God; nor do they refer to the promise; nor do they teach how it serves to exercise faith, how it serves to comfort consciences. Therefore, the chief purpose—the consolation of consciences—must be maintained.

Afterwards, other purposes should also be added, such as thanksgiving, in that we who have obtained the forgiveness of sins should give thanks for such great mercy. There is also the purpose of exhortation to doing good works, lest we pollute the bodies that have now been joined to the body of Christ. Likewise, the purposes pertaining to charity: Since we all are made members of one body of Christ, we should be devoted to one another with mutual love.

Concerning the use of this Sacrament, if the ancient practice of the Church had not been abolished, the judgment would be easy. For long ago there was one common Mass on fixed days in every one of the Churches, where the presbyter distributed the body and blood of the Lord to those who asked. I understand that in the Greek parishes, not even today are more Masses held than the one which is held by the pastor. They also argue over a metaphor, but I believe that Christ is truly present in His Sacrament and is efficacious there, as Hilary says, "The things which are taken and consumed cause Christ to be in us and us in Christ." And Cyril says, commenting on John 15, "From this it must be considered that Christ is in us, not only with regard to a disposition (*habitudine*), which is understood as love, but also by natural participation." Surely it is an amazing and enormous pledge of the highest love toward us, of the highest mercy, that Christ means to testify by means of this very Supper that He imparts Himself to us, that He joins us to Himself as members, that we may know that we are loved, cared for, and saved by Him. Minds should be convinced that Christ is efficacious in us in this way. The ancient writers diligently teach these things whenever they preach about the Sacrament.

If only we learned to measure with the mind and to contemplate the magnitude of this enormous gift so that we were truly grateful! Then we would both be strengthened in faith and, at the same time, become terribly frightened, considering what a great offense ingratitude is, what horrible punishments will follow the manifest abuses and profanation of the Sacrament. Nor should a person imagine that those solemn threats found in Paul's writings are in vain. God has always punished idolatry with great calamities, even in this life. Therefore, I think that the greatest part of the public sins in these last days must be reckoned to the profanation of this most holy gift. But in the last judgment, when the impiety of the world is publicly and openly seen, these abuses will cause a horrendous spectacle and will be punished with penalties more atrocious still, which human speech is unable to express. I once read about a certain pious man's vision two hundred years ago. Christ appeared to him with the appearance of one who had been thrashed with a scourge, with wounds and blood all over His body. The man was at first frightened and dismayed by this appearance. Afterward, when He had collected himself, he recognized that it signified every kind of abuse with which Christ is being afflicted. And when he asked what these wounds chiefly signify, Christ replied that this is how He is being thrashed by those who violate His body through the abuse of the Sacrament and of the Masses.

It is also reported that a vision was given to St. Anthony in which he saw pigs standing at altars around the world, administering the Sacrament. This vision signified also the abuses which later spread into the Church after his time. And it seems that the profanation will endure until the end of the world, as Daniel indicates, even though it will be partially revealed beforehand. May Christ grant that it also be felicitously corrected!

The Mass is discussed under a separate topic. I reject the opinion that has especially given birth to that unending profanation. For they have imagined that the offering in the Mass is a sacrifice which, when it has been applied on behalf of others, for the living and the dead, merits for them the forgiveness of guilt and punishment—and that, by simply performing the deed. By this sacrifice, they have even promised deliverance for the dead from the punishments of purgatory. These things not only contradict the Scriptures; they were also unknown to the ancient Church, and they obscure the doctrine of faith. But since I have decided under this topic to pass by this debate, I will say a few things about the matter of sacrifice, for it will be helpful for forming a judgment in this controversy, even as it is helpful to know the nature of sacrifice for judging many other things. But even if it seems childish to distinguish between the terms "sacrament" and "sacrifice," the issue at hand requires that a distinction be observed in the ceremonies, for they have different purposes. Some ceremonies are signs and marks of promises in which God offers us something, while others are not properly signs of promises, but works which we render to God.

It is necessary to observe these distinctions among ceremonies, no matter which terms we end up using. And since these terms, "sacrament" and "sacrifice," are in common use, we shall also retain them. Therefore, a sacrament is a ceremony which is the sign of a promise, through which God promises us something or offers us something. Circumcision was a sign by which God promised to receive the circumcised. Baptism is a sign by which God deals with us and receives us into grace, as if He were the one baptizing us. For the minister baptizes in the stead of Christ. A sacrifice is a ceremony or a work of ours which we render to God, that we may honor Him, that is, that we may testify that we acknowledge that the One to whom we furnish this obedience is truly God, and that we are, for that reason, furnishing this obedience to Him.

Moreover, the following two things are types of sacrifice; there are no more than these two. There is a propitiatory sacrifice, namely, a work which merits the forgiveness of guilt and eternal punishment for others; in other words, a work that reconciles God and appeases the wrath of God for others and makes satisfaction for guilt and eternal punishment. The other kind is a eucharistic sacrifice, which does not merit the forgiveness of sins or reconciliation, but is done by the reconciled in order that we may give thanks to God for the forgiveness of sins that we have received, and for His other benefits; that we may return thanks by means of this obedience of ours. This distinction can be sufficiently demonstrated from the Epistle to the Hebrews. For there it teaches that there was only one propitiatory sacrifice in the world. It remains, then, that all other sacrifices are works in which the reconciled should demonstrate their obedience.

Indeed, all the Levitical sacrifices can be divided into these two types that I have mentioned. For certain things in the Law were called propitiatory sacrifices on account of the thing they pointed to or the thing they resembled. They did not merit the forgiveness of sins before God, but pointed to the future sacrifice of Christ. But they did merit the forgiveness of sins in the people's external life, that is, that they should not be excluded from the civil society of Moses. Therefore, the sacrifices for sin, for trespasses, and the whole burnt offering were said to be propitiatory. But the other sacrifices were thanksgivings: offerings, drink offerings, retributions, first fruits, tithes.

There was, in fact, only one propitiatory sacrifice in the world, namely, the suffering and death of Christ, as the Epistle to the Hebrews teaches, "It is impossible for the blood of bulls and goats to take away sins" [Hebrews 10:4]. And a little later concerning the will of Christ, "By that will we were sanctified, through the offering of the body of Christ once, etc." [Hebrews 10:10]. For Christ Himself also applies His sacrifice to us when He prays for us in John 17, "I sanctify Myself for them, that they, too, may be sanctified in the truth. And I do not pray for them only, but also for those who will believe in Me through their words." Behold, these are the words of our Pontiff and Priest with which He offers Himself for the whole Church and prays for it. We should always keep these words in view and in the forefront of our mind. Isaiah also interprets the Law in this way, that we may know that the death of Christ—not the ceremonies of the Law—is truly the satisfaction or expiation for our sins. Therefore he says in chapter 53, "After He gives His soul as an offering for trespasses, He will see His seed prolonged, etc." In other words, "Another offering remains which will truly take away sin and death. Therefore, the customary ceremonies do not take away sin and death." Paul referred to this passage when he said, "He was made a curse" [Galatians 3:13]. Likewise, "Concerning sin, He condemned sin" [Romans 8:3], that is, He punished and erased sin through His offering for sin. For the Hebrews call the offering itself "sin" or "trespass," just as the Latin calls it a "crime" (*piaculum*). Therefore, let us maintain that there was only one propitiatory sacrifice in the world. For those things which were called propitiatory in the Law, as I have said, were so called on account of the thing they resembled. Therefore, they were abolished after Christ appeared. Furthermore, since the Gospel was promised in order that it might offer the true propitiation, it is necessary that the Levitical ceremonies were not true propitiations, since they came to an end when the Gospel was revealed.

EUCHARISTIC SACRIFICE

The sacrifices that now remain are eucharistic sacrifices, which are called "sacrifices of praise": the preaching of the Gospel, faith, invocation, thanksgiving, confession, the afflictions of the saints—indeed, all the good works of the saints. These sacrifices are not satisfactions for those who do them, nor can they be applied to others in order to merit for them the forgiveness of sins or reconciliation simply by performing the work. Therefore, besides the one propitiatory sacrifice, namely, the death of Christ, the other sacrifices in the New Testament are only eucharistic, as Peter teaches in 1 Peter 2, "A holy priesthood, that you may offer spiritual sacrifices." Spiritual sacrifices are contrasted not only with animals, but also with human works offered simply by performing the work, that is, without faith and a good attitude of the heart. For "spiritual" signifies the impulses of the Holy Spirit in us. The Epistle to the Hebrews, chapter 13, also speaks of these sacrifices: "Through Him let us always offer to God a sacrifice of praise." And he adds the interpretation: "The fruit of lips which confess His name," that is, invocation, thanksgiving, confession, and similar things. These things avail, not by simply performing the work, but on account of faith. This is taught in the phrase, "through Him let us offer," that is, by faith in Christ. It is, moreover, a notable comfort for the Christian mind to know that all our good works and all our afflictions are sacrifices, that is, works that please God and with which God declares that He is honored.

Indeed, concerning this kind of sacrifice there are many statements in the Psalms and Prophets, such as Psalm 50, "Offer to God a sacrifice of praise… Call upon Me in the day of trouble, etc." Likewise in Psalm 51, "The sacrifice to God is a broken spirit, etc."

Second, we must understand that the worship of the New Testament is spiritual. That is, it is the righteousness of faith and the fruits of faith. For the New Testament brings righteousness and life that is spiritual and eternal, according to that passage, "I will place My Law in their hearts" [Jeremiah 31:33]. And Christ says, "The true worshipers will worship the Father in spirit and truth" [John 4:23], that is, with the true affection of the heart. The Levitical worship forms have been abrogated, for they must be replaced with spiritual acts: with the worship that takes place in the mind and with the fruits and signs of such worship.

From these things it follows that there is no sacrifice or worship of the New Testament that merits anything for the doer by simply performing the work or that merits the forgiveness of sins for others. For such would disagree with the saying, "The true worshipers will worship the Father in spirit and truth, etc." Indeed, it is a Pharisaical persuasion, that a certain act of worship merits the forgiveness of sins simply by performing the work. And since, by this persuasion, the Jews accumulated their own forms of worship so that many things merited grace and other benefits, the prophets sharply cried out in protest against the heaping up of sacrifices. Psalm 50, which repudiates sacrifices and requires invocation, condemns this persuasion. "Surely I will not chew on the flesh of bulls, etc." And Isaiah 1, "To what end is the multitude of your sacrifices to Me?" Also Jeremiah 7, "I did not speak with your fathers, and I did not instruct them concerning burnt offerings and sacrifices." Now, clearly the Law does give instructions about sacrifices. But the Prophet here condemns the persuasion about simply performing the work; God does not require sacrifices like these. Now Masses have been accumulated in the Church according to a similar opinion, that they are sacrifices which please God simply by performing the work, and that they merit for the doer and for others the forgiveness of sins. For they taught that the application of Christ's sacrifice takes place through the Mass. But each one applies to himself the sacrifice of Christ by his own faith, and this, indeed, is done gratis, that is, not on account of the work of another.

Besides this, there can be many purposes for a single work. We use the Lord's Supper as a Sacrament, insofar as it is a testimony by which faith is strengthened. Second, this very faith, combined with the external work, is a kind of sacrifice, for God declares in the New Testament that this faith and other such exercises are sacrifices of praise and acts of worship. So this same spiritual obedience becomes a sort of sacrifice by which the honor that God requires and approves is given to Him. In the third place, there is necessarily combined with this faith the giving of thanks for that supreme benefit which has been conferred on us and the whole Church. This is also where the name "Eucharist" comes from. Fourth, the same work is also a confession. For we show that we believe the Gospel and invite others to believe by our example. All these things are eucharistic sacrifices, which is why the ancients called this ceremony a sacrifice.

Moreover, they are wrong who claim that it is the nature of every sort of sacrifice that it can be applied on behalf of other people. For our afflictions are sacrifices, and yet, they should not be applied on behalf of others, according to that passage, "Each one will receive the reward for his work" [1 Corinthians 3:8]. Likewise, "Let each one examine his own work, and thus he will have glory in himself" [Galatians 6:4]. Also, "The just shall live by his faith" [Romans 1:17]. The same thing is proven in the parable of the foolish virgins, etc. In addition, our works cannot be applied on behalf of others, because our works are acts of worship which we ourselves owe to God, as Paul says, "We are debtors" [Romans 8:12]. Likewise, "Woe to me if I do not preach the Gospel" [1 Corinthians 9:16]. Furthermore, they cannot be applied on behalf of others, because they are insufficient in and of themselves, and faith is needed, which asks that our weakness not be imputed to us. This would be pure arrogance if we thought that such works are not only rewards for us, but also for others. For Christ says, "When you have done everything, say, 'We are useless servants'" [Luke 17:10]. Likewise in Psalm 50, calling upon God in the day of trouble is called a sacrifice and a thanksgiving. Furthermore, when we give thanks, that work is not a work which we ourselves can apply on behalf of others so that it profits them because the work is so worthy. Therefore, it is a false opinion concerning the nature of every kind of sacrifice, that it can be applied on behalf of others. For only the propitiatory sacrifice of Christ is to be applied on behalf of others; our sacrifices, which are eucharistic, benefit those who do them, just as anyone's own good work benefits the doer. They are not to be applied so that they merit the forgiveness of sins, etc., for other people.

It should be added that prayers for others consist in something different than the nature of works. For they do not bring to God some work which serves as the price for others, but only desire to receive from God. God has promised, moreover, that He will give both to us and to others for whom we ask. These things can easily be distinguished. In prayer, we do not set some work of ours before God, nor do we offer anything to God as a price for others; we merely wish to receive from God, and that, of course, for the sake of Christ the Mediator, as the text says, "Whatever you ask the Father in My name, He will give you" [John 16:23]. It is one thing to deal with God by faith, not on account of some work of ours; it is another thing to set before God the merit of a work and to do so for others. Therefore, the application of our works on behalf of others, especially for the forgiveness of sins, should never be conceded, for it is written, "The just shall live by his faith" [Romans 1:17].

Something else must be understood. Just as some are punished for the sins of others, so also the righteousness of a few bestows many blessings on others. There are many testimonies and examples of each of these cases in the Scriptures, as in Jeremiah 49: "Behold, those who were not under judgment to drink the cup, drinking they will drink." Isaiah speaks about public and private benefits in chapter 33, "He who walks in righteousness and speaks the truth, who abandons greed and injustice and keeps his hands from all bribery, who hardens his ears, lest he hear bloodshed, and who closes his eyes, lest he see evil, he shall dwell on high; the rocky heights will be his fortification; bread will be given to him; his waters will not be lacking. His eyes will see the king in his beauty, and distant ends of the earth." Here, among other rewards, he promises a more tranquil public state, that is, a common benefit pertaining to many people. There are other examples. On account of David's sin, the people were punished. For the sake of a few righteous men, God would spare Sodom. For the sake of Naaman, Syria benefited. Therefore, let us learn that penalties and rewards extend far and wide, in order that we may be stirred up to good works.

However, in such passages, these two things must be remembered. First, that these passages do not pertain to justification. That is, the foreign works of the saints do not benefit the unrighteous for justification. But they do bestow many common blessings on the righteous, because we are members of one body. Second, it does not belong to us to apply our merits to others, for this would be a kind of trust in our own work. But we should allow God to decide which common or individual rewards He will give us. However, prayer is applied on behalf of others, for it depends not on our own worthiness, but on the gratuitous promise of Christ. From these things, it can easily be determined what should be concluded with regard to the application. As it pertains to justification, there is no application without a person's own faith. But faith uses instruments—the Word and the Sacraments—which testify that the benefit of Christ pertains to us. And this benefit does not depend on the worthiness of some other human work.

Let it suffice to have provided these reasonable comments about the Mass.

REPENTANCE

It is useful to list the Sacrament of Penance also among the Sacraments, so that, having been made more illustrious in its own topic, it may be better known and appreciated within the Church. First, however, the Novatians and the Cathars[29] must be refuted in this place. They denied that those who had fallen away after Baptism could again obtain the forgiveness of sins. This heresy, too, was born of an ignorance of sin and of the righteousness of faith. For since the Cathars did not acknowledge that sin inheres in man's nature, they imagined that they were without sin. And, therefore, they pretended that they were righteous by means of their own cleanness. They also failed to understand the righteousness of faith, which affirms that we continually need the forgiveness of sins.

First, then, we shall list the testimonies which demonstrate that those who have fallen away after Baptism can again obtain the forgiveness of sins, and that the Church should impart absolution to them when they repent. Innumerable examples can be gathered from the Old and the New Testaments. David, Manasseh, and Peter obtained forgive-

---

29   The Cathars (also known as the Albigensians) were a twelfth century Gnostic sect which flourished in southern France.

ness after their denials. Peter obtained forgiveness again after he had fallen and was reproved by Paul. The Church of the Galatians also fell and was called back to repentance by Paul. Similarly, Paul himself commands that the Corinthian man who was guilty of incest be received back after he repented (2 Corinthians 2). Let us add also some sayings of Scripture. Ezekiel 33, "As I live, I do not desire the death of the sinner." Indeed, there are many sermons of this kind which exhort those who have fallen after justification to repentance. But this one from Ezekiel is notable, for the solemn oath is added, "As I live," that consciences may be the more powerfully strengthened by it when they hear, not merely a promise, but also a promise that has been confirmed by an oath. Therefore, the Novatians accuse God of perjury when they deny that sins are remitted to the fallen. It is a great comfort in the face of despair when we see how solemnly God requires us to believe that we are forgiven by adding a sworn oath. Nor is there any weight to that sophistry which claims that the Old Testament had this benefit, while the New Testament lacks it. For the prophet's sermon pertains to the whole Church. There is not one kind of forgiveness of sins in the Old Testament and another in the New, nor is the spiritual Church a different one.

Now let us take up the proofs from the New Testament. Christ says in Matthew 18, "If your brother sins against you, rebuke him, etc. If he listens to you, you will win your brother." When Christ says, "You will win your brother," He clearly declares that He is talking about those to whom that correction is beneficial. And He also attests that He is speaking about brothers, that is, those who have fallen away after justification, in that He only wants him to be cast out of the Church if he fails to listen. And then, when Peter asks, "How many times shall I forgive?", Christ responds, "Seventy times seven." Therefore, those who have fallen away after justification can obtain forgiveness. For when He commands the Church to forgive, He means that He Himself forgives, as noted above, "You will win your brother." Likewise, the Church prays daily, "Forgive us our debts." Therefore, even after he has been justified, the one who has fallen away obtains forgiveness. Galatians 6, "If a man is caught in some sin, you who are spiritual correct him with a spirit of gentleness." Here the apostle teaches that those who have fallen are to be called back to repentance. Therefore, he understands that repentance is profitable to them. In Luke 15, Christ says, "There will be joy for the angels over one sinner who repents, etc." And, in that sermon, He is speaking about the repentance of the lost son, that is, about people who were previously righteous. Revelation 2, "Remember from where you have fallen, and repent, and do the former works." These passages sufficiently prove that those who have fallen after justification can again obtain the forgiveness of sins.

But the Novatians counter with two passages from the Epistle to the Hebrews. Hebrews 6, "It is impossible for those who were once enlightened, etc., to be restored to repentance." While this passage may seem harsh, yet, if the conscience is fortified ahead of time with the true testimonies cited above, it will not allow itself to be disturbed by this passage. Indeed, the whole epistle would better be rejected than to deny forgiveness to the fallen. For there was also some doubt among the ancients concerning the author of this epistle. Once we know, then, from the above testimonies that forgiveness is not to be denied to the fallen, it can easily be determined that the saying here cannot simply be accepted at face value, but that a proper interpretation must be added. Another passage softens this one, as is done in obscure or ambiguous passages. In Greek it does not sound so improper, for it says, "It is not possible for those who crucify Christ anew and hold Him in derision to be restored." This can most simply be understood in this way: Such people who no longer listen to the Gospel, but despise it, nor are zealous to retain those beginnings of piety of which he spoke, namely, the doctrine of Baptism and repentance, cannot be restored. It seems to me that this is the genuine interpretation of this passage, and there is nothing improper about it. At the present time, they cannot be restored while they do not listen to the Gospel but are crucifying Christ. If anyone does not find this interpretation satisfactory, let him understand that the writer to the Hebrews is speaking of blasphemies. For he has used extraordinarily frightening words when he says that those who crucify Christ again and hold Him in derision cannot be restored. These are not sins of weakness; they are blasphemies, such as the sayings of the Epicureans and obstinate men who, against their conscience, persecute the Word of God. They reject admonition and repentance from God, securely celebrating their triumph and congratulating themselves for this piece of wisdom, that they dare to deride God. Nor is it valid to reason that, since the sin of blasphemy is not forgiven, therefore, no sin is forgiven. Indeed, Christ adds a distinction in order to testify that other sins are forgiven. Matthew 12, "Whoever says a word against the Son of Man, he will be forgiven." The passage in John's Epistle can then be understood, "He who sins a sin toward death, for him I do not say that you should pray" [1 John 5:16].

But we shall speak about blasphemy soon. First we must say something about the second passage. Hebrews 10, "To those who sin intentionally after receiving knowledge of the truth, there no longer remains a victim for sins, but the terrible expectation of judgment." There is nothing at all troublesome in this passage. For it does not deny that those who have fallen away can be restored; it simply makes an immediate antithesis between the benefit of Christ and judgment, namely, so that it excludes other victims and new sacrifices, etc., in this sense: After we have obtained the benefit of Christ, if we do not retain it, then the alternative necessarily follows, namely, that we pay the penalties in judgment. This passage does not deny that the fallen can return to the benefit of Christ; it merely sets up the benefit of Christ on the one hand, and judgment on the other hand, as the two alternatives. He who loses the benefit of Christ is subject to judgment. What is more, it says this for the purpose of exhorting men to do good, lest they securely go on doing evil under the notion that they can easily expiate their sins with new forms of worship and works, as they were expiated under the Law for uncleanness against the Law. Therefore, it commands men to retain the benefit of Christ and to beware lest they lose it or be prohibited from returning to it. This is the simple and genuine understanding.

THE SIN AGAINST THE HOLY SPIRIT

Augustine sometimes understands the sin against the Holy Spirit to be final impenitence among the enemies or despisers of the Church. At other times, he understands it to be despair, adding the following rationale for this interpretation, which seems very reasonable: "These sins are properly at odds with grace. For when we flee for refuge to grace, the other sins are forgiven. But persecution on the one hand, or despair on the other, rejects grace." Therefore, this is how he interprets the saying of Christ, "He who speaks a word against the Holy Spirit" [Matthew 12:32]: He who finally rejects the word of grace, which has been preached and confirmed by the testimonies of the Holy Spirit, etc., is guilty of an unforgivable sin. This understanding of Augustine is reasonable. For not every falling away after a person has acknowledged the truth should be judged to be an unforgivable sin. For above we recounted examples and testimonies which teach that such fallen ones can be forgiven. Nor should every persecution of the Gospel be judged to be an unforgivable sin, for Manasseh, Paul, and others obtained forgiveness.

Indeed, both statements should be retained. First, we should consider the following statement to be certain: All sins are forgiven to believers. For the forgiveness of sins is universal, according to that passage, "that everyone who believes in Him should not perish" [John 3:16]. Likewise, "Grace abounded more than sin" [Romans 5:20]. Also, "He is the propitiation for sins, not for ours only, but for the whole world" [1 John 2:2]. Therefore, if anyone denies that the sacrifice of Christ is valid for his sins, he hurls insults at Christ. This, too, is an insult, to conclude that the reign of sin is more powerful than the reign of grace and of Christ. Therefore, we should consider this statement to be sure and certain: All sins are forgiven to believers.

Now I come to the second statement, and this one, too, should be upheld: There is a certain sin that is unforgivable, or, as John calls it, a "sin unto death" [1 John 5:16]. But what that sin is is not for us or for the Church to decide. For that must only be established *a posteriore*: Such a sin does not exist in those who come to repentance and faith.

From these things it is quite clear that men are not deterred from repentance by that threat of Christ, for it applies only to those who do not return to faith. And the corollary is also true, that forgiveness of sins is promised to all who come to faith. This comparison shows in general what the unforgivable sin is, or rather, in whom it is, namely, only in those who do not come to repentance and faith. Many passages testify to this. In the Epistle to Titus, "You shall shun a heretical man after one and a second admonition, for he is condemned by his own judgment" [Titus 3:10]. Likewise, concerning the hardened in Romans 11, "The rest have been hardened. He gave them an enraged spirit, eyes that they may not see; they always bend their back." These passages describe obstinate men who persevere in persecuting the Gospel, who, although they have been warned and convicted by the testimonies of the Holy Spirit (that is, by miracles or clear passages of Scripture), yet they do not stop defending and confirming their manifest impiety, just as Pharaoh, undeterred by so many miracles, continued to rage and rave against the Israelites, as the Jews also did against Christ and the apostles. One after another, the obstinate enemies of the Gospel are similar in every age. This is a simple and, in my judgment, useful interpretation, drawn from a comparison, namely, since this universal statement is certain—that all sins are forgiven to believers—therefore the unforgivable sin must be transferred to those who do not come to faith.

Therefore, since the Church has this testimony—that all sins are forgiven to believers—and since it likewise has the command to absolve them, may our consciences not be troubled over what the unforgivable sin is, but let them obey the commandment of God concerning repentance and faith. When we do this, we will know with certainty that we are not guilty of the unforgivable sin, according to that notable passage, "This is a faithful saying and worthy of all acceptance, that Christ Jesus came into this world to save sinners" [1 Timothy 1:15].

I return now to a description of repentance. There is no need to quarrel over the word, for in accord with the Church's custom we use it for conversion, or renewal. The word may otherwise be aptly applied to that part which they call contrition, for to the grammarian, repentance (*poenitentia*) means to think differently than before; or to disapprove of that which was formerly pleasing; also, to be sorrowful for having gone astray. The Scriptures refer either to contrition or to the whole renewal as repentance. The Scholastics have numbered three parts of repentance: contrition, confession, and satisfaction. We shall explain in order what the right understanding is concerning each of these parts. For the sake of instruction, we treat repentance in two parts: contrition and faith. If someone wants to add a third, which is really the effect of repentance, namely, the whole newness of life and behavior, I will not object. But we have found it expedient to place faith between the parts, so that this very division may immediately teach people about faith. For when the forgiveness of sins is treated, it is necessary to speak at the same time about faith. But the Scholastic teachers make practically no mention of faith in this topic, and for this reason they have passed along errors which should not be ignored.

Let us speak first, then, about contrition. We define contrition as the true terrors and pains of the conscience which thinks that God is angry with sin, and which is grieved that it has sinned. Scripture preaches about this aspect when it says, "Repent!" Likewise, "The Holy Spirit will convict the world concerning sin, etc." [John 16:8]. And 2 Corinthians 7, "You were grieved unto repentance." And Romans 1, "The wrath of God is revealed against all wickedness." Joel 2, "Rend your hearts and not your garments." And Isaiah [57:15], "Where will the Lord dwell? In the contrite and humbled spirit." Likewise, "Cease to do evil" [Isaiah 1:16]. The Psalms are full of examples. Psalm 38, "For my iniquities have gone over my head; like a heavy burden, they have weighed me down." Likewise, "The fear of the Lord is the beginning of wisdom" [Psalm 111:10]. And in several places the Scripture joins fear and faith. "The Lord is well-pleased with those who fear Him, and toward those who trust in His mercy" [Psalm 147:11].

These and similar passages testify that contrition is necessary, and, indeed, should increase in such a way that we acknowledge, not only our external offenses, but also our inner uncleanness. Therefore, there is no repentance in secure hypocrites who are not affected by any grief and who, meanwhile, flatter themselves as if they had no vices. Christ condemns this security often and most severely: "Unless you repent, you will all likewise perish, etc." [Luke 13:3]. Moreover, these terrors and griefs are worked in us through the Word of God, which rebukes sins. Sins are also rebuked by the Gospel, as Paul says, "Now the wrath of God is revealed, etc." [Romans 1:18]. The Gospel uses the ministry of the Law for the same purpose, as Paul says, "Through the Law is the knowledge of sin" [Romans 3:20]. This is how repentance begins. But unless faith, which cheers and comforts the mind again, is added to these terrors, contrition—that is, these sorrows—will result in eternal death. Therefore, consciences must be taught not only about contrition, but also about faith.

The second part, then, is faith, which is not only a knowledge of history and of the Law, but the trust with which each one believes that sins are forgiven to him gratis for the sake of Christ. This faith is necessary for obtaining the forgiveness of sins, as the testimonies which we will gather shortly will reveal. This faith distinguishes between the contrition of Peter and of Judas, of David and of Saul. The contrition of Judas and Saul was not profitable, because they did not add this faith. The contrition of Peter and David was profitable, because faith was added, with which they grasped the promised mercy and comforted themselves.

This faith distinguishes between servile and filial fear. For there is no need here to subtly argue about attrition or contrition, when fear arises from love and when it is a fear of punishment, for these impulses are also commingled in the saints. But the description is simple and clear. Servile fear is fear without faith. Filial fear is the fear to which faith is added, which, in the midst of distresses, cheers and comforts the mind.

From these things it is clear that we retain and absolutely require contrition, and yet we must assess the labyrinthine errors which are destructive to consciences—the errors taught by the Scholastics with regard to contrition. For what they claim about contrition is false; namely, that the forgiveness of sins is granted on account of the worthiness of contrition. For consciences would be driven to despair if, in genuine terrors, they were to think that they did not have the forgiveness of sins unless their sorrow were sufficiently worthy and adequate.

In the second place, those inextricable labyrinths must also be rejected in which they say that contrition merits the forgiveness of sins only when it comes from the love of God, not when it comes from fear of punishment. And yet they admit that it is uncertain when it comes from the love of God. Thus they leave consciences uncertain. Even the creators of these labyrinths are unable to unravel them. Therefore, we affirm that contrition is necessary. Then we add that this contrition does not merit the forgiveness of sins. That is, the forgiveness of sins is not granted on account of the worthiness of contrition, but faith should be added, which is convinced that sins are forgiven gratis, for Christ's sake. And, of course, this faith should be convinced in particular that sins are forgiven to you. It is not enough to believe in general that God forgives certain people. The devil also believes that. For he is not unaware that there is forgiveness of sins in the Church. But each one of us should be convinced that we ourselves are forgiven. We are speaking about this special faith with which each one applies the benefit of Christ to himself.

I offer the following testimonies.

Acts 10, "To Him all the prophets testify that all who believe in Him receive the forgiveness of sins through His name." This is a plain and clear statement that the forgiveness of sins is given for Christ's sake and that by this faith we should be convinced about Christ.

Romans 5, "Having been justified by faith, we have peace," that is, peaceful and tranquil consciences, etc.

But someone will say, "I know that faith is needed, but it must still be proven that sins are forgiven gratis." This is the crux (*epitasis*) of the matter, in the conscience, too. For no one is unaware that God is merciful and forgives sins. What we doubt is whether He will forgive us our sins in spite of the fact that we are unworthy. Therefore, it is necessary to keep in view the testimonies which confirm us so that we are convinced of these two things, namely, that the promise is universal, and then also gratuitous. Romans 3, "Having been justified gratis by His grace, through the redemption that is in Christ Jesus, whom God set forth as a propitiation by faith." This passage clearly adds the exclusive little word "gratis," which does not exclude good works, but transfers the cause of the forgiveness of sins from our worthiness to Christ, that the promise may be certain. Therefore, we must be certain that the forgiveness of sins is granted, not on account of the worthiness of our contrition or of our works, but only by trust in the benefit of Christ. Ephesians 2, "By grace you have been saved… It is the gift of God, not from yourselves." Romans 8, "Since it was impossible for the Law, God sent His Son, etc." That is, since we never satisfy the Law, the Law always accuses us. Therefore, we cannot set our worthiness against the wrath and judgment of God, but we should only set against it Christ the Mediator, as it says in Romans 5, "Through Him we have access to the Father, etc." Paul also argues thus in Romans 4, "Gratis by faith, that the promise may be firm." For if reconciliation depended on the worthiness of our contrition or of our works, since we never satisfy the Law, the promise of reconciliation would be in vain.

Many passages from the Psalms and Prophets apply here. Psalm 32, "I said, I will confess against myself my unrighteousness to the Lord, and You forgive the wickedness of my sin." Psalm 143, "No one living will be justified in Your sight." These and similar passages teach that we cannot set our worthiness against the judgment of God, but that we need gratuitous mercy.

It is clear, then, that faith is needed in the forgiveness of sins, and that faith should rely, not on our own worthiness, but only on the benefit of Christ. By this faith, hearts are freed from the terrors of sin and from hell, and, in that consolation, the Holy Spirit is bestowed on us and we are made alive. Therefore Paul says, "The sting of death is sin; the power of sin is the Law. But thanks be to God, who gives us the victory through our Lord Jesus Christ" [1 Corinthians 15:56].

I have thus far spoken about contrition and the faith by which we obtain the forgiveness of sins. I have divided repentance into these two parts all the more gladly for the sake of teaching, so that, as with a sort of summary, I might indicate the two chief parts of the whole Scripture, which at times rebukes sins, and at times promises comfort, etc. Moreover, when we have been reconciled in this way, then the righteousness of a good conscience should ensue, as John says, "Produce fruits worthy of repentance" [Matthew 3:8]. And Paul writes, "We are debtors, not to the flesh, etc." [Romans 8:12]. And yet, since we do not satisfy the Law, the conscience meanwhile should always retain this benefit, that a person is righteous—that is, acceptable—by faith, for Christ's sake, and that the works that follow are pleasing and are righteousness, because the person is reconciled. These things have been treated more fully above. Therefore, I shall move on to the remaining parts which they include here: confession and satisfaction.

CONFESSION

Ordinary confession and satisfaction arose from the ecclesiastical rite of public repentance. For long ago, those who were guilty of public crimes were excommunicated and were not taken back unless they first confessed; that is, unless they first testified in the presence of the pastors that they would mend their ways, seeking absolution, etc. Satisfaction was also added, that is, a certain public chastisement, either for the sake of example, so that others, having been cautioned, might be careful not to fall, or so that the mind of those who were returning to the Church might be investigated to see whether they were truly sorry. From these rites, ordinary confession arose, and now the term "satisfaction" is left.

But let us speak first about confession. Confession is not necessary. Nor is the enumeration of sins commanded by divine Law, for there is no command in the Scriptures concerning this matter. Not only that, but such an enumeration of sins is impossible, according to that passage, "Who understands his trespasses?" [Psalm 19:12]. The more prudent canonists also testify the same thing, that this enumeration is not a matter of divine Law. Finally, the Greek Church already abolished this practice long ago on account of a certain woman who was defiled by a deacon, as the *Historia tripartita* recounts. But this practice could not have been abolished if it were of divine Law. Since, then, it is clear how greatly tortured consciences were by the harsh requirement of enumeration, it is useful to warn pious minds so that they know that the canon which gives instructions about enumeration is only a human tradition.

Furthermore, it is useful to retain confession in the churches, first, on account of the absolution, of which we will speak shortly. Secondly, also on account of discipline, for it is an opportunity for the unlearned to be heard and better instructed about all doctrine. Indeed, it is shameful that those who are entirely unexamined go to Communion. And yet consciences must know that they are not to be burdened with an enumeration of trespasses, for they can also seek both absolution and counsel without it.

But someone will object, "The judge does not absolve anyone unless he first makes an inquisition. Here an absolution is taking place. Therefore, it is also necessary that there be an inquiry and enumeration of crimes."

To this one should respond as follows. There is a twofold authority of pastors. The one is called the ministry by which they impart to us the Gospel and the Sacraments and announce the forgiveness of sins publicly and privately. This authority is not a command to make an inquisition nor is it a judgment, but only a command to impart the benefit and absolution. Therefore, it also pertains to secret sins, even those which we ourselves do not remember. Therefore, this administration does not require an inquisition, for it is not a judgment.

The other authority is called jurisdiction. This is a certain external judgment of the Church which pertains only to manifest crimes. It is the power to excommunicate and absolve. Here a sentence cannot be rendered unless an inquisition is made. For no one should be excommunicated in the presence of the Church unless his crime is known, nor should anyone be absolved unless the matter is investigated, that is, unless it is clear that he has changed his ways for the better. But even this is not a judgment of the conscience, but of the external behavior.

This distinction between the ministry and external jurisdiction must be carefully observed. For the ministry of the Gospel pertains to the conscience. The fact that the Gospel can be publicly and privately applied to all is attested in the very passage, "Whose soever sins you forgive, to them shall they be forgiven" [John 20:23]. Likewise, "How many times shall my brother sin against me and I forgive him?" [Matthew 18:21]. He is speaking about the forgiveness which God approves. Therefore, private absolution brings great comfort. For it applies the Gospel and testifies that the benefit of the Gospel pertains to us. Some people cry out that men cannot forgive sins. That is true, except insofar as they announce the Word in the place of God. But the Gospel is a command to forgive sins, both publicly and privately. For in the Sacraments, too, men forgive sins as ministers. To say, "I baptize you," is no different than to say, "I forgive you your sins." For the Sacraments, too, are applications of the Gospel which testify that the benefit of the Gospel pertains to us. Faith should believe, not only that forgiveness is granted to some people in general, but each one should believe that forgiveness is granted to him, etc. As Christ says, "Your faith has saved you" [Luke 7:50]. And Paul, "Having been justified by faith, we have peace, etc." [Romans 5:1].

The remaining arguments concerning confession can easily be settled. It should be observed that the word "confession" is repeated several times in the Scriptures. The confession of sins most commonly and properly signifies the recognition of sins, that is, the immense sorrow with which we acknowledge sin before God from the heart and seek mercy. For example, "For I know my iniquity, and my sin is always against me." And Psalm 38, "There is no health in my flesh from the face of Your wrath; there is no peace for my bones from the face of my sins." And later, "For I shall announce my iniquity." This confession, described in such passages, is properly that very contrition of which we spoke above. For it signifies the confession of the heart; that is, the sorrows which exist when we truly acknowledge sin. Moreover, these passages teach that there are true sorrows in this confession or contrition.

Therefore, there is no repentance in those who are, as Paul calls them, *apelgekotes* – "past feeling," nor are they afflicted with any sorrow or fear of the wrath of God, but indulge securely in their own sinful desires, like brute beasts born for slaughter. For this is how Peter describes men who are wickedly secure.

SATISFACTION

Long ago in the Church, infamous sinners were not taken back without some sort of public chastisement, which they called "satisfaction." Although this custom has already been out of use for a long time, the term remains, along with a certain trace of the old custom which has given birth to many debates. Those ancient spectacles of public repentance were a sort of external and societal discipline of the Church, instituted by human authority, which did not pertain to the conscience or to the forgiveness of sins before God. But unlearned men—as happens in many other affairs—turned a societal matter into a spiritual one and pretended that satisfactions were necessary for the forgiveness of sins before God. We will mention briefly what should be thought of this whole affair, for it is also beneficial in this matter to refute the errors which place consciences in peril. Certain things should be said here concerning the difference between the forgiveness of guilt and of punishment, for it is useful for these things to be taught in the Church.

First, then, it must be understood that no mention is being made here of civil satisfactions, as when we say that satisfaction must be made to those whose property we have seized. These works are not unjustified, but are necessary and pertain to contrition, according to that passage, "Cease to do evil" [Isaiah 1:16]. For satisfactions in this topic define works that are not owed—works by which the punishment of purgatory or certain other temporal punishments are supposed to be paid off. For this is what the Scholastics say: "Since God is merciful, He forgives guilt; but since He is also just and an avenger, He changes eternal punishment into the temporal punishment of purgatory." Then they add that some of those punishments are forgiven by the power of the Keys, while some must be paid off with satisfactions. This is the sum of their fabrication. On the one hand, they rightly admit that guilt is not forgiven on account of satisfactions. But then they proceed to fantasize about paying off eternal punishment. It is an error to think that eternal punishments are forgiven on account of our compensations, and it is still more absurd for them to imagine that such penalties are forgiven on account of works that are not owed.

Therefore, we combine the forgiveness of guilt and of eternal death; we teach that both are the gratuitous benefit of Christ. By faith, we are delivered gratis for Christ's sake from guilt and the wrath of God, that is, eternal death, according to these passages: "The sting of death is sin, etc. … But thanks be to God, through whom we have the victory" [1 Corinthians 15:56–57]. Likewise, "O death, I will be your death" [Hosea 13:14]. Also, Romans 6, "The gift of God is eternal life through Jesus Christ, etc." And in that very forgiveness we are reassured with faith; we are delivered from eternal death, according to that passage, "Having been justified by faith, we have peace" [Romans 5:1]. Therefore, Christ is insulted if anyone transfers the forgiveness of eternal death to an act of compensation on our part.

Secondly, although the forgiveness of guilt and of eternal death should not be separated, nevertheless, the forgiveness of guilt should be distinguished from the forgiveness of temporal penalties. For the saints suffer the common hardships of the human race. In addition, God punishes certain sins with specific penalties, such as David experienced on account of his adultery. Indeed, whoever fails to shudder as he ponders how horribly God punished that sin of David surely has a heart harder than iron! There was sedition; many thousands of citizens were killed;

and then the kingdom of Israel was torn away from Judah. This change within the kingdom caused the permanent ruin of that people—the ruin of their religion and endless wars. That single lapse on David's part was the cause of so many sins. Likewise, the people of Israel were punished with the most terrible disasters on account of their idolatry. Nor is there any doubt that the world even now is being punished on account of idolatry, lust, debauchery, and other vices. Peter says even of the saints of God, "Judgment begins with the house of God" [1 Peter 4:17]. Therefore, temporal penalties should be distinguished from guilt, and one must learn what to think of these penalties and how they are mitigated.

First, then, it must be understood that these penalties, being divinely imposed, have nothing whatsoever to do with the power of the Keys; the Keys neither forgive nor impose these penalties.

Second, the afflictions of the saints should not always be considered punishments, as the sufferings of John, Paul, and similar men were not penalties for specific offenses. Indeed, God Himself excuses Job and testifies that he is not afflicted on account of past misdeeds. Then, although they are sometimes punishments, we must take comfort and see another purpose behind the cross and afflictions. For if they were only to be considered punishments, then only the wrath of God would be presented to the conscience. Therefore, the Gospel sets forth another purpose. It teaches that the cross is an exercise whereby the sin in us may be done away with and a newness of spirit should increase, as Paul says, "Our outer man is being corrupted so that the inner man be renewed day by day" [2 Corinthians 4:16].

Third, it has yet to be learned that these penalties are mitigated by our repentance. Here it is beneficial to distinguish the forgiveness of guilt from the forgiveness of punishment in this life. Public and private calamities are mitigated by our repentance as a whole, according to that passage, "If we judged ourselves, we would not be judged by the Lord" [1 Corinthians 11:31]. Likewise, "Turn to Me, and I will turn to you"

[Zechariah 1:3]. The meaning of this is, "If you repent, I will do good to you. I will give great rewards." Here belong such proclamations as, "Alms deliver from sin," namely, as it applies to the forgiveness of punishment. In other words, alms merit the mitigation of calamities in this life.

Indeed, it is useful in the Church to teach both things: that penalties have been set forth for misdeeds, and that they are mitigated by our repentance. For we are speaking about repentance as a whole, not about those ridiculous satisfactions which are supposed to be valid even when they are made in a state of mortal sin. The absurdity of such a thing can easily be determined, for the worship of the ungodly does not please God, according to that passage, "You are not a God who takes pleasure in wickedness" [Psalm 5:4].

Fourth, the Scholastic satisfactions obscure the Law and the Gospel and magnify the worthiness of human traditions, for in satisfactions they pretend that something greater than the Law is being done, and they dream that the Law is fulfilled by means of these remaining works. But even the saints are far from the perfection of the Law. This teaching must exist prominently in the Church. Scholastic satisfactions also obscure the Gospel, because they pretend that eternal death is abolished by our own doing. Such satisfactions also make it easy for the unlearned to transfer the forgiveness of guilt to the satisfactions. Third, they magnify human traditions, for they admit that satisfactions are works, not things that are duly owed; that is, the human traditions concerning fasting on certain days, abstaining from certain foods, reading certain prayers, etc. If these things are satisfactions, then there is much value in traditions and the monastic life. But in the Church one must find this teaching of Christ: "In vain they worship Me with the commandments of men" [Matthew 15:9]. We must beware, lest the truly good works be buried under the praises of traditions.

From all these things, it is sufficiently clear that consciences should not be burdened by those customary satisfactions. For, first of all, the

Keys have the command of forgiving sins, and they teach about the gratuitous forgiveness of sins. They do not have the command of imposing a penalty. Second, it is false that eternal death is abolished by our doing. Third, the opinion about satisfactions obscures the Law and the Gospel and falsely magnifies human traditions. Nevertheless, it must be concluded that temporal punishments are mitigated by our repentance and by the works which are duly owed. Therefore, zeal for doing good should be increased also by the admonition that troubles will be mitigated by our repentance.

If someone asks whether diligence in restraining the flesh is required, or fasting, or other exercises, I answer: These exercises must certainly be required and furnished. But it must be done to this end: not that they should serve as compensation for past sins, but that they should restrain the flesh so that a person sins less going forward. Indeed, this diligence in restraining the flesh is a work that is duly owed. It is commanded by God; it is not a work that is not duly owed. Those who indulge the flesh excessively, who do not practice the basic exercises of temperance, continence and prayer, certainly sin. For Christ says, "Take care, lest your hearts be weighed down with drunkenness" [Luke 21:34]. Likewise, "This kind of demon is not cast out, except by fasting and prayer" [Matthew 17:21]. And Paul writes, "Put to death your members, etc." [Colossians 3:5]. Likewise, "I discipline my body and force it into servitude." [1 Corinthians 9:27]. Similarly, "The people sat down to eat and drink and got up to play" [1 Corinthians 10:7]. But how anyone should exercise himself is left to the conscience of each one. For the same form cannot be prescribed to all people or to every time, nor are traps to be laid for consciences. Besides, these exercises should be continual, not only performed from time to time. Therefore, the Church is continually giving instruction about them in her sermons.

It may also happen that some pious person performs works that are not duly owed. For example, he is generous where he could have not been generous without offense to conscience. Paul preached the Gospel for free, although it was lawful for him to demand a livelihood. These are noteworthy works of the Spirit of freedom, and they are great merits. I do not even forbid that they should be called "works of supererogation." Nonetheless, Paul understands that he is still, in other respects, far from the perfection of the Law, since in his flesh there still remain ignorance and covetous desires, which impede fear and faith.

Concerning works of satisfaction, they cite the saying of Paul, "If we would judge ourselves, we would not be judged by the Lord" [1 Corinthians 11:31], which they interpret in this way: If we would punish ourselves, we would not be punished by the Lord. From there, they reason that the punishments which God threatens are removed by our self-punishments.

To this I reply: Paul cannot be understood to be speaking about those satisfactions which are not duly owed; he must be understood to be speaking about repentance as a whole. Indeed, it means to judge rightly and to condemn sin from the heart. That is done in contrition and repentance as a whole. Furthermore, he said above that temporal punishments are mitigated or removed by repentance as a whole and by the works that are duly owed. It is helpful to teach this, as Isaiah also teaches in chapter 58, where he also disparages traditions and requires the works that are duly owed. "Behold, you fast for quarrels and contentions, etc. Is not this the fast that I have chosen? Break bread for the hungry, etc. Then you will be like a well-watered garden" [Isaiah 58:4, 6–8]. The prophets often preach in this manner. Micah 6, "Surely God cannot be appeased with thousands of rams, etc. I will show you what is good and what God requires: to do justice and to love mercy and to walk in fear before your God."

But they object: "Sins merit penalties; no sin, then, is forgiven unless the penalties are paid. Therefore, since sins are forgiven through repentance, repentance itself has penalty and compensation in view, and therefore must be enhanced with many penalties, etc." A good many people now color satisfaction with this new dye. But both consequences must be denied. For it is not true that no sins are forgiven without penalties. Indeed, God often promises forgiveness, even for temporal punishments, to those who repent. The Ninevites are a notable example. Furthermore, repentance obtains the forgiveness of sins, not because repentance is a compensation for sins, but for the sake of the divine promise. "Turn to Me, and I will turn to you" [Zechariah 1:3]. But I do not wish to pursue this sophistry too far. I have only desired to warn the student about how some people defend satisfaction with this new sophistication, for it is full of manifold craftiness of hypocrisy. It is simpler and more pious not to think arrogantly about our repentance, nor to attribute to it the notion of a price or compensation for higher crimes. For this is a new and due obedience. It is sufficient to attribute the cause of forgiveness, that is, the mitigation of penalties, to the mercy and promise of God.

They also cite examples. After David's guilt was forgiven, he was punished with exile and civil war. After Adam's guilt was forgiven, he was subjected to bodily death and the other afflictions of this life. It was mentioned above concerning these examples that penalties are often divinely inflicted. But such punishments do not pertain at all to the Keys, nor does it follow in any way from these examples that those penalties are removed through rites of satisfaction, but (as said above) they are mitigated by repentance as a whole. In fact, I admonished above that those afflictions which the saints endure are not always punishments for certain offenses.

But when the ancient Church writers and councils mention satisfactions, they are talking about the rite and spectacle of their own time. Nor did they think that men by that rite merited the forgiveness of guilt or of penalties, whether of purgatory or otherwise, but they knew that it was a civil custom of the Church, instituted by human authority for the sake of giving an example in order to discourage the rest from shameful behavior, or to scrutinize those who were returning to the Church to see if they had truly come to their senses. Indeed, Ambrose expressly says, "It is enough if this public penance takes place once in a person's life." With these words, he demonstrates that those satisfactions are not required for the forgiveness of sins, or else he would have ordered that they be repeated as often as there was need of repentance.

Indeed, from that ancient custom arose indulgences, as they call them, which were and remain nothing other than the forgiveness of those public penalties. Afterwards, unlearned (or even wicked) men sold indulgences by making astonishing promises, as if they were some kind of forgiveness for great offenses and penalties—indeed, a more certain and more generous kind of forgiveness. They falsely claimed that, with the indulgences, they were imparting to some people the excess merits of the saints. Thus, there were many things among those imposters which can easily be judged to be absurd, both by the pious and by those who have been moderately educated. For since indulgences are merely the relaxations of the ancient canons, those very indulgences are now outdated, together with those canons. Moreover, those canons and customs were human traditions and did not pertain at all to the forgiveness of guilt or of penalties before God. Therefore, much less do those indulgences pertain to the forgiveness of guilt or of penalties, nor is it necessary that those canons be reinstated, since they were merely human traditions.

ECCLESIASTICAL POWER: THE KEYS

"Keys" signify a certain domestic administration. And since the Gospel is like a certain kind of domestic ministry, and since this ministry does not curb with bodily force, but only with words, we use the name "Keys" to signify the ecclesiastical ministry. So then, "ecclesiastical power" and "the Keys" signify the same thing. However, there is an ancient division which is highly useful. It divides ecclesiastical power into the power of order and of jurisdiction. The power of order is what they sometimes call the ministry of the Gospel; that is, the command to teach the Gospel, and to announce the forgiveness of sins, and to distribute the Sacraments, either to individuals or to many. But jurisdiction is the power to excommunicate those who are guilty of public offenses and again to absolve them, if they are converted and seek absolution. Therefore, according to the Gospel, ecclesiastical power properly includes, first, the command to teach the Gospel, to announce the forgiveness of sins, and to distribute the Sacraments to individuals or to many; and second, it also includes jurisdiction, but without bodily force, as we have said.

But this power is not tyrannical. That is, it is not without a definite command or a definite law. Nor is it permissible for those who hold the ecclesiastical power to invent new doctrine; they have a defined doctrine handed down by Christ which they ought to set forth purely. This is the command Christ gives in the last chapter of Matthew: "Teaching them to observe all the things that I have commanded you" [Matthew 28:20]. And Paul says, "If an angel from heaven teaches something other than what we have taught, let him be cursed" [Galatians 1:8]. This is a rather serious threat. It forbids the establishing of new articles of faith beyond the Scripture or of a new doctrine which disagrees with the Gospel as it stands in Holy Scripture. It also forbids the Church to listen to any doctrine that disagrees with that Gospel.

Again, jurisdiction does not have the power to curb by bodily force, but only to curb with words, that is, to excommunicate, as Christ taught in Matthew 18, "Let him be to you as a Gentile." He does not command the apostles to punish with the sword. And He says in John 20, "As the Father has sent Me, I also send you, etc." But He says in another place,

"My kingdom is not of this world" [John 18:36]. And Paul says in 2 Corinthians 1, "We do not rule as lords over your faith, but are assistants of your joy."

From these things, it is clear that ecclesiastical power must be distinguished from political power; that is, from the kingdom of the world. Civil power in the world makes laws about the defense of the body, about the distinction of ownership, about contracts, about crimes. And it curbs with bodily force. On the other hand, ecclesiastical power bestows eternal and spiritual things; that is, the heavenly doctrine. And it curbs with words. For this reason, it neither condemns nor abolishes civil power. Indeed, it approves of it and subjects the bodies of the saints to it. And yet one must know the difference, lest ecclesiastical power infringe on the offices of political power; that is, the kingdom of the world.

When, in His passion, Christ is crowned with thorns and is led forth to be ridiculed in royal purple, it signifies that in the future, after the true spiritual kingdom is scorned (that is, after the Gospel is oppressed), another earthly kingdom will be established under the pretext of ecclesiastical power.[30] As some unlearned men have written, "The Roman pope is, by divine right, the lord of the kingdoms of the world." Also, the Anabaptists (and others like them) attempt to spread their doctrine by force of arms, thus transforming ecclesiastical power into an earthly power. Thus they crown Christ with thorns and lead Him forth in a purple robe and cover Him with wounds. Therefore, the powers must be prudently distinguished, lest the kingdom of Christ be obscured. This false persuasion afterward produces many errors, for the doctrine of faith and of spiritual righteousness and of the cross is obscured when men imagine that Christian righteousness is merely that external and civil way of life. And those who ought to have taught and borne the cross seize the reins

---

30   These words are later included in Melanchthon's *Treatise on the Power and Primacy of the Pope*.

of power, contrary to the will of God. We must beware of these errors and offenses.

There are also other errors. Wycliffe contended that the ministers of the churches are not allowed to hold property and wealth. He made no distinction between offices or authorities; he made a distinction between resources. We teach that the offices are to be distinguished, and that it is lawful for any ecclesiastical minister to use the resources of the civil realm, such as food and drink. In other words, it is lawful for him to hold property, wealth, the donations of princes, and to have control over his own property, just as it is lawful for a church's pastor to be at the same time the father of a family, just as Paul was at the same time a tent-maker and apostle. The minister must simply see to it that he performs his office correctly. He must not use the offices of the secular kingdom under the pretext of ecclesiastical authority. He should not incite rebellions. He should not take up arms for the purpose of spreading the doctrine. He should not tear the authority away from others as if the Gospel commanded it, as Monetarius did and as the Anabaptists are currently doing in their madness. I wanted to warn the reader briefly about these things. For that Wycliffian superstition is also pernicious and rebellious as it drives the ministers of the churches to beggary and denies them the right to hold property.

Up to this point, I have spoken of the proper office or mandate of ecclesiastical authority. There still remains the question of what kind of obedience is owed to the ministers of the Church; likewise, whether it is permissible for bishops to institute traditions.

First, I will answer the question about obedience. Just as obedience is owed to the Word of God, so also it is owed to the ministers who teach the Word of God, as far as it pertains to the ministry. As Scripture teaches, "He who hears you, hears Me" [Luke 10:16]. Likewise, "Whatever they say, do" [Matthew 23:3]. Also, "Obey your overseers" [Hebrews 13:17]. These passages are speaking of the ministry and require the obedience that is due to the Gospel itself. But they do not establish a kingdom beyond the Gospel for the teachers. Obedience is also owed to them in the area of jurisdiction, which they have according to the Gospel, namely, in the investigation of offenses, in hearing witnesses, in legitimate excommunication, etc. But I will speak later about what one should think about ceremonies. For they have authority to ordain ceremonies to the end that matters may be carried out in an orderly manner in the public assembly of the Church, just as Paul ordains that women should cover their heads, and the Church from the beginning established Sunday and various other festival days so that there might be set times for teaching. But these ordinances should not be understood superstitiously, for they are neither righteousness nor forms of worship that are necessary for righteousness; they are by their very nature matters of adiaphora, which can be omitted without sin, as long as it does not cause offense. Therefore, obedience is owed to these traditions insofar as it touches a case of offense. But apart from a case of offense, consciences are free, and the bishops do not have the right to further burden consciences with their traditions, as we will demonstrate below.

We should say something about the call, or ordination. Paul commands Titus to appoint elders in the neighboring regions. Thus we have a Scriptural testimony that pastors are ordained by neighboring pastors. That is, they are placed in charge of other churches. But the Church has the command not to admit wicked teachers, but to seek good ones, according to that passage, "Beware of false prophets" [Matthew 7:15]. Therefore, the authority of the Church was added to the election of ministers by ancient custom, that is, by the custom of those to whom the Church committed that matter. The histories and decrees bear witness that this was the custom. The people would elect someone. Afterward the authority of the neighboring bishop was added, who would approve the one elected. These are the words in the decree of the Council of Nicaea, as they are found in the *Tripartite History*, Book 8, page 325: "Let the people make their choice, as the bishop of Alexandria joins them in ratifying and in certifying their decision."

Cyprian frequently mentions this custom, such as in Epistle 3 *Ad Cornelium:* "When the bishop is substituted in the place of the deceased, when he is chosen by the suffrage of all the people." And Epistle 4: "For which reason, the common people, yielding to the Lord's precepts and in fear of God, should separate themselves from the sinner set before them, nor should they attend the sacrifices of the sacrilegious priest, when they themselves certainly have the power either to choose worthy priests or to recuse the unworthy." And then: "For this reason, the divine tradition and apostolic observance must be preserved and retained which is also retained among us and in practically all the provinces, that for the proper celebration of ordinations, all of the neighboring bishops of the same province should meet with the people for whom the overseer is being ordained, and a bishop should be chosen in the presence of the people who have fully examined the life of each one. We see that this was also done among you in the ordination of our colleague Sabinus, so that from the suffrage of the universal brotherhood and from the judgment of the bishops who had met together at the time, the episcopate was bestowed upon him and the hand was laid on him."

Augustine testifies that the bishops in Africa were ordained by neighboring bishops, and the Roman bishop by the Ostian bishop. He writes about the votes of the people in Epistle 110: "I came, and as the Lord willed, He helped us for His mercy's sake, so that they received in peace the bishop whom their prior bishop had designated, for they willingly embraced the will of their preceding bishop. But something unfortunate had been done, on account of which some were saddened. For Brother Severus thought it sufficient that his successor should be appointed by the clerics, and so he did not consult the people. This caused a certain amount of sadness on the part of some. In the end, it pleased God. Sadness fled. Joy ensued. The bishop whom the previous bishop had designated was ordained. As for me, lest any should complain about me, I declare my will—which I believe to be of God—that you all may know it: I want Elder Eradius to be my successor. The people shouted their approval, 'Let it be so! Let it be so!'" Here Augustine clearly testifies that the bishops were elected by the votes of the people. The examples in the histories demonstrate the same thing, as we read in the life of Ambrose that the people were gathered to choose a bishop, and there Ambrose was chosen and demanded by all. And Gregory Nazanzenus says of Athanasius, "Thus, then, and for these reasons, by the vote of all the people, not in an evil way, by vanquishing the one who came before, not bloodthirstily nor tyrannically, but apostolically and spiritually, he ascends to the throne of Mark." I have chosen these examples, not to show contempt for the ordinary authority, but that we may understand the right of the Church, when necessary. For Scripture also ascribes this right to the Church when it gives commands concerning wicked teachers, "Beware of false prophets" [Matthew 7:15]. Likewise, "If anyone preaches another gospel, let him be cursed" [Galatians 1:9]. Christ intends for the supreme judgment to belong to the Church when He says, "Tell it to the Church" [Matthew 18:17].

Therefore, since the Church has the mandate to reject ungodly teachers, it also has the mandate to choose good teachers, for the Keys belong to the Church, according to that very passage, "Tell it to the Church." And wherever the Church is, there is the right to administer the Gospel. For it is impossible for the Church to exist without the Gospel, and likewise without the forgiveness of sins. Therefore, this right is proper to the Church, according to that passage, "You are a royal priesthood" [1 Peter 2:9]. These words pertain to the true Church. But the priesthood has the right to administer the Gospel. Likewise in Ephesians 4, "He ascended; He gave gifts to men," and He numbers pastors and teachers among the gifts that are proper to the Church, adding that such gifts are given for the ministry, for the edification of the body of Christ, for building up the saints.

Therefore, where the true Church is, there the right must necessarily exist to choose ministers. But the true Church is the one that has the pure Word of God, according to that passage, "My sheep hear My voice" [John 10:27]. Therefore this Church retains its right, even if those who have the title of authority to ordain do not want to provide godly teachers. For Christ forbade His Church from binding itself to certain persons and human authority when He said, "When they say, 'Behold, He is here! Behold, He is there!' do not believe it" [Mark 13:21]. And He adds, "The kingdom of God does not come with observation" [Luke 17:20]. Likewise, "Wherever two are gathered together in My name, there I am in their midst" [Matthew 18:20].

THE CHURCH

Sometimes the word "church" in the Scriptures signifies the general assembly of all who profess the Gospel (and have not been excommunicated), in which the good and the bad exist together indiscriminately, as it is written, "The kingdom of heaven is like a dragnet cast into the sea" [Matthew 13:47]. It is true that there are evil, non-excommunicated members of the Church, according to their external behavior and outward signs. But the Church properly and principally signifies the congregation of the righteous, who truly believe in Christ and are sanctified by the Spirit of Christ. And this Church has external marks: the pure Word of God and the legitimate use of the Sacraments. This is how Paul speaks of the Church when he says in Ephesians 5, "Christ loved the Church and gave Himself for her, that He might sanctify her, cleansing her by the washing of water through the Word, that He might render her glorious for Himself, not having spot or wrinkle, etc." This description includes both the inner character and the external marks. He speaks about the inner character when he says, "that He might sanctify her," and then adds the external marks, "the washing" and "the Word."

The article in the Creed also deals with this Church: "I believe in a holy catholic Church, the communion of saints." That is, I believe that there is a true Church which is the congregation of saints. The word "catholic" is added that there may be a certain mark, for it signifies the Church that is in agreement with the Gospel that was handed down by the apostles. Thus it excludes heresies and false opinions about ceremonies, lest we should think that the Church is bound to certain places and certain human ceremonies. It wants us to understand that the Church is catholic; that is, that it agrees on the doctrine of the Gospel, even if it has different human rites, being scattered as it is throughout the world. This article had to be placed in the Creed, lest we should conclude that God had entirely abandoned the Church in the midst of so many human vices. Therefore, Christian minds had to be fortified against this offense, that we might know that the Church always exists and that the promises concerning the forgiveness of sins and the other benefits of Christ always remain certain, according to that passage, "I am with you until the end of the age" [Matthew 28:20]. Indeed, this is tremendously comforting, to know that the Church is catholic. That is, it is not bound to one place or to certain human ceremonies, but we are joined together by the Spirit with the Church throughout the world, wherever there are saints.

But there are many hypocrites and evil men mixed in with this Church, that is, with the saints in the world. And sometimes the wicked rule externally in the Church and persecute the good. Therefore, there are two different understandings of the Church. The Scriptures often describe two bodies: one the true Church, the other the hypocritical Church which wages war with the true Church, as the Jews persecuted the prophets and later Christ Himself. Therefore, let us take these different understandings as referring to different Churches. Paul says, "The Church is the pillar and seat of the truth" [1 Timothy 3:15]. And it is commonly said, "The Church does not err." This cannot be understood concerning those who are in the Church, since there are also opposite sayings, affirming that horrible errors will arise in the Church, as Christ says, "There will arise false Christs and false prophets, and they will perform great signs, so that the elect—if it were possible—may be led into error" [Matthew 24:24]. This is obviously a horrible threat. And Paul says that the Antichrist will reign in God's temple; therefore, many of those who are mingled together with the Church will go astray.

It is important for the godly to observe this distinction between the two bodies of the Church, lest they be deceived by the authority of the title "Church." For that body of the hypocritical Church has a great and glorious appearance. It often has the power to ordain, so its authority must be great. It has the examples of the fathers. Therefore, the godly must also have a definite mark to determine which is the true Church. But the most certain and principal mark is the pure doctrine of the Gospel, according to that passage, "My sheep hear My voice" [John 10:27]. We should set this mark against all the titles of those who persecute and condemn the Gospel, according to that passage, "If anyone preaches another Gospel, let him be accursed" [Galatians 1:9]. The following passage is speaking about this Church, which has the pure Gospel: "The Church is the pillar of truth" [1 Timothy 3:15]. But the members of this true Church are scattered here and there. It has besides a great multitude of wicked men mingled together with it, so that the true members lie hidden and can hardly be seen. These true members also have their weaknesses, errors, and sins. This is why the true Church prays, "Forgive us our debts." This is how Paul depicts the true Church in 1 Corinthians 3: "No one can lay another foundation, etc." That is, though the foundation—that is, the true knowledge of Christ—remains, nevertheless, there will be differences among the teachers. One will build upon that foundation with gold and silver, that is, with the precious doctrine, works, and forms of worship commanded by God. Another will build with wood, hay, and stubble, that is, with useless and passing opinions and vile works, even as we sometimes find in the holy fathers certain unhelpful sayings concerning ceremonies and other matters. Thus the

Church lies hidden, concealed not only by the reign and multitude of wicked people, but also by certain foolish—or at least frivolous and useless—persuasions of the pious. For what is so peculiar to man as to be able to fall, to be deceived, and to err!

Such a Church is depicted for us in the histories of the people of Israel. For the true Church existed among that people, and yet a very great multitude of ungodly men and false prophets were commingled with it. Yes, the godly had their errors and wicked forms of worship. But the true Church was subsequently nobler, purer, and larger, after the prophets had cleansed the doctrine. Christ, Paul, and Daniel point to a future time in which ungodly men would hold dominion in the Church and seduce the majority. From this, it can easily be judged how the argumentative statements about the Church should be settled. The statement which says that the Church is the pillar of truth is speaking, not about men of a certain location, or about a certain human society, but about the spiritual assembly of the godly who are scattered throughout the world. The other statements teach that individual members can err, and that mingled together with the truly godly is a great multitude of men who are contaminated with pernicious errors. I have recounted these things, not as one who is zealous for contention, but in order that we ourselves might fortify our minds, together with those who understand rightly: The ungodly are the ones who oppose the title and the authority of the Church.

For, just as we should not fear to disagree with the ordinary authority which holds the title "Church," so it must be understood that the clear Word of God must be preferred to the title "Church" and to the authority of all men, according to the passage, "If anyone preaches another gospel, let him be cursed" [Galatians 1:9]. Augustine speaks worthily in *Ad Ianuarium*: "The Church of God is planted in the midst of much chaff and many weeds. It tolerates many things, and yet it does not approve the things which are contrary to the faith or a good life. It is neither silent nor complicit." Let it suffice to have said these things about the question of whether the Church can err. It is truly astonishing that the priests and the teachers, who securely dream that there is nothing wicked in the Church, are not even slightly moved by the terrifying prophecies of Christ.

Now there are still two assertions for us to prove under this topic. The first is that the administration of the Sacraments is not invalid, even if the behavior of the ministers is wicked. This dispute caused great tumult and strife in the Church on more than one occasion. Wycliffe, in recent times, and the Donatists, in ancient times, removed the authority from the Sacraments on account of the bad behavior of the ministers. At the present time, the Anabaptists are similar to the Donatists. They try to establish a Church in which there are no wicked men. Therefore, the godly must be instructed, so that they know that the use of the Sacraments is valid on account of the divine command and ordinance, even if the behavior of the ministers is evil. (To be clear, we are speaking of evil men in the Church, not about open blasphemers, like the Jews or Turks, to whom the Church has not commended the ministry at all.) For if the power of the Gospel or of the Sacraments depended on the worthiness of the ministers, consciences would always be uncertain about Baptism, about absolution, etc. Indeed, the Word and Sacraments require faith. Therefore, they cannot depend on the worthiness of the ministers. This argument is sufficiently plain and firm and was practically presented in just so many words in the edict of Constantine against the Donatists, as Augustine relates in Epistle 166.

The statement of Christ teaches the same thing: "The scribes and Pharisees sit in Moses' seat, etc. Do whatever they say, etc." [Matthew 23:2–3]. This statement does not condemn the ministry of wicked men, but rather confirms it. Christ also says that in this life the Church is like a net cast into the sea, in which both good and bad fish are caught indiscriminately. But where the Church is, there, too, is its ministry. Therefore, since there are wicked men in the Church, they must also have a ministry, etc. Indeed, Christ prophesies that there will be wicked men in the Church until the end of the world. Therefore, wicked men cannot be entirely separated by human judgment, etc. John distinguishes his office from the effect of the Sacraments. "I baptize with water; but He will baptize you with the Holy Spirit" [Mark 1:8]. Therefore, the gift of the Holy Spirit does not depend on the worthiness of the minister; it is the benefit of Christ, who is efficacious through the Gospel. Indeed, Christ transfers the authority of the ministry from the ministers to Himself. "He who hears you…" [Luke 10:16]. That is, "The ministry is valid because of Me." Nazianzus says neatly that the Baptism is the same, even if the ministers are different, just as the shape made by the signet ring in wax is the same, whether the ring is made of gold or of iron. "But note this: One ring may be of gold, the other of iron. But if they are both engraved with the same royal image and then pressed into wax, what difference is there between this seal and that? None."

Therefore, the error of the Donatists and their ilk must be rejected. On account of the wicked behavior of the priests, they condemn the ministry and depart from the rest of the Church, causing schisms. But the godly should know that they owe it both to the concord of the Church and to the dignity of the ministry not to depart from ministers on account of their behavior, as long as their teaching is not ungodly. For we owe obedience to the ministry itself, since it was ordained by God. We should recognize it as a divine benefit and, for that very reason, we should put up with the behavior of the ministers, even if their behavior is highly problematic. Deliberate caution should be taken in this matter, for persnickety and angry men will always find something blameworthy in the ministers, if we allow the Church to be agitated on account of the behavior of the priests. To undermine the dignity of the ministry rashly is a sin against the Second Commandment. For the honor of the divine name is injured by contempt for the ministry. Besides this, as we owe honor to parents, so also we owe honor to the ministers of the churches and to that very ordinance of the Church which preserves public concord. In addition, it is impossible for any multitude—for any church—to exist for long in this life without evil men in it. Finally, schism itself produces innumerable sins: the scattering of the Church, hatred, factions, and bloodshed, as the Donatists themselves used to advance with violence against their adversaries.

Therefore, neither the current ministers of the churches nor the Church itself should be abandoned, as Augustine solemnly said. "In fact, when the influence of sin takes hold of the multitude, the severe mercy of divine discipline is necessary. For discussions of separation are not only inane, but pernicious and sacrilegious, ungodly and arrogant, doing more to disturb good men who are weak than to correct evil men who are strong."[31]

The second assertion we must prove under this topic concerns traditions: For the unity of the Church, it is not necessary that human traditions be the same. Men must be admonished in this regard, for great tumults have often arisen in the Church over differences in tradition. The Roman pontiffs excommunicated the Eastern ones because they celebrated Easter at another time; also, because they abolished images in the temples; because they use leavened bread in the Lord's Supper; and other unworthy things of this nature—things over which Christians quarrel. The Council of Nicaea itself made a pious decree concerning differences of tradition, that each church should retain its own ancient customs, and not quarrel among themselves concerning rites. Indeed, Ambrose answered Augustine's mother that she should observe Roman rites in Rome and Milanese rites in Milan. Such prudence is necessary for Christians lest they rashly stir up discord. There should be a consensus on the doctrine of the Gospel and the use of the Sacraments, which is ordained in Scripture, as Paul says: "One God, one faith, one Baptism" [Ephesians 4:5]. However, although the people in each

---

31 Augustine, *Contra epistulam Parmeniani*, lib. 3.

church should use the customs of that church, and although a similarity of traditions has some benefit since it is helpful for the unlearned, men must be taught, nonetheless, to understand that having different rites among various churches does not conflict with Christian righteousness. As Paul teaches in Romans 14, "The kingdom of God is not a matter of food and drink." But this topic will be better understood when we explain how one should think about human traditions as a whole.

HUMAN TRADITIONS

We call "human traditions," not those things which are commanded by the civil magistrates, but the ceremonies in the Church which have been instituted by men, not commanded by an express word of God. There are three kinds of human traditions. First, there are traditions which command that something be done that is openly contrary to God's commandments, as are the traditions concerning the abuse of the Mass or the ungodly worship of the saints; or traditions which command something which cannot be practiced without sin, such as the tradition concerning celibacy, since it is imposed on those who are not suited to celibacy. Furthermore, the Scripture says, "It is necessary to obey God rather than men" [Acts 5:29]. Therefore, divine authority clearly excuses the conscience that violates these traditions. We have examples of this in Scripture. Daniel did not obey the royal edict commanding that the statue be worshiped in place of God, nor did the apostles obey the Jewish rulers who forbade them to teach the Gospel.

The second kind of tradition concerns matters that are by their very nature adiaphora, like traditions concerning festival days, fasts, and vestments. In these matters, the purposes must be considered. For if the purpose is civil, they are lawful. Such is the case when festivals are instituted or observed for the sake of the neighbor, not so that the work itself should merit the forgiveness of sins or should be righteousness and a true act of worship which God requires for His honor and not for other reasons. But the purpose should be the neighbor, for the purpose of order, so that the people may know at what time they should come together to hear and learn the Gospel and to use the Sacraments. Fasts may be prescribed, not so that the work itself merits the forgiveness of sins, or is by its very nature an act of worship, but so that a day is set aside by such a ceremony, or so that the people may be more soberly prepared to pray and hear and meditate on the Gospel. Certain songs may be designated in the temples, lest there be confusion that is unworthy of the churches.

Bishops or pastors can create such ordinances for this civil purpose. For Paul commands that all things be done decently and in order in the Church, and thus he himself makes ordinances about the readings among the Corinthians, and about coverings for the women. Indeed, by means of such pedagogy in the world it is necessary that the people learn the stories depicted in the rites and become accustomed to treating sacred things reverently. For as there is a need in this bodily life for the other laws, so, too, ceremonies are necessary. For ceremonies are by nature a certain part of discipline or of the law. Therefore, those who want to abolish all ecclesiastical traditions are making war against human nature itself, which cannot be ruled without ceremonies. In domestic affairs, it is necessary that the father of the family establish times for prayer, for learning, etc. As in the schools, so also publicly in the Church there is a need for such ordinances. And Paul speaks in favor of this understanding. "The Law is a tutor." He goes so far as to add, "toward Christ" [Galatians 3:24]. This is no trivial accolade. He hereby attests that ceremonies are of great benefit, namely, because they teach the youth and common people and train them to learn the Gospel, through which Christ is efficacious, etc.

However, although there is certainly a need for ceremonies as pedagogy, we must take care, lest superstitious opinions about them creep in, lest the benefit of Christ and this doctrine about faith be obscured, lest consciences thus be tortured. For this reason, we must conclude that these rites do not merit the forgiveness of sins, nor are they a matter of Christian righteousness, nor are they acts of worship—that is, things which God requires only that He may be influenced by this honor and not for civil reasons. Besides this, although these traditions whose aim is civil should be observed for the sake of example, they should not be imposed on consciences as nooses, but Christian liberty must be recognized, of which we spoke above. Consciences should consider these rites as matters of adiaphora. They should not consider them either to be sinful or to be righteousness, but should know that they can be omitted without sin, except where offense would be given, as Paul says when he wants women to be covered. He did not think this work was righteousness before God, nor did he think that a woman sinned if she uncovered her hair without giving offense.

There are countless such things in daily life. Since human beings alone understand good order, it is of greatest benefit to human nature to establish distinctions of places, times, and persons. Stage clothing is not fitting for the student. But it would be a ridiculous superstition if the student thought that he were righteous on account of the clothes he wore, or that he sinned mortally if he were to use other clothing, apart from giving offense. This reasonableness in traditions is highly necessary. For otherwise traditions are accumulated beyond measure by superstition, since they are thought to be matters of righteousness and acts of worship to God and perfections. This is how they once grew in the Church and among the monks. Likewise, consciences are tortured and thrown into despair by not understanding their liberty. Therefore, it is necessary that there be a firm consolation in the Church concerning the use of traditions. There is certainly a need for particular prudence, lest traditions either be barbarically despised or superstitiously observed. But we shall add testimonies concerning freedom a little later.

The third kind of tradition concerns matters of adiaphora which are prescribed, but with ungodly or pernicious opinions attached to them. Many false opinions are attached to traditions. First, there is the Pharisaical opinion that men merit the forgiveness of sins by these works, or that such works embody Christian righteousness, or that God requires these works, not for a civil purpose, but only that He may be influenced by such honor. Christ condemns this opinion when He says, "In vain do they worship Me with the commandments of men" [Matthew 15:9]. The doctrine concerning faith is hidden when men transfer the benefit of Christ to these traditions. This is the main reason why Paul preaches so vehemently against Mosaic ceremonies and human traditions, in order that the benefit of Christ may not be obscured, but that this understanding might be present in the Church, that the forgiveness of sins is granted gratis for Christ's sake, and that it is to be received by faith, and that we are declared righteous for Christ's sake, not on account of traditions or ceremonies. Likewise, true acts of worship are spiritual—fear, faith, love, and the other works commanded by God.

The second error that clings to traditions is born of the first. People have imagined that those traditions comprise perfection. It is all the more absurd to prefer human traditions to God's Law, since obedience is the perfection of the divine Law.

The third error concerns necessity, which is wrongly drawn from the Mosaic Law. For since men noticed that there were a multitude of ceremonies in the Law of Moses, they dreamt that there must also be similar ceremonies at the time of the Gospel. Then they claimed that faith, apart from those ceremonies, was useless, and that men were righteous on account of the ceremonies. Thus they imagined that Christianity was an external society of this kind, as was the Levitical society. From there arose more fantasies, because they rightly understood neither the doctrine about faith in Christ nor the use of the ceremonies of the Law. For although, in the Law, it was necessary that ceremonies be observed on account of God's command, they still needed another righteousness before God, a spiritual righteousness; namely, a righteousness by faith in the coming Christ, etc. Afterwards, God did not want the Church to be burdened with such servitude, as Peter says, "Why are you tempting God by imposing a yoke, etc.?" [Acts 15:10]. Likewise, he taught that the kingdom of Christ is a spiritual life and a life of righteousness.

The fourth error concerns the authority of bishops, who create traditions through superstition and defend the errors which I have recounted. Likewise those who think they have the authority to burden the Church in such a way that all who violate the traditions sin, even when they omit them apart from the case of offense.

The fifth error arises from the opinion of necessity. Consciences are cruelly tortured, and the unlearned condemn churches because of a difference in traditions. In this way, discord arises within the Church. These errors must be opposed, so that the pure doctrine concerning faith, concerning true acts of worship, and concerning spiritual worship may be preserved, and so that snares are not set for consciences, lest the concord of the churches be disturbed for no good reason.

It is necessary to dispel the false opinions, but the customs themselves in matters of adiaphora may be retained, and charity should govern their use. Then, since there is a need for some ceremonies and rites for the sake of good order, it is helpful to retain the usual rites which have no impiety associated with them, for change—and especially unnecessary change—offends the minds of many. It is even better to practice and to foster a mutual benevolence in the Church. But they are not to be condemned who cast aside certain useless rites, especially for the sake of example, as Paul also refused to have Titus circumcised for the sake of example. But I will explain shortly how offense is to be taken into account.

Furthermore, it is necessary in the Church to retain this doctrine of freedom; namely, that traditions are not righteousness before God, and that it is not a sin to omit them, apart from the case of offense. We use these testimonies to prove as much. Colossians 2, "Let no one judge you in food, drink, Sabbath, etc." Likewise, "If you died with Christ to the elements of the world, why do you make decrees as if you lived for the world? Do not touch, do not handle, etc.!" In Acts 15, Peter says, "Why are you tempting God by imposing a yoke, etc.?" In Galatians 5, "Stand in the freedom in which Christ called you and do not subject yourselves again to a yoke of servitude." He forbids that consciences should be burdened with the opinion that human traditions are necessary in the same way that the Jews were obliged to observe their ceremonies. Pastors neither can nor should abrogate this freedom, for it is a divine ordinance. In Matthew 15, Christ excuses the apostles for violating traditions, etc. He adds, "In vain do they worship Me with the commandments of men." Likewise, "Nothing that enters the mouth contaminates a man." Thus He embraces both things. He denies that they are acts of worship, that is, righteousnesses. He also denies that consciences are polluted if the traditions are violated. In 1 Timothy 4, Paul calls traditions about food and similar things "doctrines of demons." Here he does not prohibit abstinence of a certain kind, which is an indifferent matter. What he condemns are the false opinions, namely, that such things are righteousnesses or necessary things.

MORTIFICATION

If forms of worship that have been invented by human choice are useless, what should we think of voluntary abstinence and similar exercises? Here is my answer. A distinction should be made between mortification, as Paul calls it, and exercises which may be referred to as discipline. For the true and unfeigned mortification is done through the cross and affliction, as Paul says, "We carry around the mortification of Christ in our body" [2 Corinthians 4:10]. Likewise in Romans 8, "The body is mortified on account of sin." In these cases, we are talking about true terrors, about the cross and death itself, not about voluntary exercises. And this obedience—to put up with afflictions—is necessary. Indeed, it is the chief form of worship of the saints. As David says, "The sacrifice to God is a crushed spirit" [Psalm 51:17]. Also, "We must be made in the image of the Son of God" [Romans 8:29]. Again, "Offer your bodies as a living sacrifice" [Romans 12:1].

However, in addition to this mortification, there is another exercise which is voluntary, and it, too, is necessary. Christ speaks about it in this way: "Beware, lest your hearts be weighed down with drunkenness" [Luke 21:34]. Likewise, Paul says, "I discipline my body and I drive it back into servitude" [1 Corinthians 9:27]. The purpose of this exercise should not be to make satisfaction for sins, as if God required it as a form of worship and for no other reason, but to restrain the flesh, lest we should be overtaken by prosperity and rendered secure and lazy. This is why it happens that men indulge and obey the desires of the flesh.

Moreover, there should be many exercises of this kind: abstinence, a more ardent zeal for studies, labors, sacred readings. Therefore, Paul commands, "Teaching and admonishing one another with Psalms and spiritual songs" [Colossians 3:16]. All discipline, finally, pertains to this. But the world now most arrogantly rejects this and assumes for itself an immoderate license, because of which God will eventually issue serious penalties. For besides the fact that license itself is mixed with intemperance and many other vices, it also involves another evil: that while young people are involved in such a barbaric life, they cannot be taught, or made accustomed to, religion. Indeed, little by little they grow to despise religion. Afterwards, at an older age, they have neither understanding, nor reverence, nor any exercises of religion.

Paul commands parents to bring up their children in the discipline and admonition of the Lord. Now, discipline applies to one's whole behavior, and to this he means to add the admonition of the Lord, that is, the doctrine or Word of God. And since God is efficacious through His word, He will aid those who have these exercises of learning and meditating on the Word of God and praying. Therefore, this training is not in vain.

In addition, force of habit is strong. Those who are not trained from an early age will neither understand nor adopt these exercises when they are older. Therefore, as much as we can, let us encourage these exercises and stir up the young, not only with words, but also with our own examples.

Indeed, these exercises which have the immediate purpose of restraining the body are already works commanded by God. This discipline should be continual, and therefore it does not pertain properly to human traditions. For as useful as some traditions may be for this and for as much as they may admonish the youth, the observance itself must be without superstition; no opinion of righteousness or necessity must be added. Indeed, let us consider that these exercises should be undertaken, not on account of this or that tradition or time, but only that we may be admonished by this tradition, so that diligence may be continual. But now, for the sake of example, these customs should be observed, as should others, such as the ceremonies of the festival day. And yet here also it is helpful to learn the boundaries, knowing that some things are helpful to those of one age while other things are helpful to those of another, and knowing that the health of the whole must be preserved, as Paul says that one must have honor for the body, etc.

But Taulerus[32] rightly complains that most people prematurely reject the images or "shadows," as he calls these exercises, alluding to Paul, "which things are a shadow of things to come, but the body is of Christ" [Colossians 2:17]. For this discipline is not the righteousness

---

32 Johannes Tauler (1300–1361), a German mystic who was occasionally referred to in favorable terms by Martin Luther and several early Lutheran reformers.

of the Spirit. These exercises are, rather, shadows or images by which men are to be admonished, restrained, and trained so that they may be taught, that they may become better suited for contemplating the Gospel and preaching, as Christ says, "This kind of demon is not cast out except by fasting and prayer" [Mark 9:29], that is, by the prayer of sober men. This is why Paul does not say that bodily exercises are entirely useless, but makes a comparison between these exercises and spiritual righteousness. These exercises are somewhat useful, but there is another step that is far superior and more excellent, namely, piety—that is, true repentance, true sorrow, true exercises of faith, prayers, and patience. I have said these things that we may remember that this kind of exercise should not be rejected, and that we may know for what purpose it should be carried out, without superstition.

SCANDAL

"Scandal" means an offense by which the spirit of another is disturbed, that is, either discouraged from imitation or incited to it. There are, moreover, two kinds of scandal. One is Pharisaical, which is commonly referred to as "received." It is when hypocrites are offended, either by right doctrine or by a necessary deed, and begin to hate the Gospel and the godly, as, for example, the Pharisees hated the Gospel and the teachers of the Gospel and had great causes, drawn from human reason, for their sorrow and hatred. For what person, gifted with even a bit of decency, does not hate to see the form of religion shaken, concord disturbed, dissensions caused in the Church, empires and commonwealths destroyed? Moreover, the Pharisees saw that their forms of worship were being diminished; they saw their commonwealth being destroyed and the authority of the leaders being despised. And yet, for however great these causes were which understandably move men, it must be understood that the commandment of God must come before these causes, that is, before all things, according to the rule, "It is necessary to obey God rather than men" [Acts 5:29]. Therefore, this Pharisaical scandal must not be avoided, for the commandment of God excuses us. No, this type of scandal must prevail, that the doctrine may be true, certain, and beneficial for the Church. For it is a very grave sin to disturb the Church with evil disputes that are either uncertain or unhelpful.

The other kind of scandal is that which is "given." Indeed, ungodly doctrine is a bad example which harms others, either because they imitate it, or because it deters men from the Gospel. All ungodly dogmas are scandals of this kind, as are the idolatrous forms of worship and human traditions which could not be observed without sin. Christ especially threatens the perpetrators of these scandals. "Woe to the man through whom scandal comes, etc." [Matthew 18:7]. Therefore, these scandals must be guarded against with the utmost vigilance, lest we be either perpetrators or supporters of ungodly doctrine, or imitators of ungodly forms of worship, etc.

Also to be guarded against is another kind of scandal: when an indifferent work is done inappropriately, such as the inappropriate use of Christian freedom. People often argue over this use—when it is permitted and when not. I said above that it is a sin to violate human traditions in the case of scandal. Therefore, Paul's rule must be observed concerning the use of freedom. Paul commands the learned to put up with the weak and to indulge them for their good and for their edification, that is, that they may invite them to the Gospel by their own helpfulness, not deter them from it. For not only hypocrites, but also godly and temperate men, especially those who are not sufficiently educated, when they see ancient customs being violated, judge that men are brutalized and rendered profane by that kind of teaching, and thus they are deterred from knowing the Gospel.

Therefore, one must not make use of freedom among those who have not yet heard this kind of teaching, or among brothers who have not yet been sufficiently established. Instead, the example of Paul must be followed: "To the weak I became weak. If food offends a brother, I will never eat meat, lest I offend a brother" [1 Corinthians 9:22]. But where the Gospel has already been taught clearly and where the Church has been reasonably established, the strident observance of unhelpful traditions should not be required. Indeed, Paul was unwilling to circumcise Titus in order that he might provide an example of freedom. And Christ excuses the apostles for violating the tradition, saying, "Let them alone. They are blind and leaders of the blind, etc." [Matthew 15:14].

But in this very matter, we must understand that restraint is beneficial. For even among enemies, there are some who are to be not so much provoked as reconciled, and it is beneficial for Christians to direct all their works, not to their own desires or to the domination of others, but to the benefit of others and the glory of Christ. But many people violate the usual customs, not in order to benefit or serve others or in order to do better things, but because this freedom delights them. It is tyrannical to despise public customs and laws. It is not Christian. Besides, the violation of public customs easily stirs up great tumults. But such commotion should not be incited rashly, for it is difficult afterward for the conscience to bear the fact that you have provided the cause for public calamity.

The second rule. It is also necessary in duly-established churches to take scandal into account, lest by our examples we bring harm to others, whether it be by often neglecting the public custom or the public ceremonies of the Church, or by signaling some sort of contempt, or by rendering others more negligent by that example. Likewise, to furnish an occasion for discord or factions without necessary cause. If anyone violates traditions in this way, he surely sins. Apart from such cases of scandal, traditions should be understood to be free.

It is highly beneficial to retain this even-mindedness in traditions, for it retains the authority of traditions and preserves public customs and discipline, and yet it frees consciences from that ancient torture, since they know that traditions are external and indifferent matters and can be omitted without sin, except where it would cause scandal.

Furthermore, doctrinal scandals are much more harmful than bad examples in customs. Therefore, we must beware with the utmost diligence, first, that we do not teach anything impious or uncertain or unbeneficial. Then, even when we teach rightly, we must beware so as not to teach in such a confusing way that the hearers conceive false opinions in such confusion, as we see how urgently the people need to be admonished, to what extent human traditions must be rejected, and again for what purpose and for what benefit traditions are to be preserved and loved. Unless we explain these things properly and expressly, the unlearned will hold all laws and customs in contempt.

The same is true for the other articles as well. Unless they are truly, properly, and clearly explained, terribly pernicious persuasions tend to creep in. When we say that men are justified by faith, the most absurd opinions arise if the hearers are not admonished how it should be treated: both that a person is reconciled by faith, and that afterwards our obedience is necessary, and that such obedience is righteousness in the reconciled. Likewise concerning free will, that God is not the cause of evil. The same can be said of many other things that we have treated in their place. Merit is not removed from works because we do no works, but because the promise is a gift, so that the forgiveness of sins may be certain. What is more, good works in the reconciled are also meritorious. Thus in all these topics, diligence must be shown so that they may be explained properly and distinctly, without sophistry.

This is why Paul wanted the bishop to be a good teacher, that he may teach aptly and properly. Indeed, Christ wants the clerk in the kingdom of heaven to be educated and similar to a good father of the family, who chooses wisely in teaching new things and old. For unless the teachers exhibit this prudence and diligence, consciences will be disturbed, and depraved opinions will creep into men's minds which are harmful to religion and to morality. Tumults will arise and all sorts of scandals. Therefore, let us not only see to it that our customs bring praise to the Gospel, but also that logic and perspicuity accompany our teaching, that it may aid consciences, disentangle those who are doubt, and heal the erring.

THE KINGDOM OF CHRIST

The Gospel plainly teaches that the kingdom of Christ is spiritual, that is, that Christ sits at the right hand of the Father and intercedes for us and gives forgiveness of sins and the Holy Spirit to the Church, that is, to those who believe in Him and call upon Him, and that He sanctifies them in order that He may raise them on the Last Day to life and eternal glory. That we may obtain these benefits, the ministry of the Gospel has been ordained, through which men are called to a knowledge of Christ, and the Holy Spirit is efficacious through the Gospel, etc. But meanwhile, before the Last Day, the Church suffers persecution in the world and there will be wicked men mixed in with the good in the Church. This is the true and genuine sense of the Gospel concerning the kingdom of Christ and the Church. And that Jewish error of the Anabaptists must be abhorred and condemned when they imagine that the Church will be an earthly society before the Last Day, in which the godly reign and destroy all the ungodly with weapons and seize all the reins of power, etc.

Let us assemble some testimonies about the spiritual kingdom, not only to refute the fanatical spirits, but also because it is helpful to have these sentences in view so that they may comfort us and spur us on to spiritual exercises: to faith, to prayer, and to patience. For that Jewish error, in addition to other problems, also has this one: that it obscures and entirely buries spiritual consolations. It also abolishes spiritual exercises, since minds do not understand that the forgiveness of sins and grace are the characteristic benefits of Christ. Instead, they look for bodily benefits. They do not sustain themselves by faith in the midst of terrors and afflictions, but require bodily benefits.

John 17, "Even as You gave Him authority over all flesh, in order that all that You gave Him, to them He might give eternal life. And this is eternal life, that they may know You, the only true God, and Jesus Christ whom You have sent." Here Christ testifies that His benefit and His kingdom is eternal life. And He defines what eternal life is—not some worldly domination, but the true knowledge of God and of our Lord Jesus Christ.

Romans 8, "Who is at the right hand of God and intercedes for us, etc." And Isaiah 11, "The root of Jesse will stand; Him the nations will entreat, etc." These passages describe the priesthood and kingdom of Christ, and they testify that both of these things are spiritual. Christ does not set up some kind of earthly government, but intercedes with the Father for us; and He reigns in such a way that He wishes to be called upon, to hear, to sanctify, to guard by His Holy Spirit those who call upon Him, as it is also written elsewhere, "Those who walk by the Spirit of God are sons of God" [Romans 8:1,14]. Likewise, "I will put My Law in their heart" [Jeremiah 31:33]. These benefits are obscured when we look for a bodily kingdom, etc.

Romans 8, "Coheirs with Christ, if we suffer in a similar way, we will also be glorified in a similar way." Likewise, "We were saved by hope." Also, "Those whom He foreknew, these He wishes to be made in the image of His Son." Again, "For Your sake we are sacrificed all day; we are counted as sheep for the slaughter, etc." These passages testify that the glorification does not happen in this life; in this life, we must suffer afflictions and persecution. Matthew 16, "If anyone would follow Me, let Him deny Himself and take up his cross and follow Me." John 16, "In this world you will have trouble." And 2 Timothy 3, "All who wish to live piously in Christ will suffer persecution." These sentences very clearly teach that the Church in this life is subject to afflictions. Colossians 3, "Your life is hidden with Christ in God. When Christ is manifested, who is your life, then you also will be manifested with Him in glory." 1 John 3, "Now we are children of God, but it has not yet been manifested what we will be. We know, however, that when He is manifested, we will be like Him, for we shall see Him as He is, etc." This passage also teaches that the glory of Christ's kingdom is not in an earthly government, but in a spiritual one; that is, that when we are raised from the dead we may have new and eternal righteousness and life, like the glory of the risen Christ.

Similarly, Paul clearly says that the Antichrist will rule until the Last Day, when Christ will come and destroy the kingdom of the Antichrist. Therefore, the true Church will not seize the reins of power, but will much rather find itself in grave dangers and afflictions. And 2 Peter 3 says that scoffers will come in the latter days who will openly mock religion. Therefore, there will be people who persecute the Church. And Daniel clearly says that beasts, that is, governments, are cast into the fire when Christ appears for judgment. Therefore, there will be ungodly governments up until the Last Day. In John 20, when Christ sends the apostles, He only gives them the commandment to teach, saying, "As the Father has sent Me, so do I send you." But it is clear that Christ was sent for the ministry of the Gospel, not to seize the reins of earthly power, as He Himself said, "My kingdom is not of this world" [John 18:36]. And He forbids the apostles to take over the government when He says, "The kings of the Gentiles rule. But not so you" [Luke 22:25–26]. Likewise in Matthew 5, "But I command you, do not resist an evil person," that is, do not take up arms under the pretext of establishing the Gospel and a new kingdom. Therefore, the apostles were sent for the ministry of the Gospel; that is, to teach, not to seize the reins of earthly power. Therefore, Paul also says, "The Gospel is the ministry of the Spirit" [2 Corinthians 3:8], that is, in the Gospel are offered spiritual and eternal goods. We are not establishing new spiritual governments. And in 2 Corinthians 10 he says, "The weapons of our warfare are not carnal, but powerful in God for demolishing intentions." Likewise 2 Corinthians 5, "We function in the ambassadorship for Christ, commending ourselves as God's ministers in afflictions." Also, "We do not rule over your faith as lords" [2 Corinthians 1:24].

Therefore, since the apostles have such a great command to teach, it is wicked to conclude that the teachers of the Gospel should employ weapons in order to establish new governments, as the Jews and Anabaptists imagine, or that the kingdom of God is to be established in the last days on earth in this way, wherein the saints should rule as lords and wipe out all the ungodly with weapons; likewise, to pretend that there will not be any hypocrites in the Church. Indeed, this Jewish delirium has often wormed its way into the Church, for long ago there were also fanatical spirits called Chiliasts and Pepusians who dreamed of this sort of Anabaptistic kingdom.

It still remains for us to bring together the testimonies which teach that there will be a mixture of good and bad men in the Church right up until the Last Day. Luke 17, "As it was in the days of Lot, so it will be on that day when the Son of Man is revealed." Likewise, "On that night there will be two people in one bed. One will be taken up and the other left, etc." Matthew 13, concerning the weeds, "Let them both grow until the harvest, etc." And a little later, the end of the age is compared to a harvest. "The Son of Man will send His angels and gather from His kingdom all causes of offense and those who do iniquity, etc." Likewise, "So will it be at the end of the age. The angels will go forth and separate the evil from the just and will cast them into the fiery furnace, etc." These passages testify that the separation of saints from hypocrites will not occur until the Final Judgment.

In addition, one must also consider that pastors have a mandate to excommunicate those guilty of manifest crimes by means of the Word, without physical violence. It does not belong to human judgment to examine the heart and to pass judgment on those who are not guilty of manifest offenses. Therefore, Paul says, "Do not admit an accusation against an elder except with the testimony of witnesses" [1 Timothy 5:19]. Therefore, those who cannot be convicted by testimonies should not be excluded by human judgment. It is, therefore, impossible to establish the kind of Church before the Last Day in which there are no hypocrites. But pastors should carry out their office, teach purely and faithfully, and commend the glorification of the Church to Christ. Meanwhile, in this life there will always be bad men mixed in with the Church, and many ungodly men will rule in the world, and they will cruelly persecute the Church until the glorious coming of Christ. And yet, in these persecutions, Christ, according to His own counsel, preserves a remnant, lest the Church be completely wiped out. Such is the kingdom of Christ in this life.

There is also the fact that, even if there were to be some new Church such as this, the teachers should not take up arms by their own counsel to establish such a Church, etc. Indeed, no such command should ever be expected, for Christ would not command something that is contrary to the Gospel.

But to the Jews and Anabaptists who cite the prophets as they speak about the kingdom of Christ and often use analogies taken from the governments of the world, I respond first in this way: The Gospel is the interpretation of the prophets. Therefore, since the Gospel clearly teaches that the kingdom of Christ is spiritual, that it brings spiritual and eternal benefits and does not seize dominion over the world, but rather suffers persecution, we should also understand the prophets according to the Gospel. Therefore the apostles, in the Book of Acts, clearly apply the passages about the kingdom promised to David to this spiritual kingdom, which is subject to persecution, etc. And Christ Himself rebuked the apostles when they held that Jewish persuasion and thought that they would seize control of the world.

Second. Although the prophets use various analogies, they themselves also expressly testify at the same time that the kingdom of Christ will be spiritual. Daniel clearly says that the Christ will be killed [cf. Daniel 9:26]. And Isaiah says, "He will give His soul for sin" [Isaiah 53:10]. Therefore, He will not have bodily dominion in this life. In addition, the prophets affirm that the kingdom of Christ is eternal. But no bodily society is eternal in this life. Therefore, the analogies of a bodily society which sometimes apply to the eternal kingdom of Christ must be understood allegorically.

Indeed, that eternal kingdom begins in this life in the Spirit and by faith, and then endures forever after this life. Therefore, the prophets sometimes speak in such a way that they do not discern between the period of this life and that of the life to come. But sometimes they do discern and openly prophesy that the Church will suffer persecutions in this life. Psalm 2 teaches this. "The kings of the earth have taken a stand and the princes have convened as one against the Lord and against His Christ." And Psalm 116, "Precious in the sight of the Lord is the death of His saints." And Psalm 72, "Precious is their blood before Him." And Isaiah beautifully describes the Church in this life in chapter 30, "The Lord will give you a short supply of bread and little water, and He will not withdraw from you your teacher any longer, etc." Here he testifies that the Church is to be preserved, but it will be in the midst of afflictions. Daniel openly prophesies about persecution before the Last Day: "And the learned among the people will teach many, and they will ruin by the sword" [Daniel 11:33]. And he adds immediately after, "At that time all your people will be saved who are written in the book, and many of these will sleep in the dust of the earth; they will awaken, some to eternal life, others to eternal reproach."

These and similar passages must be remembered, that we may have comfort under the cross and learn to understand the spiritual kingdom rightly; that is, to seek spiritual consolations and to exercise faith. Indeed, these passages quite clearly refute the Jewish and fanatical persuasion concerning a bodily dominion of the saints in this life.

THE RESURRECTION OF THE DEAD

The article on eternal life and the resurrection of the dead is among the chief articles of the Gospel. Therefore, it is set forth very clearly in the New Testament and is often treated. It is dealt with in several public discourses of Christ. In Matthew 25, He clearly affirms that the just will have everlasting happiness, while the ungodly will suffer everlasting sadness, being tormented without end. Likewise in John 5 and 6. "This is the will of My Father who sent Me, that everyone who sees the Son and believes in Him should have eternal life, and I will raise him up on the Last Day." And Paul defends this article vehemently in 1 Corinthians 15. But it is beneficial to keep many testimonies in view, that we may stir up and strengthen fear and faith. But since the passages from the New Testament are sufficiently well-known, we shall gather several especially clear passages from the Old Testament, for there are clear and perspicuous testimonies found in the prophets.

Isaiah 25, "Your dead will live; My slain will rise again. Awake and rejoice, you who dwell in the dust, for your dew will be like the dew of the meadows, and the earth will give up its dead. Go, My people, within your sleeping chambers. Shut up your bones, hide for a little while, until My indignation passes. For behold, the Lord will go out from His place that He may scatter the iniquity of those who inhabit the earth against them, and the earth will reveal its blood and will conceal its slain ones no longer." This prophecy speaks very clearly about the raising of the dead, about the joys of the saints, about the punishment of the ungodly, and about the present affliction of the Church. Therefore, it must be diligently considered. "Your dead will live," he says. He calls the saints "the dead of God" in order to signify that the Church here is afflicted for God's sake. In other words, Your sons were slain for Your sake, and those whom You care about will live again. But what will eternal life be like? "Rejoice!," he says. That is, the godly will ever be verdant and will bloom with everlasting happiness, with the perfect knowledge of God, and with perfect righteousness, without sin or death, even as the meadows turn green again because of the dew. At this point, he adds a little comfort because of their afflictions. But the Church must be afflicted for a time and endure death. They will be enclosed as in a sleeping chamber; namely, because they will be preserved in the Church and in the Word until the judgment. Then he prophesies about the punishment of the ungodly and repeats the sentence about the resurrection: "The earth will conceal its slain ones no longer, etc."

Isaiah 66, "'As the new heavens and the new earth, says the Lord, so will your seed stand, and your name before Me, and it will be from month to month and from Sabbath to Sabbath, and all flesh will come to worship before My face,' says the Lord. 'And they will go out and see the corpses of the men who sinned against Me. Their worm will not die, and their fire will not be extinguished, and they will be a loathsome sight to all flesh.'" This passage, too, describes both the eternal punishment of the ungodly and the joys of the righteous, and it teaches what eternal life will be like when it says, "Perpetual months and perpetual Sabbaths," that is, a perpetual feast day on which all the saints perpetually worship the Lord. Therefore, eternal life will be a perpetual act of worship, that is, the knowledge of God and righteousness, without sin and without death.

Isaiah 65, "Behold, I am creating new heavens and a new earth. And the former things will not be remembered, nor will they ascend upon the heart. But you shall rejoice and be glad forever in these things which I am creating. For behold, I am creating Jerusalem to be gladness and its people a joy, and I will be glad in Jerusalem and rejoice in My people, and there will not be heard in it any longer the sound of weeping or the sound of shouting. There will no longer be an infant who does not grow up or an old man who does not reach old age. For a boy will die at a hundred years, and a sinner who lives a hundred years will be cursed." Some sentences here are clearer than others. But this one also testifies that all creation will be renewed and that the godly will have perpetual joys: "There will not be heard in it any longer the sound of weeping, etc." Therefore, they will be without sin and death. Likewise, the infants and old men will live forever. But the boys of a hundred years and the sinners of a hundred years, that is, those who persevere in ungodliness, will be punished. And since these passages teach that the Church will be afflicted before the resurrection and that it will not be glorified until after the resurrection and after the renewal of all creation, the prophets clearly testify that the kingdom of Christ is spiritual, not an earthly society before the resurrection, as the Jews and Anabaptists imagine.

Isaiah 25, "And the veil of those who are enshrouded will be swallowed up on this mountain, the veil with which all peoples are enshrouded, and the covering with which all nations are covered up. And death will be completely swallowed up, and the Lord God will wipe away every tear from every face, and He will remove His people's reproach from all the earth." This passage also teaches clearly that death will be abolished and that God's people will be delivered from reproach and tears, that is, from sin, death, and persecutions. Now, what it says at the beginning ("The veil of those enshrouded") is also a reference to death, for the dead used to be wrapped in a shroud when they were buried. These coverings will be removed. That is, death will be taken away.

Isaiah 24, "And it will be on that day that the Lord will visit upon the host of heaven and upon the kings of the earth. And they will come together as the gathering together of a single bundle into a pit, and they will be enclosed there in prison, and after many days they will be visited and the moon will turn red, and the sun will be disfigured, for the Lord will reign, etc."

Isaiah 35, "Those who are delivered and redeemed by the Lord will come into Zion with praise and eternal happiness." In Isaiah 9, Christ is called, "Father of eternity," that is, the Author of eternal life.

Daniel 12, "And many of these who sleep in the dust of the earth will awaken, some to eternal life, others to reproach, that they may see always."

Hosea 13, "I will deliver them from the hand of death; from death I will redeem them. O death, I will be your death; O hell, I will be your sting, etc."

Ezekiel 37, "Behold, I will open your tombs and bring you out of your graves, My people, etc." This passage from Ezekiel 33 also applies here, "As I live, I do not desire the death of the sinner, but that he be converted and live." All the passages from the prophets apply here which speak about the eternal kingdom of Christ and the saints.

From Psalm 16, "My flesh will rest in hope. You will not abandon my soul to hell, nor will You give Your Holy One to see corruption." For when the prophet speaks of Christ, he also includes Christ's members. He knows that the reign of sin and death is destroyed by Christ.

Psalm 22, "The poor will eat and be satisfied, and those who seek the Lord will praise Him. Their hearts will live forever."

Psalm 34, "The death of sinners is very harmful." Therefore, even when sinners are not punished in this life, they must be punished afterward.

Psalm 116, on the other hand: "Precious in the sight of the Lord is the death of His saints." Therefore, it will go well for the saints after this life. Another passage also applies here. "Many are the tribulations of the righteous, but the Lord will deliver them from them all" [Psalm 34:19].

In Psalm 49, the ungodly, who are fortunate, are compared with the godly, who are afflicted. This teaches that in death the condition of both is reversed. Concerning the ungodly it says, "Like sheep they are laid in the pit, and death will devour them. They will never again see light." On the other hand, it says concerning the godly, "But God will redeem my soul from the hand of hell, for He will receive me." The comparison in Psalm 4 also pertains to this, "They abound in grain and wine. But I shall sleep and rest in peace." Here also belong all the passages that speak of the eternal kingdom of Christ.

Job 19, "I know that my Redeemer lives, and that I will rise from the earth on the Last Day. And I shall be surrounded again by my skin, and in my flesh I shall see God, whom I myself will see and my eyes will behold, and not another." This is a noteworthy passage which testifies that we will truly receive the same bodies, but renewed, as Paul teaches, etc. Likewise, it teaches what eternal life is like, namely, the knowledge of God, etc.

Christ makes an argument based on the passage from Moses, "I am the God of Abraham, etc." [Matthew 22:32]. Therefore, Abraham lives, for God does not have regard for things that are nothing.

And we can surely draw similar conclusions from the promises and examples in which this article of eternal life is enfolded, as it were. For example, God promised that He would guard Abraham and other saints. "I am Your protector, etc." [Genesis 15:1]. But the saints in this life are terribly afflicted and appear to be abandoned, although, in reality, they matter very much to God. Therefore, another life remains, together with the tremendous glory with which they will be glorified after this life, in consideration of which they think that all injustices, troubles, and calamities are to be scorned and in no way compared with that marvelous prize.

Likewise, it is said in the first prophecy, in Genesis 4: "If you do well, you will receive. If you do badly, your sin will keep quiet until it is revealed." Therefore, there must be another life in which Abel receives a prize. This, too, follows, that there must be a judgment of all sins, including especially those which were not punished in this life. Indeed, the flood is an example of this universal judgment. Likewise, the destruction of the Sodomites and similar accounts which show that God will undoubtedly punish the sins of all men.

So, too, the first promise in Genesis 3 prophesies the destruction of the devil's kingdom, that is, the destruction of sin and death. Therefore, man's nature will be renewed. And Jacob prophesies about the Savior of all nations, whom the fathers understood to be the Author, not of some bodily kingdom, but of righteousness and eternal life. They saw that the Church in this life would exist in the midst of afflictions and the remnants of sin, even as they had seen that Abel was murdered, and that Abraham was ordered to slaughter his son as a sacrifice. In this type, he understood well enough that the Seed which had been promised would be a sacrifice.

Enoch and Elijah were taken to God alive, as the text clearly says about Enoch. These facts are certainly manifest testimonies of eternal life. For if they had been destroyed, then they would not be with God, for to walk with God is to live with God in a divine sort of life. Therefore, these examples make a stronger case than if the promise had been set forth with words only, without examples. Nor is there any doubt that the holy fathers explained abundantly both the promises and these examples. The words spoken by the angels to Abraham and the other fathers also testify that there is another life. Indeed, the angels indicate that we are their associates in that eternal life in which they live, since they care for us and defend us, etc.

In Numbers 23, Balaam says, "Let my soul die the death of the righteous, and may my end be like theirs." And in chapter 24, "I shall see Him, but not now. I shall regard Him, but not near."

AFFLICTIONS: BEARING THE CROSS

Since it has been said that the Church in this life is subject to the cross and afflictions, it seemed best to add a few things concerning this topic. It is helpful to prepare the Church diligently in this matter, so that, in the midst of every kind of affliction, we may have godly and useful consolations at the ready. There are four main divisions of this consolation.

First, we must determine with certainty that we are not afflicted by chance, but according to a certain counsel and permission of God. For the first question that arises in the mind of man in the midst of any affliction is, "Are these things happening because of good or bad luck, or are they taking place under God's guidance?" Indeed, the greatest comfort in the midst of the afflictions we commonly suffer is to know for certain that these troubles are not happening to us by chance. For we know that God must be obeyed. Therefore, here the mind must be strengthened and confirmed with definite testimonies against Epicurean opinions. Jeremiah says in Lamentations 3, "Who has said that it came to pass apart from the Lord's command? Who has claimed that from the mouth of the Most High neither good things nor bad proceed? How is it that man grumbles against God?" To this pertain all the passages about providence. Matthew 10, "Not one of these sparrows falls to the ground apart from the will of the Father." Acts 17, "In Him we live, we move, and we exist." Psalm 100, "He Himself made us, and not we ourselves." Psalm 94, "He who made the eye, does He not see?" Psalm 33, "Who made each one of their hearts, who understands all their works, etc." And when Paul says to the Corinthians, "When we are judged by the Lord, we are being chastened" [1 Corinthians 11:31], he testifies that afflictions do not happen by chance, but by the counsel and will of God. And in the song of Hannah in 1 Samuel 2, "The Lord kills and makes alive; He brings down to the dead and brings back."

The second division of consolation. It must not only be determined that afflictions take place by God's counsel, but it must also be added that God punishes, not to bring us to ruin, but to call us to repentance and to exercise our faith. Thus, afflictions must be transformed into signs of mercy and God's good will. This is the chief consolation. For in the midst of utmost grief, we acknowledge that we are being divinely punished. But this very thing increases the sharpness of the pain and causes despair unless we hold on to this consolation which teaches about the will of God: that He punishes, not to bring to ruin, but to call us back to repentance or to exercise us. Indeed, this is how the Gospel interprets afflictions.

Therefore, the Scriptures often emphasize this consolation. 1 Corinthians 11, "When we are judged by the Lord, we are being chastened, lest we be condemned with this world." Proverbs 3, "Whom the Lord loves, He chastens." Hebrews 12, "He disciplines every son whom He receives." Psalm 119, "It is for my good that You humbled me, that I may learn your justifications." Revelation 3, "I discipline those whom I love." Isaiah 28, "Trouble produces understanding." Likewise, "To whom will He teach knowledge? To those who have been weened from milk, who have been torn from the breasts." Isaiah 26, "O Lord, they visit You in tribulation. The anguish with which they cry out is their discipline." Nahum 1, "The Lord is good; He comforts in tribulations and acknowledges those who hope in Him." Jeremiah 31, "You have disciplined me, O Lord, and I learned like an untamed beast of burden. After You converted me, I repented, etc." Likewise in the Gospel, "Blessed are the poor in spirit. Blessed are those who mourn, etc." [Matthew 5:3–4]. Luke 6, "Woe to you who are full." Likewise, "Woe to you who laugh now." In summary, afflictions are part of the Law, for they are punishments added to the Law.

Therefore, as the Gospel teaches that the Law was given to humble us, in order that we may seek Christ, so it also teaches that punishments were added, not to bring us to ruin, but to call us back to repentance, in order that we may bear the cross. Therefore, those universal statements also apply here: "He has confined all under sin, that He may have mercy on all" [Galatians 3:22]. For to be 'confined under sin' means that we are subject, not only to present calamities, but to condemnation, etc. And yet, even in the face of this greatest of all afflictions, the Gospel teaches that we are not destroyed, but admonished, so that we may acknowledge the benefit of Christ, etc. The passage also pertains to this, "I do not desire the death of the sinner, etc." [Ezekiel 18:32].

In addition, there are many testimonies concerning the Church, proving that it must be exercised in order that fear and faith and the other fruits of the Spirit may grow in the saints, etc. 1 Peter 1, "You must be grieved by various temptations in order that the testing of your faith may be made purer than gold." 2 Corinthians 1, "We have had the response of death within ourselves, lest we should trust in ourselves." 2 Corinthians 4, "Although our outer man is being corrupted, nevertheless the inner man is being renewed daily, etc." Romans 5, "Tribulation produces patience, patience testing, and testing hope, etc." James 1, "Consider it pure joy when you are faced with various temptations, knowing that the testing of your faith produces patience." Genesis 22, with regard to Abraham, "Now I know that you fear God." Therefore, it must be established, concerning the purpose or usefulness of afflictions, that they are signs of God's good will. In other words, God allows us to be afflicted, not to bring us to ruin, but to call us back to repentance or to exercise us. This consolation fortifies the afflicted against despair and shows us the good purpose behind afflictions.

The third division of consolation. By his very nature, man, especially when he seems to suffer without deserving it or when he is afflicted too harshly, bears calamity impatiently. He groans, he resents, and he becomes angry with God's judgment, which seems unjust. For while the ungodly and the tyrants live in peace, with the greatest opulence and pleasure, we are oppressed with much misery. Men must be taught in the face of this temptation not to indulge in resentment or grief, but that this resentment or impatience is a sin and that God requires obedience and wishes for His Church especially to be exercised in this way.

To this pertain the statements about the afflictions that are proper to the Church; they require this obedience and unique form of worship. But extraordinary consolations should be drawn from this. First, that God has demanded this obedience of the Church. Second, if afflictions are a form of worshipping God, then one ought not conclude that the afflictions are signs of wrath, or that we are afflicted because we are rejected, but that we are being made members in the image of Christ. Likewise, that we should furnish the worship that is due to God. Third, since it is the Church that is most greatly afflicted, then certainly afflictions are not signs of wrath, since God dearly loves the Church and will deliver it, even as He also raised up Christ.

But the reason why the Church is afflicted is this: the kingdom of Christ will be new and eternal justice and life. But the remnants of sin cling to our body. Therefore, He wants this body to be destroyed, and He has subjected it to afflictions and death in order that we may afterward be clothed and finally glorified with a new and spiritual nature which is free of sin and death. And, meanwhile, He wants to use afflictions as an opportunity to exercise our faith. Paul teaches this in Romans 8. "The body is put to death because of sin"; namely, the sin that is present in the flesh. And Romans 6, "Our old man has been crucified at the same time, in order that the body of sin may be destroyed."

Human reason will be exercised by the following argument: It should go well for the righteous; the Church is righteous; therefore, the Church should not be afflicted. But first we should respond to the minor premise: The Church is righteous by imputation, but it still has sin in the flesh. Therefore, afflictions and death remain. Next, we must respond to the major premise: It should go well for the righteous. This statement is the voice of the Law, which the Gospel interprets in this way: it teaches us that, because of the sin that clings to our body in this life, we are subject to afflictions, and yet, since the Church is righteous, it will be delivered from these afflictions and receive rewards in due time.

Now, therefore, we will add some passages about the Church's afflictions. First, we should set forth for ourselves the examples of Christ and of the whole Church from the beginning of the world—of Abel, Abraham, Isaac, the people of Israel in Egypt, the prophets and apostles, etc. These examples should admonish and encourage us. If it is the Church, it must be made like the body of Christ. Therefore, it is necessary that there be persecutions and that the Church be afflicted. Therefore, let us not become disheartened in spirit, for when we think we are in the midst of great dangers and troubles, we will remember that this is how it will be for the Church. Let us focus on Christ crucified, on Abel, on the prophets, on the apostles who were put to death, etc.

Therefore, Paul says in Romans 8, "We must be made in the likeness of God's Son." Peter writes, "Judgment begins with the house of God" [1 Peter 4:17]. Also, "Do not marvel at your affliction which is happening to test you, but rejoice as those who share in the afflictions of Christ." And Christ says, "Whoever wants to follow Me, let him take up his cross, etc." [Mark 8:34]. 2 Timothy 3, "All who want to live a godly life in Christ will suffer persecution." And Paul says that the apostles are considered by the world to be *catharmatis*, that is, sin offerings. This is the most extreme and heinous of all the curses that can be imagined. Psalm 126, "Those who sow in tears will reap in gladness, etc." Likewise Psalm 118, "Chastening the Lord has chastened me, and He has not given me over to death." This is a prophecy about affliction and about deliverance. And Psalm 116, "Precious in the sight of the Lord is the death of His saints."

But the most beautiful consolation is set forth in those passages which testify that afflictions are sacrifices. For sacrifices signify something which is properly dedicated to God, so that through it He may be honored—something especially pleasing to God. Psalm 51, "The sacrifice to God is a troubled spirit. A contrite and humbled heart, O God, You will not despise." Romans 12, "Present your bodies as sacrificial offerings, even your reasonable worship, etc."

Yes, God also requires this obedience and very much approves of it as a true and magnificent form of worship. Therefore, He does not cast off the afflicted. We should not grow resentful, as if God had abandoned us, but we should bear in mind the good things which afflictions bring along with them, that we may be able to offer this obedience with a quiet spirit. As Peter says, "Rejoice as those who share in the afflictions of Christ, etc." [1 Peter 4:12]. First, obedience itself is good, for God commands us to obey patiently, according to the saying of Paul, "Patient in tribulations" [Romans 12:12]. Likewise, "Do not complain, etc." [1 Corinthians 10:10]. Second, the purpose is good, for afflictions train us, or they call us back to repentance. Third, there is also another far greater purpose; namely, that afflictions become acts of worship and sacrifices, for nothing more honorable can be said about any work than that it is a sacrifice. Moreover, afflictions become sacrifices when we focus on the will of God; namely, when we prefer to suffer in order to obey God, and when we believe that such suffering is pleasing for Christ's sake. Now, we are not speaking here about the afflictions which we have willingly brought on ourselves, but about those which happen apart from our decision or will, either by nature or by the cruelty of men. For the things that are naturally displeasing are also punishments added to the Law and are done by God's will. Therefore, Peter expressly said, "Suffering according to the will of God" [1 Peter 3:17]. But that pagan persuasion must be rejected which pretends that afflictions willingly summoned are sacrifices—and that, apart from faith—as the priests of Baal slashed their own bodies with blades, etc.

Therefore, since, in bearing afflictions, not only is obedience required, but it is required in such a way that we do not become angry and resentful, but willingly and steadfastly obey God, we should set against this resentment and impatience the commandments which I have cited and the passages which testify that it is God's will that the Church in particular should be exercised, etc. The advantages of the afflictions, which I have already mentioned, must also be set against such resentment and impatience.

But there must be added a fourth division of consolation which is very beneficial to know and greatly alleviates that resentment. Not only should the above divisions be maintained—that afflictions do not happen by chance, that they are not signs of wrath, that resentment is a sin, that God requires obedience, etc.—but faith and invocation must also be added. Therefore, we must continue to believe that God will be present with us and that He will help us and deliver us at the time determined by His own wisdom. With this faith, we must call upon Him. For this, too, is a purpose of afflictions; namely, that we should have occasion to exercise faith and invocation, and that our deliverance from afflictions, or the strengthening we receive through them, testifies that God is present, and that we matter to God, etc.

So it is that, through this outcome, the knowledge of God grows in us and becomes brighter, as the notable example of Manasseh teaches in 2 Chronicles 33. "After he was afflicted, he prayed to the Lord, and God heard his prayer. And Manasseh acknowledged that the Lord is God." And Psalm 50, "I will deliver you, and you will honor Me." That is, you will acknowledge and proclaim Me more, etc. Psalm 69, "Let the poor see and rejoice, for the Lord has heard the poor, etc." Examples of deliverance testify that God is present to help us. There is a very beautiful sentence in 2 Corinthians 1, where Paul commands many people to pray, so that many may again give thanks to God for the blessing given; namely, so that the mercy and knowledge of God may become brighter.

Here, therefore, let us set two things before ourselves: the commandments and the promises. The commandments order us to seek and to expect aid. "Call upon Me in the day of trouble, etc." [Psalm 50:15]. Psalm 4, "Offer the sacrifice of righteousness and hope in the Lord." Likewise, Christ says, "Ask and you will receive, etc." [John 16:24]. In Luke 18, He commands His disciples to pray always. 1 Thessalonians 5, "Pray always." Philippians 4, "Do not be anxious, but in every prayer and supplication, with thanksgiving, let your requests be made known to God." And Psalm 55, "Cast your care upon the Lord, and He will sustain you, etc." Commandments of this kind should stir us up to call upon the Lord.

Then let us also consider the promises. John 16, "Whatever you ask the Father in My name, He will give you." Matthew 7, "If you who are evil, etc." And there are innumerable promises in the Psalms. "To You the poor man is wholly abandoned; You will be the Helper of the orphan" [Psalm 10:14]. "Call upon Me in the day of trouble, and I will deliver you, and you will honor Me" [Psalm 50:15].

Indeed, these are the true exercises of Christians: to understand public and private perils; to fortify the mind with faith, and to ask God to guide the Church; to deliver it from impiety and from scandals; to defend the commonwealth; to give peace, crops, and nourishment; to rule the behavior of the people so that God may be glorified, etc. By these exercises, faith should grow, whereas it is extinguished by idleness and pleasures. For since minds are not accustomed to seeking good things from God, the opinion creeps in that all things happen by mere chance, without divine help. Therefore, the Scripture teaches that in times of prosperity, men become blind and impious, for they miss the opportunities to seek aid from God, as Moses says, "The people sat down eating and drinking, and rose up to play" [Exodus 32:6]. And Deuteronomy 32, "He grew fat and became recalcitrant." And Hosea, "The princes began to grow mad with wine, etc." [Hosea 7:5]. Perils are never lacking, but the drunk fail to perceive them due to their present state of tranquility. Therefore, perils must be considered, so that we may exercise faith and call upon God, etc.

But one must learn by experience how powerful these four divisions of consolation are. It is not in vain that the Scriptures so carefully inculcate in us these consolations; God wants us to use them and testifies to their efficacy. And when we set these topics before our eyes, then we are truly able to furnish patience. For in the end, true patience is this: not only to obey in the midst of afflictions, but also to conquer—or at least to fight against—the resentment of our weak nature.

What is more, we should carefully consider how beautiful this virtue is and how necessary, especially for Christians. Not only the books of the philosophers, but also the public judgments of good men teach us how highly human judgment esteems an evenness of mind in the midst of adversity. For reason itself teaches men that moderation of one's resentment is highly beneficial to one's nature, as opposed to being crushed in spirit or overly disturbed, so that we should either act contrary to justice or depart from that temperance which is suitable in one's nature. From this, come those famous words of brave and mighty men.

"All fortune, whatever it may be, must be overcome by bearing it."[33]

And again: "Face adversity with stout hearts."[34]

And Aristotle says, "Virtue shines at its brightest in adversity." Even as he says *in Tragoedia*: "Nevertheless glory shines through hardship." And Cicero says *in Tragoedia*, "Fortune must be squeezed from a mighty spirit like water from a rock."

But much more beautiful is the Christian virtue of patience. This can be understood if we compare it with the corresponding vices. For impatience arouses God's anger; it first drives obedience from the spirit, and then also faith. For the angry spirit thinks it is being neglected by God and imagines that it seeks and expects help from God in vain. Therefore, in great afflictions, many people become utterly blasphemous

---

33   Virgil, *The Aeneid*, Book V, line 710.
34   Horace, *Sermons of Quintus Horatius Flaccus*, Book 2.2, line 136.

and go looking for God's plans, contrary to God's command, as Saul consulted the medium. Impatience gives birth to such sins against the first table. Then, against men, the pain of injustice gives birth to hatred. It incites a person to vengeance, and from this arise, not only private dissensions, but also seditions and public riots, even as the pain of injustice compelled Coriolanus to make war against his homeland. Scipio acted much more honorably. With a remarkable spirit, he scorned the barking tribunes, and he, too, yielded to spite. But he withdrew into the countryside, lest, remaining, he should be further inflamed with hatred. He could easily have defended himself against injury by means of weapons, but instead he forgave the republic for these private injuries. He was, therefore, a better citizen than Marius and many others were afterwards, who avenged their private injuries with public treachery. After Thrasibulus the Athenian had recovered his homeland, he enacted a law of amnesty. That is, he established the practice that the conquering citizens could not seek their goods back from the conquered citizens, in order that the republic might return to peace. This was a great and salutary regulation for that city. But when Marius returned to Rome, he killed all the rulers of the opposing faction, and the impotence of his spirit gave birth to much evil. Likewise, many bring death upon themselves. Let us consider for a moment what great danger there is in the Church when, after terrible violence has been provoked by the teachers, they seek to avenge their private grievances by publicly inciting tragedies against the teachers. Heresies have often arisen from such hatred. Therefore, patience is necessary, first before God, that we may retain obedience and faith; second, for the sake of the tranquility of the Church and of the commonwealth; and finally, for the sake of private tranquility. Therefore, the Holy Spirit frequently gives instruction concerning patience. Paul said to the Colossians, "May the peace of God govern your hearts" [Colossians 3:15]. The "peace of God," that is, the patience which concludes that God must be obeyed and which expects help from God. Therefore, it does not cause an uproar. It does not seek vengeance or incite sedition or civil war, etc. Isaiah, "In quietness and hope will be your strength" [Isaiah 30:15]. That is, God helps those who suffer patiently, who expect help from Him, who do not forget about God and murmur, seeking to stir up heaven and earth to rebellion, seeking refuge in forbidden places. The Psalm teaches the same thing. "Be angry and do not sin" [Psalm 4:4]. Let us train our spirits, therefore, and let us learn to bear adversity, that we may exercise obedience and faith and especially suppress the stirrings of our spirit when, provoked by injury, we are inflamed with a longing for vengeance. This virtue is necessary in the Church and in the commonwealth, to forgive private grievances for the sake of public tranquility, lest discord should arise in the Church on account of private enmity. So let us fortify our minds to consider that it is better to endure all punishment and all torment than to disrupt public tranquility on account of private injury. But this entire philosophy is unknown to rulers and teachers who stir up public discord with their private dispositions. Think especially of Ulysses, who, when he was warned not to go into the territory lest he be struck, said: "For I am unaware neither of the blows nor of the injuries."

Thus our minds should become accustomed to enduring blows and ignoring injuries. And let us meditate on this: "Suffer to the end and endure. This pain will profit you one day."[35]

PRAYER

We use the common word "prayer" both for invocation and for thanksgiving. Therefore, two types of prayer should be recognized: invocation and thanksgiving. Invocation is to ask God for something. Thanksgiving is to give thanks to God for His blessings, to acknowledge that divine help has been given, etc., to celebrate and to

---

35   Ovid, *Amores*, Book III, Elegy XI.

proclaim God as the Author of the benefit. The Scripture often joins these two types of prayer together. Psalm 50, "Call upon Me… and you will honor Me." Likewise Philippians 4, "Do not be anxious, but in every supplication and petition, with thanksgiving, make your requests known to God." But let us speak first of invocation, that is, a supplication or a petition. Four main things should be found in a supplication: a command, a promise, faith, and the thing to be asked for.

First, we must look at the commands which enjoin us to call upon God. Therefore, let us learn right from the beginning not only that things like murder, theft, and adultery are sins, but that it is a sin not to render to God this worship of invocation—not to ask, not to expect help from God in the midst of danger, not to give thanks for His benefits, etc. Let us set the command against both our unbelief and against our unworthiness, for men naturally doubt both that they matter to God and that they are heard by God. Those who despair fail to practice invocation, since the mind thinks that it will accomplish nothing by calling upon God, as that saying in Virgil goes, "We cherish a useless rumor."[36] As a result of this darkness and stupor in the minds of men, they do not seek refuge in God. Therefore, God's command should be set against such darkness and one must think, "Behold, it is necessary to follow God's command. He Himself has commanded us to call upon Him, and He has not commanded in vain. He certainly hears those who obey Him, and He punishes those who disobey Him. The authority of the command must not be dismissed." Next, the commandment must also be set against one's unworthiness. The mind reasons thus—and not altogether impiously—"Even if I think that some people are heard by God, He surely will not accept my prayers. I feel that I am unworthy to be heard." Thus, the person's unworthiness prevents him from praying. But against this notion one must set forth the command: God requires this worship from all people. What madness it would be to apply this logic to the other commandments, to say, for example, that we

---

36   Virgil, *The Aeneid*, Book IV, line 218.

do not want to abstain from theft or from murder because we are not worthy to obey God! If any head of the household gives his servant a legitimate task, he will not accept the servant's excuse if he says that he is unworthy to obey. Therefore, the authority of the commandment must be diligently impressed on men's minds so that we know that we are not left free to pray or not to pray, but that it is a necessary work. Then, when our unworthiness creeps in, let us consider that the authority of the command is not to be minimized on account of our unworthiness. We should obey. We should not elude the divine command by arguing about our worthiness or unworthiness. First of all, then, the authority of the divine command should motivate us to pray. To that end, let us gather for ourselves a few passages in which we are commanded to pray. Matthew 7, "Ask and it will be given to you, etc." A universal saying is then added: "Everyone who asks receives." Luke 18, "You must always pray and not give up." Matthew 26, "Watch and pray, that you may not fall into temptation." 1 Timothy 2, "I urge you to offer prayers, etc." 1 Thessalonians 5, "Rejoice always, pray without ceasing, give thanks in all things. For this is the will of God in Christ Jesus toward you." Psalm 50, "Call upon Me in the day of trouble, and I will deliver you." I have spoken about the commandment, for these passages pertain to the Second Commandment of the Decalogue. Invocation is a work of the Second Commandment. Indeed, it is the chief form of worship.

Second, one must consider the promise which testifies that prayers are answered and that prayers are effective. Moreover, the promise is often repeated in the Scriptures. John 16, "Truly, truly I say to you, whatever you ask the Father in My name, He will give you." Luke 11, "How much more will your Father who is in heaven give the Holy Spirit to those who ask Him?" Psalm 50, "Call upon Me and I will deliver you, etc." It is a tremendous kindness that God invites us to call upon Him both with promises and with commands. If we were to match our hearts against this generosity, we would find that they are harder than iron, that they neither obey the commands nor are moved by the greatness of the promises. They are paralyzed with a terrible numbness, neither trying nor daring to call upon God. As Taulerus famously said, "The spirit of man can never be so eager to receive that God is not much more eager still to give." For He is truthful and keeps His promises.

Third, faith must also be added. This faith should hold onto the consolation of justification first and foremost, for immediately our own unworthiness creeps into prayer and this sentence breaks in: "God does not hear sinners." If we repent and believe that we are forgiven, then we must conclude that we are certainly pleasing to God for Christ's sake, even though some diseases still remain in us. Therefore, Christ says, "Whatever you ask in My name…" [John 14:13]. In other words, you cannot bring your own worthiness to the Father. You need an Intercessor and a High Priest. Therefore, take refuge in Me and know that you are certainly pleasing, that you are certainly heard for the sake of Christ the Intercessor and High Priest. Let us consider that the promises were made to Christ, and that He is most certainly heard. This is a true and firm consolation against our own unworthiness. The Church preserves it best in the ancient prayers, in which it always adds, "… through Christ our Lord."

Therefore, in every prayer let us first include this faith, namely, faith in the forgiveness of sins or justification, and let us believe that the prayers are acceptable because of Christ. Then, let the faith also be added which expects the things that have been promised. But faith only expects unconditionally that which is promised. It only concludes that our specific request is granted to us when God expresses His will and commands us to believe that the particular thing which has been promised is given to us, such as when we ask for the forgiveness of sins, or to be delivered from ungodliness and from eternal death. In this case, a particular faith is called for which concludes unconditionally and undoubtedly that these benefits are granted to us, for God has commanded us to believe that these things are granted to us, just as He affirms with an unbreakable oath, "As I live, I do not desire the death of the sinner" [Ezekiel 33:11]. There is no need to discuss predestination here, for we have the command to believe the promises, and we should neither make judgments about God's will that are contrary to the promises, nor should we seek God's will outside of, or apart from, His Word. But, as stated above, the promises are universal.

In bodily danger, when obedience would bring some sort of affliction along with it, we must understand both that God requires obedience and that He wants to come to our aid. Therefore, we should always start with a general faith, as I call it, which believes that our sins are forgiven and that our prayers are heard and acceptable to God for Christ's sake, that they are not an annoyance to Him, but that they will obtain either deliverance from the present danger, or the mitigation of it, or some other good result. Indeed, this general faith remains certain and soothes our hearts.

But the specific faith which asks for deliverance from a specific, present peril is held a little differently. For it expects deliverance in bodily danger so as to add the condition: if it does not displease God, if God sees fit. So, in this case, the two things should be joined together: the will which is prepared to obey, and a certain expectation of deliverance, but with the aforementioned condition. So David also expects to return, and yet his mind is set to obey. 2 Kings 15, "If I find grace in the eyes of the Lord, He will bring me back. But if He says to me, 'You are not pleasing,' I accept it. Let Him do what seems good to Him." And the leper said, "If You are willing, You can make me clean" [Matthew 8:2]. And Christ said, "Father, if it is possible, let this cup pass from Me, but not as I will, etc." [Matthew 26:39]. And Paul said, "We do not know what to ask for, as we should" [Romans 8:26]. That is, the flesh, oppressed by the magnitude of afflictions, asks for deliverance and shrinks back from obedience. But the Spirit calls the mind back to obedience, and while it asks for, and expects, deliverance, it does not put us at odds with God's will, but desires to be delivered if and when it pleases God.

But there are other examples which demonstrate unique impulses of faith, such as the Samaritan woman or the centurion, who do not dispute whether Christ is willing, but ask and expect with tremendous vigor. Such impulses are like this: "If you say to this mountain, 'Be cast into the sea, etc.'" [Matthew 21:21]. Luther says, "These impulses are unique; no instruction can be given about them by teaching." It is sufficient to command that faith should generally conclude unconditionally that our prayers are acceptable to God for Christ's sake and will certainly obtain something good. But the specific faith which asks for deliverance from a certain peril in particular should add the condition, "if it pleases God."

This condition does not prevent us from asking for specific things. Indeed, God wants invocation and faith to be exercised on such occasions. This is the main reason why the saints are afflicted, so that, when they experience comfort in the midst of danger, they may acknowledge the presence and the kindness of God. Both dispositions must be stirred up: the will to obey—for this will is the true denial of oneself—and faith, too, must be roused which expects this specific deliverance. For although the condition must be added, one must not yield to distrust. A person should have faith, that is, the expectation that can generally exist, for as the will to obey is not at odds with faith, so that condition does not prevent invocation, that is, the request and the expectation of help. Christ said to the centurion, "As you have believed, so let it be done for you" [Matthew 8:13]. And He orders the ruler of the synagogue to believe that his daughter will live again, etc. [Mark 5:36]. These examples have been set before us so that we, too, may ask with great confidence, that faith may grow by means of these exercises. Meanwhile, there still remains the will to obey. Therefore, we also add the condition, "If it pleases God." We should prescribe to God neither the manner of deliverance nor the time, but as Paul says, "God does more that we can ask or understand" [Ephesians 3:20]. So let us understand that God will guide the outcomes and the matters themselves in a wonderful manner. For the saints, too, are thus exercised so that they may learn that God wants us not to depend on our own thinking, but to do only those things which our vocation demands, and in these things, to depend on God's help. In this way, saints like Abraham, Jacob, Moses, and David are guided. This is how God wants us to think about the Church: that God governs it according to a wonderful plan. And David says, "God makes His holy one glorious," that is, He delivers and preserves him, not with human, but with wonderful counsels. And 1 Corinthians 10, "He will make a way out together with the temptation."

There is still another struggle of faith in prayer: when the things for which we ask are not granted immediately. Let faith not grow weak, as if God did not want to hear our prayers, but let us understand that faith is exercised by this delay, such as when Abraham was promised a son, but was not given offspring until he was very old. This is why Paul commands us to "pray without ceasing" [1 Thessalonians 5:17]. In other words, even if you do not immediately obtain what you ask, do not stop asking. Christ teaches the same thing with the marvelous parable in Luke 18 about the judge and the widow.

Fourth, prayer requires something that must be requested, for prayer should not be vain babbling. This is why prayer is an act of divine worship, because in prayer we profess that God cares for us, that God is not idle, but is the Author and Giver of good things. Therefore, something must be requested of God, or thanks must be given for some gift. For thus God wants to be acknowledged, as the One who protects us in the face of danger. As it is said in the canticle, "He fills the hungry with good things" [Luke 1:53]. And Christ says, "Ask, seek, knock, etc." [Matthew 7:7]. But it must be understood that Scripture commands us to ask both for spiritual and for bodily benefits. This notion should not be rejected by unlearned men, as if bodily things were unworthy of our petitions. Indeed, let us learn that these things, too, are benefits of God. God wants faith and invocation to be exercised in asking for such things.

Therefore, let us set before ourselves the private perils and private necessities of spirit and of body. Peter says that the devil goes around lying in wait for us like a roaring lion, etc. [1 Peter 5:8]. He lays various kinds of traps, especially when, on any number of occasions, he turns the minds of all men to evil and ungodly opinions. He himself sows these wicked thoughts and holds demented minds prisoner with false persuasions. Then he incites men to shameful acts, heresies, sedition, murder, lust, etc., and from these things he hurls them into all kinds of calamity. We have an enemy who is both powerful and cunning, while we, on the other hand, are not only feeble, but also astonishingly lazy and sluggish. Now consider the innumerable bodily calamities of men: an infinite number of plights, scarcity, sickness, exile, murder, etc.

However, we should not only be moved by private perils, but much more by public ones. Therefore, the Scriptures command us to pray for the Church, that it may be set free from ungodliness and from scandals, so that more people may obey the Gospel and be saved. Likewise, in 1 Timothy 2 we are ordered to pray that God would grant peace to kings and to the commonwealth, along with a pleasant and pious administration, the preservation of discipline and of good behavior. Likewise, we are commanded to ask for sustenance and the other necessities of the body. Indeed, all these things are included in the Lord's Prayer.

Our Father in heaven. That is, You who are truly present everywhere, You who hear and care for us, etc.

I. *Hallowed be Your name.* That is, cause Yourself to be acknowledged in truth. Cause those true things to be taught through which Your glory is truly revealed. Cause men to call upon You and to worship You rightly. Thus the first petition prays about the glory of God, that is, about the doctrine and success of the Church, for God's name signifies knowledge of God.

II. *Your kingdom come.* That is, rule us by Your Holy Spirit, so that we may believe Your Word. Establish Your kingdom in us, that we may become heirs of Your kingdom. The second petition, therefore, speaks of the effect of the Gospel and how we are to be governed by it.

III. *Your will be done.* That is, cause all men on earth to obey You. Cause pastors, kings, magistrates, teachers, and subjects to fulfill their office. And cause all men to obey You and to live the kind of life that pleases You, as the angels obey and please You in heaven. Thus, these three petitions encompass all the spiritual things, both public and private, which pertain to the glory of God and our salvation. Then follows a petition about bodily things.

IV. *Give daily bread.* That is, sustenance, peace, protection, success in our daily lives, the education of children, and finally, all the interests of life.

V. *Forgive us our debts.* This petition teaches that, in every prayer, we must employ the faith that believes in the forgiveness of sins and grasps Christ the Mediator and Intercessor, so that we may know that we are approaching the Father through this High Priest and are heard for His sake. Indeed, there is a notable confession in this petition, for in it, the Church acknowledges that it has sin. There is also a consolation, for if Christ commands us to ask for forgiveness, then He will certainly give it. There is even a sacrament added: "as we forgive." For it does not say that our sins are forgiven because we forgive, but our act of forgiveness is the sign by which we who have been admonished should conclude that we, too, are forgiven by God.

VI. *Lead us not into temptation.* That is, do not permit us to be led into temptation. Defend us against the snares of the devil, lest we be led astray toward ungodliness, toward sin, etc.

VII. *Deliver us from evil.* This is a general petition which asks for deliverance from all the sins and calamities of this life. In summary, it asks that we be delivered from the misery and hardships of this present life, and that eternal life and righteousness should be given to us.

Therefore, the Lord's Prayer teaches us what to ask for: spiritual and bodily things, private and public, present and future. Whenever we recite this prayer, the magnitude of the dangers and of the benefits should arouse us to pray earnestly and always to include, in the proper place, those things which are troubling our minds at the present. These are Christian exercises which are useful for strengthening faith. God especially requires this act of worship. Therefore, Zechariah most aptly embraced the sum of Christ's benefits and the true forms of worship: "I will pour out upon the house of David the spirit of grace and of prayer" [Zechariah 12:10]. It is the spirit of grace by which we acknowledge that God is pleased, and that we, in turn, are pleasing to God. So, in the first place, grace and justification are described. Then the true forms of worship are described, for it is the spirit of prayer by which we who have now been reconciled offer the highest form of worship: true invocation, thanksgiving, confession, etc. But even as we have thus far spoken of petitions, so we shall also remember that thanksgiving must always be added. For many tremendous benefits are conferred even on those who are unaware. We would be oppressed by an infinite number of perils if we were not divinely protected. Therefore, Paul says, "In everything give thanks" [1 Thessalonians 5:18]. And when he writes to the Corinthians, commanding that many should pray for him, so that many may give thanks when he is preserved [2 Corinthians 1:11], he indicates that this form of worship in particular must be exercised.

CIVIL MAGISTRATES AND THE DIGNITY OF CIVIL AFFAIRS

It is highly beneficial to have in the Church the true and certain doctrine concerning magistrates and the dignity of civil affairs. For fanatical spirits have often arisen who have denied that Christians may hold civil office, serve as judges, or exercise authority. In sum, they have barred Christians from all the offices of civil life, from owning property, and from making contracts. They have also condemned the civil laws which the commonwealth now uses. These delusions have not only given birth to sedition, but have also obscured the Gospel, for they spread darkness over the mind, as if Christian righteousness and life consisted in an external, novel, barbaric form of government, unlike other humanly instituted governments. Thus they have confused the distinction between spiritual and civil life.

The mind must be fortified against errors of this kind. The true doctrine concerning the distinction between spiritual and civil life must be upheld, and the dignity of civil affairs must be extolled. This is beneficial for piety and for public tranquility. For it is a great comfort for the godly to understand that the civil life is pleasing to God, that it is a gift of God, that God has commanded each one to comply with the demands of his vocation in civil life as well, that all offices of civil life—to govern the republic, to serve as judges, to wage war, to serve in the military, to comply with the magistrates, to marry, to own property, to strive to improve and protect one's personal property with work and legitimate contracts, to honor the useful arts of life, to teach the young rightly, and similar things—all these are true forms of worshiping God among the godly. It is likewise a great bond of peace, to know that God has commanded us to comply with the governing magistrates, not to tear the authority away from the them, that God requires us to preserve and to honor this civil life with great zeal. Therefore, the praises of civil life should be diligently inculcated in men. The very young especially should be taught with great care and skill to think reverently of the magistrates, laws, and all civil affairs. This reverence is useful for the commonwealth. Indeed, it is the nursemaid of the greatest virtues.

Celsus, Julianus, and many others denounce the Gospel, claiming that, since it forbids vengeance, it utterly destroys the republic, as it removes the right to wage war, to pass judgments, to inflict punishments; it encourages theft and grants license and impunity to every form of crime. But with this denunciation they have horribly twisted the Gospel. Therefore, it behooves Christians to uphold the proper understanding of the dignity of civil affairs, both in order to deliver the Gospel from this most unjust and venomous calumny and to establish their own consciences properly concerning civil offices. The monks do not want to seem as if they utterly condemned civil life, and yet they obscure its dignity when they pretend that it is evangelical perfection not to hold private property, not to take part in civil affairs, etc. They have troubled the consciences of many people with these dreams. Therefore, the mind must be fortified against errors of this kind by observing several rules.

The first rule is this: The Gospel teaches about a spiritual and eternal righteousness in the heart. Meanwhile, it does not abolish home or society in the bodily life, but teaches that the home and all societal matters established by reason are good ordinances of God and are gifts of God that are necessary in this bodily life. It commands us to preserve and to extol these gifts of God and to exercise faith and love in these situations. Therefore, just as architecture or music is not at all contrary to the Gospel, so civil affairs are not at all contrary to the Gospel. For as architecture is used in constructing buildings for sheltering the body, so the State sets the limits of possessions, of bodily matters, of contracts, of penalties, of grades of persons for the preservation of external society, all of which is necessary for bodily life.

The second rule is this: The works of domestic and societal life which each one performs for his own vocation are good works and are true acts of divine worship among the godly, for they are works which have been commanded by God. Therefore, the prophets often compare these works with sacrifices, so that sometimes they greatly prefer civil works to sacrifices, and sometimes they entirely condemn the sacrifices of human traditions. Such is the comparison of Isaiah 1. He says of sacrifices, "Who requires these things from your hands, etc.?" But of civil works he says, "Seek judgment. Aid the oppressed. Defend the widow." And he adds the greatest rewards: "Although your sins were as scarlet, they shall be made as white as snow." In Zechariah 7, "Judge with right judgment, etc." And in Hosea, "I desire mercy, not sacrifice" [Hosea 6:6]. The voice of Paul on domestic duties is notable: "The woman is saved through childbirth, if she remains in faith, etc."[1 Timothy 2:15]. Here he commends marital duties with such great honor that he says that the faithful are saved on account of them, for he combines faith and the works of one's vocation, even as it is clear that each kind of righteousness is necessary. Therefore, Paul teaches here that the works of vocation—the works of a wife—are a sort of righteousness and an act of worshiping God which God rewards. Thus Peter preaches about obedience toward magistrates: "Obey every human ordinance." And he adds, "for the Lord's sake" [1 Peter 2:13]. Likewise, "This is the will of God" [1 Peter 2:15]. Therefore, these duties are pleasing to God. And Paul says, "It is necessary to obey, not only because of wrath, but also because of conscience" [Romans 13:5]. Therefore, he teaches that this obedience is judged by God, etc. These and similar passages testify clearly enough that all civil duties are good works and acts of divine worship among the godly.

The godly should uphold this rule against the opinions of hypocrites who admire and praise monastic works, who either condemn civil life outright, or certainly disparage it, and who trouble the consciences of those who take part in this civil life.

It is an entirely peculiar wisdom worthy of the Christian to understand the dignity of this common civil life and to prefer such duties to monastic works. First, because they have God's command and vocation. Second, because they are duties of love, for they are destined for the common benefit of men. Third, because they are subject to common perils and the cross, and therefore require the exercise of faith.

On the other hand, monastic ceremonies do not have God's command or vocation, wherefore they are worthless acts of worship, according to that passage, "In vain do they worship Me with the commandments of men, etc." [Matthew 15:9]. Second, those who do not teach do not help others, but enjoy the sweetest leisure. Finally, they do not experience any part of common perils. Therefore, the common, civil life should be placed far above monastic ceremonies.

These things must be diligently impressed on the mind, so that each one may learn to understand his own vocation and know that it pleases God. Everyone should be zealous to honor his vocation for the sake of God's glory, and no one should seek or admire other works, although they appear to be more beautiful, as men otherwise naturally admire hypocrisy and peculiar ceremonies.

The third rule. Christians are permitted to hold the magistrate and to rule, to serve as judges, to establish penalties according to the current laws and customs, to wage legitimate wars, to serve in the military, to make contracts, to buy, to sell, to hold property, to accuse and defend in court, to bring one's own lawsuit or that of another, etc. The fanatical spirits bar Christians from all these civil activities. First, because they do not understand that Christian righteousness is spiritual, but pretend that it is a certain novel, external and barbaric state. Second, because they do not know that the governing authority is an ordinance and work of God, but judge that it is an unjust power which has only arisen from the ambition and evil desires of men. The Manichaeans once condemned civil affairs in like manner, whom Irenaeus splendidly refuted with a long disputation. Thus, in a single matter the fanatical spirits make two mistakes: They transform spiritual righteousness into an external, civil affair, and they judge that civil affairs are an unjust power.

But since we demonstrated above what the kingdom of Christ is, namely, that Christian righteousness is spiritual, we shall only say something here about the second misunderstanding of the fanatics. It is fundamental to these rules which we have set forth that the magistrates—that is, the State or secular authority—are good creations of God and affairs that are not only permitted by God, but approved by the Word of God and instituted by God. They have also been ordained by a certain work of God and are preserved by God, even as the celestial movements have been ordained by a work of God and are preserved by God. This is the meaning of Paul when he says in Romans 13, "The authorities which exist have been ordained by God." Likewise, "He who resists the authority resists the ordinance of God." And again, "He is God's minister." The Scriptures often teach the same thing in other places. Daniel clearly says, "God removes and establishes kingdoms" [Daniel 2:21]. The Psalm says, "I have said, 'You are gods'" [Psalm 82:6]; that is, those who carry out the office ordained and commanded by God. Second Chronicles 19, "You are not exercising the judgment of man, but of the Lord." And Wisdom says through Solomon, "Kings reign through Me" [Proverbs 8:15]. Proverbs 16, "The scales and weights are judgments of the Lord."

These passages all testify that the magistrates and civil ordinances are not said to be from God in the same way that evil things are permitted by God, but they teach positively that civil ordinances are affairs which God has effectively instituted by a certain work of His and still preserves and approves by His Word. Therefore, they are good creations of God, like crops, wine, etc. And God is not only to be considered the Author of authorities because He is the Creator of human reason and has given it a light by which it distinguishes right from wrong and ordains civil affairs. For although this reasoning is not to be rejected, nevertheless, it must be added that God, by His own work, truly moves and governs the minds of magistrates in producing just laws and in carrying out vital affairs, and that He preserves authority in the world. For human reason is much too weak to be able to preserve civil affairs against the great power of the devil, who seeks to destroy authority, or against the infinite desires of men, unless they are restrained by the help of God. Therefore, Daniel expressly says, "He has established kingdoms" [Daniel 2:21], that is, He causes them to exist so that they endure and are preserved, etc. And the Psalm says, "Unless the Lord guards the city, etc." [Psalm 127:1].

Therefore, the highest and most extraordinary praise of civil affairs is this: that they are truly works and benefits of God. The Scriptures which I have noted testify to this and provide many proofs of it. For it is clear that murderers also, though they try to slip away, are divinely brought back to punishment and very rarely escape, as it says in Ecclesiastes 8, "The ungodly cannot escape in war, etc." Tyrants, although they appear safe because of their own strength, are divinely swept away to punishment, to such a degree that there have been very few who have avoided it. The same thing happens with other notable crimes. For God preserves civil justice in the world in such a way that He regularly punishes in this life those who violate civil justice, just as He regularly causes storms, sometimes in winter, sometimes in summer. Therefore, even though in the storms He sometimes does something unexpected, outside the rule, and delays the penalties and rewards by His hidden counsel, nevertheless, the rule must be acknowledged that God is the Preserver of civil righteousness in the world, so that the unjust may always fear the penalties. They should not imagine that they will avoid the penalty, even if they see one person or another avoiding it. For the rule must be upheld, in spite of rare exceptions.

To this notion Isocrates issues a grave response—to those who, because of a few examples, hope to have impunity for their crimes. He says,

"Even if these things do not always happen, nevertheless this generally tends to be the outcome. But since the future is always uncertain, a wise man looks rather at that which is more often advantageous. And since you understand that justice is more pleasing to God, it would be most foolish to imagine that the just will end up in a worse state than the unjust."[37]

Third, it is a manifest sign of the presence of God in government that no government can be instituted or upheld without heroic men whose virtue and fortune are unquestionably marvelous works of God. Wise men have always seen this in the republic. For example, Plato says in *De legibus*, book 4, "As cattle are not ruled by cattle, nor goats by goats, but by a more excellent nature, namely, by us, so human nature is too weak to be able to rule itself. Therefore, God did not place mere men in charge of cities, but a more excellent and divine race, namely, heroes to preserve peace, decency, freedom, and righteousness." And he adds, "The saying is true: where not God but a mortal is in control, there is no way to escape ills and toils."

The Psalm also teaches that kings are divinely aided. Psalm 144: "He gives salvation to kings." The efficient cause, therefore, testifies that the magistrate is not a sin or something that is condemned. For it is an ordinance made by God, wherefore it must necessarily be a good creation, just as the ordinance of winter, of summer, of life, and of living things. Second, the divine approval has also been added through the Word, as the above-cited passages testify.

Third, the formal and final causes prove the same thing. Paul names the formal cause when he says, "It is an ordinance of God" [Romans 13:2]. Likewise, "He is God's minister" [Romans 13:4]. For robbery is not something God has ordained, that is, it does not follow the sure rule of justice; it is disorder, and it does great harm to good men. In addition, robbery is not a ministry of God. Therefore, the magistrate is not robbery, but a good thing that pleases God.

---

37   Isocrates, *On Peace*, section 8, par. 35.

The final cause is the defense of good men, so that good men may be able to live in peace, with godliness and honesty, as Paul says in 1 Timothy 2.

Therefore, the magistrates should do these things and see to it that they are done, first, that there may be peace for good men. But then it is not enough to bring about peace; the two things must be added which are the goals of peace or the things for which peace is to be sought; namely, discipline and godliness. That is, the magistrates should see to it that men use peace properly, not for luxurious living, for pursuing lust, and for other vices, but behavior must be ruled by laws and discipline. Likewise, men should be prepared for godliness and the knowledge of God. These goals testify that the magistrate is a blessing from God. For robbery is not devoted to good purposes. It destroys honorable behavior and does not preserve the nation, etc.

Finally, the commandment also teaches the same thing—the commandment in which we are ordered to pray for the magistrates; namely, that their governments may be preserved. But we are not to pray for robbers, that they may be preserved, etc. All these reasons give high praise to the magistrate and confirm consciences in the understanding that the magistrate is a divinely ordained office and that it is lawful for Christians to serve in government office. For since the office is a good thing, it is permissible for Christians to hold it, just as it is permissible to use other good creations of God, like food, drink, etc.; or just as it is permissible to practice other arts, such as medicine, architecture, etc. This is why the Scriptures number kings among the godly in the Church of Christ. Psalm 102, "When the peoples gather together, and kings to serve the Lord." And Psalm 47, "The princes of the peoples gather together with the God of Abraham." And John says, "Be content with your wages" [Luke 3:14]. He therefore approves of the office itself. In addition, it is clear that Christians are permitted to use the law. But the magistrate is part of the law. As Paul says, "The law is good, if it is used lawfully, etc." [1 Timothy 1:8]. Likewise, the Gospel approves of bodily life. At the same time, then, it approves of civil authority, without which it is impossible to retain bodily life. And the examples testify that it is permissible for the saints to serve as magistrates. The centurions in the Gospel and in Acts were soldiers. Joseph and Daniel held the reins of power among the Gentiles.

As for the passages from the Gospel which are cited in opposition, namely, those which forbid vengeance, it must be understood that in all those passages it is only private vengeance that is forbidden, that is, vengeance that is not exercised by the magistrate or by command of the magistrate. But public vengeance is not forbidden. For Paul calls the magistrate "God's minister" [Romans 13:4], and it pertains to this passage, "Vengeance is Mine" [Romans 12:19]. For civil vengeance, which is legitimately exercised by the magistrate, is done by God's command. Therefore, the Gospel zealously protects public tranquility when it also commands the magistrate to exercise vengeance; that is, to restrain, drive out and punish the unjust, by means of laws, penalties, sword, and wars. On the other hand, it commands private individuals not to exercise vengeance privately, that is, not to take up arms without the authority of the magistrate, not to incite rebellion, etc.

Some also raise the following objection, that wicked men often grab hold of the reins of power, that there is much wickedness among the authorities. Because of this, the fanatical spirits argue that the authorities are not ordinances of God. But one must respond in this manner: The persons should be distinguished from the matter itself, that is, from the ordinance. The ordinance, that is, the preservation of civil justice and of the civil state is a work of God, even if the persons abuse the ordinance, etc. But I have abundantly treated these and many other things that are here being discussed in my commentary on Paul's Epistle to the Romans.

The fourth rule. The Gospel has not set up a new earthly commonwealth, but commands us to comply with the governing magistrates and laws. It commands us to preserve and to honor the current authorities. Thus it teaches in general that the civil authorities are lawful, divine blessings. It commands the magistrates to carry out their office diligently. It commands subjects to obey, and that for conscience' sake. It teaches in general what kind of laws there should be, namely, laws that honor good works and that forbid evil works. As for which works are good and which are evil, that is determined by natural reason, that is, the law of nature, and by the magistrate.

Let the teachers of the Gospel, then, understand their duty and teach about spiritual righteousness. Let them not hurl accusations against civil ordinances. Let them not speak of new laws about the ownership of property, about tributes, about penalties for criminals, about contracts, etc. But let them teach that the governing authority and the current laws are to be preserved, for the Gospel forbids rebellion. And Paul says, "Let every soul obey the authority that governs" [Romans 13:1], that is, the governing authority. And when he says that the magistrate is a divine ordinance, he includes every aspect of the civil estate. Just as he approves of the governing magistrates, so he also approves of the governing laws, courts, penalties, the military, and distinction of private property. And since he orders us, not only to obey, but also to honor the magistrate, we will be sure to instruct people to think most reverently of all civil affairs. They should understand that every aspect of the civil estate—laws, courts, contracts, etc.—is a blessing of God, and that they should be zealous to honor and preserve them, praying that God Himself would preserve these vital affairs that are so necessary for earthly life. We will teach them to flee from and to despise the meddlesomeness with which private citizens, forgetful of their own vocation, intrude on public affairs, etc. These clever men are not, by nature, suitable for tranquility, either because of their curiosity or because they are by nature unruly, tyrannical, and seditious. Not only is there danger for the commonwealth from the clever devices of men, but much more from the devil, who, since he is a murderer, delights in rebellion and slaughter. He is zealous to cause disorder, and especially to twist the Gospel, to incite the ignorant, and to destroy civil affairs under the pretext of religion. But we should also correct the vices of nature and know how to beware of the devil's traps. Godly teachers should warn about these things and should honor the dignity of civil affairs with genuine praise, both for the sake of public peace and for the glory of the Gospel, and so that everyone's conscience may understand that this kind of civil life is pleasing to God.

Monetarius, then, was acting madly when he wanted to reinstitute the Mosaic form of government, when he denied that thieves were to be penalized with capital punishment, when he wanted matters to be judged from the laws of Moses. For the Gospel does not command the nations to accept the Mosaic form of government; instead, it approves of the governing magistrates. Therefore, it also approves of their laws and gives them power to make laws. Therefore, thieves are to be punished according to the laws of the governing magistrates, and matters should be adjudicated on the basis of the governing laws.

The fifth rule. The Gospel is so serious about obedience that it teaches that it is a mortal sin not to obey the commands of the magistrates. Therefore, Paul says, "It is necessary to obey, not only on account of wrath, but also for the sake of conscience" [Romans 13:5]. First, he teaches that it is a necessary work. Then, that this necessity may be understood concerning conscience, he speaks not only of civil penalties, but adds, "Not only on account of wrath," that is, not only on account of the bodily penalty with which the magistrate punishes those who are disobedient, but "for the sake of conscience." In other words, obedience is necessary in such a way that in those who do not obey, the conscience becomes guilty before God. There are many other similar passages in the Scriptures, but since this word of Paul is perfectly clear, I will not add further testimonies here. I will simply admonish Christian readers to consider how seriously the evangelical doctrine protects the authority of rulers when it teaches so sternly about obedience. Second, there should be a greater zeal for obedience among us, since we understand that those who do not obey will undoubtedly give account to God, even if they imagine that they will escape the wrath of the magistrates. Again, Paul speaks not only of the external duties or external obedience, but also of the judgment and will of the mind. That commandment is full of wisdom, both civil and Christian. For it is most beneficial to the commonwealth that minds should be imbued with a truly reverent opinion of the authorities, of laws, of patriotism, that is, of obedience, as the secular writers have often taught as well. But I will pass over their statements at this time. Let us simply consider the saying of Paul, which contains the weightiest doctrine. For he insists that the magistrates be honored. Now honor is not only an external sign of reverence, but the more genuine judgment and will of the mind. First, it means to acknowledge that the magistrates have been ordained by God, and that through them God bestows great blessings on men. Second, it means to recognize these blessings: peace, the whole of civil society, laws concerning marriage, courts, contracts, discipline. For this earthly nature has nothing more lovely, nothing better than societal order, and to have these assemblies of men associated with justice, temperance, and the other virtues. Third, it means to fear and love the magistrates for God's sake and to understand that we owe both God and the magistrates a debt of gratitude for these blessings. This judgment of the mind is the true honor that is owed to the magistrates. Finally, this honor should also be added: to pray, namely, to pray for the magistrates that God would grant peace to the commonwealth, that He would preserve religion and discipline, that He would guard the good rulers and govern their minds for the glory of God and the salvation of the people. For among so many snares of the devil, in the midst of so much wickedness of men, the commonwealth could not stand if it were not preserved by divine providence. For the devil is a murderer and seeks to trouble and destroy the commonwealth. Therefore, Paul commands Timothy to pray for the magistrates. Which books of the philosophers speak of these honors? There is absolutely no literature that honors the magistrate more than Christian doctrine does. But these great matters lie buried beneath the inept opinions which the monks have spread in the Church. Therefore, good men are to be admonished diligently to promote the praises of magistrates and civil affairs, that they may become accustomed to obedience and pray to God with greater zeal for the commonwealth and for rulers.

In addition, Paul requires other earthly duties, namely, tributes and taxes. For the commonwealth can be neither defended nor ruled without great expense, without garrisons, without wise governors. Therefore, since there is need of wages and of civil works, Paul commands that the due earthly responsibilities be provided, namely, tributes and military service. And he teaches most severely about the penalty, that those who do not comply will be divinely punished, for it is mortal sin to disobey the magistrates. But when the magistrates command their subjects to do something against God's commandments, the subjects should obey God rather than men, as the story in the third chapter of Daniel teaches.

I will add also a sixth rule. It is not our intention to include here the entire doctrine concerning civil affairs. For there are many books of philosophers and jurists who (although the subject matter is infinite) have gathered together many precepts which are useful for those who rule the commonwealth. I have only briefly mentioned a few of them here, the ones which are most necessary for the consciences of all men. And since I have spoken about the obedience of citizens, I shall add one precept concerning the duty of magistrates. Their power is not infinite, whether they are kings or princes. For first, they should not command or do anything contrary to divine Law and the law of nature. Second, they also sin when they command something against the laws of their own kingdom or against the form of their own government, as, for example, it was not permissible for Ahab to tear the vineyard away from the citizen Naboth against his will. For the laws of the Israelites recognized private ownership and granted freedom and private property to their citizens. So the laws which we use today distinguish between freedom and slavery. They grant property and the ownership of private property to free men. Therefore, citizens are properly the owners of their own things. Nor is it lawful for princes to seize on a whim as much as they want from the fortunes of their citizens. Therefore, John says, "Be content with your wages. Do not harass anyone. Do not accuse falsely" [Luke 3:14]. Thus the passage about the law of the kingdom in the story of Samuel does not grant infinite license to the princes. It speaks of wages. That is, it allows wages to be taken from the fortunes of private individuals for public use. But I do not wish to pursue these things further.

This must be added. The magistrate is the guardian, not only of the second table, but also of the first table, as far as it pertains to external discipline. That is, it belongs to the magistrate not only to see to the tranquility of the citizens and to prevent injuries to body and fortune, but also to retain discipline in religion. For even though bodily penalties do not bring about godliness in the mind, the magistrate should, nevertheless, for the sake of discipline, forbid external abuses of religion, manifest idolatry, blasphemies, wicked dogmas, and perjury, even as we see in all moderately established republics that perjury and violations of religion have been punished with severe examples. The Decalogue itself proves this. "You shall not take the name of God in vain." And David says, "And now, you kings, understand; be instructed, you who judge the earth. Serve the Lord, etc." [Psalm 2:10–11]. Proverbs 25, "Remove wickedness from the face of the king, and his throne will be established with justice." And 1 Kings 2, "I shall glorify those who glorify Me, and those who show Me contempt I shall render contemptible." And lest I should only take examples from the kings of Israel, Daniel records that Nebuchadnezzar and Darius the Mede made decrees in which they forbid blasphemy to be spoken against the God of the people of Israel.

Finally, Paul says, "The law has been set in place for the wicked, the profane" [1 Timothy 1:9]; that is, so that it may restrain men, lest they perpetrate wicked and sacrilegious deeds.

Now, since the magistrate is the custodian of the law and of discipline, he should certainly see to it that external reverence toward God is shown. This is a large part of discipline, as it is clear that perjury is punished by the laws of all nations. After that, the wise magistrate should consider this to be the one chief purpose for which men have been brought into civil society, namely, that God may be known and glorified. For man was created in order that God might begin to dawn in him and be revealed through him. For this reason, a society was necessary in which some might teach others about God. Human nature was designed especially with this philosophy in mind, which is why there are so many bonds of society. Procreation, education, and the defense of life all have need of society. Thus necessity itself joins men together and brings them into association with one another. For what reason? That just as man was created in order that God might begin to dawn in him, so also, through the society of men, some men may be taught about God. And for this reason, since society was designed for such a great work, for such a great purpose, it has been created with law and order in such a way that nothing more beautiful can be envisioned than such a society. Now it is clear that the magistrate is the custodian of human society. Therefore, he should also oversee the chief goal of society. And if we want to judge truly, he should be the master and judge[38] of this most beautiful of works among men, so that with the best discipline men should be trained for religion, that God may be glorified. This goal should be chiefly set forth to the wise governor of the commonwealth. In this way, the commonwealth will truly be blessed. For God, in turn, will defend it, furnish it with all good things, as He has said, "I shall glorify those who glorify Me" [1 Samuel 2:30]. Therefore, the magistrates should forbid ungodly forms of worship and the profession of ungodly

---

38   antistes et ἀγωνοθέτης

dogmas. They should punish heretics. But they must be careful to judge rightly, and they should not become ministers of an alien cruelty or impiety. Now, the examination of doctrine belongs to the Church, that is, to those who are godly and have been rightly taught. And the magistrate himself is also a member of the Church, a fact which should continually stand before his eyes. The ancient canons concerning synods and examination of doctrine are in agreement with this. God honors the kings with the honor of His name. "I have said, 'You are gods'" [Psalm 82:6], namely, that they may know that it belongs to their office to understand divine matters and to preserve religion, justice, peace, and discipline in the world. I have listed these common precepts concerning civil matters and magistrates, the knowledge of which is necessary for all the godly.

It is the task of other skilled teachers to discuss the precepts concerning each part of the governance of the commonwealth. The Gospel highlights the dignity of civil affairs in order to foster reverence toward the magistrate and the whole civil order, and to admonish us to be thankful to God for such great blessings. In addition, it teaches both magistrates and subjects about their duty in general in order to prevent both tyranny and rebellion. Now, when civil affairs are praised, it should be understood that to them pertain laws, arts, literature, and doctrine, wherefore men are to be taught that they should also think honorably about these things, that they may consider them to be gifts of God which are necessary for retaining laws, for preserving and proclaiming the Gospel, and, finally, for an infinite number of useful purposes. It should also be understood concerning contracts, that just as it is permissible to use other civil matters, so also it is permissible to use contracts. For this life cannot exist without contracts. And the teachers of the Gospel should take care not to fear or wickedly condemn approved contracts. But I have otherwise taught this rule, that the forms of those contracts should be approved which the laws and magistrates themselves approve, that is, those which the wise and fair jurists approve.

ECCLESIASTICAL POLITY

Just as I have praised the secular polity and declared that minds must become accustomed to thinking of it reverently, loving it and being zealous to honor and preserve it with every kind of service, so also should we love and venerate the ecclesiastical polity in our minds and honor it with sincere devotion.

There are two parts of ecclesiastical polity. The one is the divinely ordained ministry. The other is good order, which has been established by the authority of the Church. I have spoken above about the divinely ordained ministry. To it pertain these things: First, the Church has the command to call, that is, to ordain ministers who are to teach the Gospel publicly and administer the Sacraments, and who are to announce the forgiveness of sins, either to individuals or to many. Second, the Church has jurisdiction to bar from Communion those who live in manifest sins. It is clear that the ministry has also been divinely ordained in order that the Gospel may be preserved on earth, and that through the Gospel eternal blessings—righteousness, the Holy Spirit, and eternal life—are offered to us, as Paul also says, "The Gospel is the power of God for salvation to everyone who believes" [Romans 1:16]. Indeed, we are commanded to preserve this ministry by the heavenly voice when it says of Christ, "This is My beloved Son. Hear Him" [Matthew 17:5]. Therefore, all men should venerate this ministry with sincere devotion and should see to it that it is preserved and exalted. The Psalm says, "Open your gates, O princes, and the King of glory will come in" [Psalm 24:7]. He commands all nations and men to receive and to preserve the ministry of the Gospel, so that even if the majority of men cares little or even shows contempt for it, nevertheless the godly are to be taught that God requires no higher duty than the preservation of this ministry. This is the pearl which we should purchase for ourselves after selling all things [cf. Matthew 13:46].

The second part must also be preserved, namely, the good order which is necessary for the Church, for discipline and tranquility. For since the divinely instituted ministry should be public and external, there is a need for certain human ordinances. We should also love and preserve those human ordinances which serve the divinely instituted ministry and are advantageous for discipline and tranquility. And since the Church holds and nourishes us just as a womb holds and nourishes a fetus (for the prophets often use this analogy), this picture itself teaches us many things. The Church is like a womb. There are vessels on all sides leading into the womb, whose openings, in order that they may be able to enclose the fetus, are like the cotyledons of a polyp. The fetus is surrounded by a membrane, which is called a chorion, enclosed by the cotyledons so that the fetus may be held in the womb. Filaments arise from the umbilical cord and stretch through the chorion to the openings of the veins. These capillaries draw the blood from the veins by which the fetus is nourished. First, the liver is made from the coagulated blood; and from the seed, the *vena cava* in the liver. Then, the heart is made from the warmer blood, together with the living breath; and from the seed, the arteries. Then, from the foremost part of the seed come the brain and the nerves; and from the blood which is drawn, the flesh.

Therefore, since the veins feed the fetus, they are a picture of the divinely ordained ministry. For the godly are regenerated and fed by the Gospel. The chorion signifies the ecclesiastical polity, or the good order instituted by the Church. For although we take nothing from this membrane when we are born, nevertheless, it ties the fetus to the womb and to the cotyledons and holds it there, lest it be expelled. And once the chorion has been breached, the fetus is able neither to be fed nor to remain in the womb. Thus human ordinances of days, places, and similar things, although they themselves are not godliness, are chains which join us to the ministers of the Gospel. Through these ordinances, as through vessels, the teachers embrace us. Each one has his own flock. We have certain places, certain times for hearing the Gospel. If these chains are broken, the Church is scattered and torn to pieces. It can no longer be fed, for the newborns can no longer reach the veins by which they are nourished, that is, there are no certain, rightly called (*rite vocati*) teachers. There is no authority among those who teach, no discipline among those who hear, and men cannot be ruled or restrained. And license gives birth to an infinite number of scandals. Sects and factions arise, because the people permit themselves to be easily separated from the true veins, that is, from the true teachers, just as a fetus cannot be saved if the chorion is ruptured prematurely. Thus let us know that the Church is also put at risk when ecclesiastical ordinances are abolished. For it is most certainly true what the wise poet Sophocles said, "There is nothing more evil than anarchy."[39] And the more important the ordinances, the more one must beware the popes, lest unjust laws or impious forms of worship be added to the good, ancient rites. For unjust laws cannot last, and when they arise, they cause the remaining polity to waver, as ulcers lacerate the stomach lining. Therefore, let us correct these vices, and let us love and preserve useful rites, especially since Paul commanded that in the Church all things should be done in a fitting and orderly way. Indeed, pedagogy itself is beneficial, as has often been said.

For whenever we hear and teach the Gospel, God is calling out to teachable minds and is efficacious through the Word. Thus the other things, too, are helpful, as the filaments which are affixed to the cotyledons transmit nutrients through the chorion. So we, too, should be taught. First, the liver is formed, that is, the doctrine and pedagogy of the ceremonies is taught. For these things are rudimentary, like milk, and are the first nutrient of godliness. Afterward, the brain and the heart, that is, the doctrine of faith and the new and spiritual life, is added. Nor should these things be idle, but both the doctrine and the new life should be exercised, should grow and spread, just as arteries and breath spread from the heart, and nerves from the brain. And these

---

39   Sophocles, *Antigone*, line 672.

things must be clothed with flesh, that is, with an external way of life that is honorable. But setting aside the analogy, let us view life itself and the nature of man, which cannot be lacking in ceremonies and rites, as has now often been said. Therefore, let us sincerely love and defend also this area of ecclesiastical polity, and let us impress upon ourselves those venerable and weighty verses of the poet:[40]

> Obedience to command saves many persons;
> Therefore, we must support the secular institutions.

May Christ direct our minds to true godliness and restore godly and perpetual concord to the Church. Amen.

Praise be to God!

---

[40] Sophocles, *Antigone*, lines 676–677.

www.ingramcontent.com/pod-product-compliance
Lightning Source LLC
Chambersburg PA
CBHW050548160426
43199CB00015B/2580